Law and Enjoyment

This book advocates, and develops, a critical account of the relationship between law and the largely neglected issue of 'enjoyment'. Taking popular culture seriously – as a lived and meaningful basis for a wider understanding of law, beyond the strictures of legal institutions and professional practices – it takes up a range of case studies from film and literature in order to consider how law is iterated through enjoyment, and how enjoyment embodies law.

Drawing on psychoanalytic theory, this book addresses issues such as the forced choice to enjoy the law, the biopolitics of tyranny, the enjoyment of law's contingency, the trauma of the law's symbolic codification of pleasure, and the futuristic vision of law's transgression. In so doing, it forges an important case for acknowledging and analysing the complex relationship between power and pleasure in law – one that will be of considerable interest to legal theorists, as well as those with interests in the intersection of psychoanalytic and cultural theory.

Daniel Hourigan is a lecturer in English Literature at the University of Southern Queensland, Australia.

Discourses of Law

Series editors: Peter Goodrich, Michel Rosenfeld and Arthur Jacobson
Benjamin N. Cardozo School of Law

This successful and exciting series seeks to publish the most innovative scholarship at the intersection of law, philosophy and social theory. The books published in the series are distinctive by virtue of exploring the boundaries of legal thought. The work that this series seeks to promote is marked most strongly by the drive to open up new perspectives on the relation between law and other disciplines. The series has also been unique in its commitment to international and comparative perspectives upon an increasingly global legal order. Of particular interest in a contemporary context, the series has concentrated upon the introduction and translation of continental traditions of theory and law.

The original impetus for the series came from the paradoxical merger and confrontation of East and West. Globalization and the internationalization of the rule of law has had many dramatic and often unforeseen and ironic consequences. An understanding of differing legal cultures, particularly different patterns of legal thought, can contribute, often strongly and starkly, to an appreciation if not always a resolution of international legal disputes. The rule of law is tied to social and philosophical underpinnings that the series has sought to excoriate and illuminate.

Titles in the series:

Nietzsche and Legal Theory: Half-Written Laws
Edited by Peter Goodrich and Mariana Valverde

Law, Orientalism, and Postcolonialism: The Jurisdiction of the Lotus Eaters.
Piyel Haldar

Endowed: Regulating the Male Sexed Body
Michael Thomson

The Identity of the Constitutional Subject: Selfhood, Citizenship, Culture, and Community
Michel Rosenfeld

The Land is the Source of the Law: A Dialogic Encounter with Indigenous Jurisprudence
C. F. Black

Shakespearean Genealogies of Power: A Whispering of Nothing in Hamlet, Richard II, Julius Caesar, Macbeth, The Merchant of Venice, *and* The Winter's Tale
Anselm Haverkamp

Visualizing Law in the Age of the Digital Baroque: Arabesques and Entanglements
Richard K. Sherwin

The Scene of Mass Crime
Peter Goodrich and Christian Delage

Novel Judgments: Legal Theory as Fiction
William Macneil

Sex, Culpability and the Defence of Provocation
Danielle Tyson

Wickedness and Crime: Laws of Homicide and Malice
Penny Crofts

Shakespeare's Curse
Björn Quiring

Exemplarity and Singularity: Thinking through Particulars in Philosophy, Literature, and Law
Edited by Michèle Lowrie and Susanne Lüdemann

Law and Enjoyment: Power, Pleasure and Psychoanalysis
Daniel Hourigan

Genealogies of Legal Vision
Edited by Peter Goodrich and Valérie Hayaert

Forthcoming:

Crime Scenes: Forensics and Aesthetics
Rebecca Scott Bray

The Rule of Reason in European Constitutionalism and Citizenship
Yuri Borgmann-Prebil

Varieties of Liberalism: Nineteenth Century Contract Between Literature, Law and History
Anat Rosenberg

The publisher gratefully acknowledges the support of the Jacob Burns Institute for Advanced Legal Studies of the Benjamin N. Cardozo School of Law to the series *Discourses of Law*.

Law and Enjoyment

Power, Pleasure and Psychoanalysis

Daniel Hourigan

Routledge
Taylor & Francis Group
LONDON AND NEW YORK

First published 2015
by Routledge
2 Park Square, Milton Park, Abingdon, Oxfordshire OX14 4RN

and by Routledge
711 Third Avenue, New York, NY 10017

First issued in paperback 2016

Routledge is an imprint of the Taylor & Francis Group, an informa business

British Library Cataloguing in Publication Data
A catalogue record for this book is available from the British Library

Library of Congress Cataloging-in-Publication Data
Hourigan, Daniel.
Law and enjoyment : power, pleasure and psychoanalysis / Daniel Hourigan.
pages cm. -- (Discourses of law)
Includes bibliographical references and index.
ISBN 978-1-138-81596-4 (hbk) -- ISBN 978-1-315-74646-3 (ebk) 1. Pleasure. 2. Law--Social aspects.
3. Power (Social sciences) 4. Psychoanalysis. 5. Popular culture. I. Title.
BF515.H68 2015
340'.19--dc23
2014047225

ISBN: 978-0-415-79223-3 (pbk)
ISBN: 978-1-138-81596-4 (hbk)

Typeset in Minion by
Servis Filmsetting Ltd, Stockport, Cheshire

Dedication

This book would not have happened without the love and support of my family and friends. Special thanks go to Sally for her love and support, John for the gift of philosophy, and William for his recognition and friendship. I would also like to acknowledge the institutional support of the School of Humanities and the Griffith Law School at Griffith University, the School of Arts and Communication at the University of Southern Queensland, and the Law and Literature Association of Australasia Inc.

Contents

Introduction

It is striking how law reaches beyond the legal profession and institutions to operate as a popular pathos of cultural narratives and social developments. In these contexts law not only expounds its legal and juridical rules, procedures and practices; it also functions as a popular trope of twentieth- and twenty-first-century narratives delivered for mass consumption on presses and screens everywhere. But there is a third place that law inhabits, a place where the commercial interest of entertainment and the political interests of professionalism part ways. This third place is the theoretical: law in theory. Legal theory and jurisprudence are the two dominant modes of this realm that draws upon minor literatures to inspect the legal canon: the words of novelists, the clinic of psychoanalysts, the letters of disciples, and the speculative realism of philosophers to name but a few. This book is interested in how the cultural and legal are inflected by the theoretical; how law is thought, how it is narrativised, and how it is *enjoyed*.

The enjoyment of law has many different stripes. It can be a judicial construction that avows the arbitrary separation of jurisdiction and power. It can also be the sexually charged erotics of a lovers' contract. It may even be the undoing of the origin of the legal in favour of the primal. To approach the enjoyment of law this book puts forward eight critical vignettes of power, pleasure and close reading. These vignettes aim to develop the idea of 'enjoying law', be it through 'more law', nilhilistically deconstructing the social contract, or even more speculative methods of retrieving that certain 'legal' flavour that inhabits popular cultural media. While the critical materials of this book vary from case law to case studies from literature, cinema, philosophy and psychoanalysis, always the focus is on how law is iterated through enjoyment and, more radically still, how enjoyment is iterated by legality.[1]

The opening chapter briefly outlines the psychoanalytic coordinates of this volume's attempt to read law in popular cultural media. It explains something of this work's connection to current trends in cultural legal studies and why the theories of a French psychoanalyst like Jacques Lacan can prove useful to unravelling the legal in the cultural and *vice-à-versa*. The critical method of how the subsequent chapters move between psychoanalytic readings of law in cultural media to a cultural–legal reading of psychoanalysis is also explained.

The second chapter examines the fundamental question: why law at all? In many a romantic vision of the State dominating the aggressive nature of human beings, the yoke of anarchy stirs. But in our postmodern era, such a vision commits itself to a fundamental legal–epistemological dilemma: once you know the law, you cannot go back to a 'no law' space. This has led some theorists to follow Robert Nozick in seeking the meagre assurances of private property and open markets to regulate in the absence of a state apparatus that is too conflict-ridden, too corrupt to be remedied. However, it is the view of this chapter that such a theoretical purview misses several crucial features of the psyche of the contemporary Australian law revealed by Lacanian psychoanalysis. In the wake of this psychoanalytic reframing, this chapter proposes a commentary on law's relation to anarchy as the path to enjoying in the law.

The discussion then moves to the ontological coordinates of law in chapter three. Drawing on contemporary philosophical debates about the necessity of contingency, the impossibility of knowing, and the logics *(logos)* of order, this chapter explores the foundation of any possible imagining of an Ur-law in the wake of law's presence. Examining the debate about contingency between Slavoj Žižek and Quentin Meillassoux in detail, this chapter connects enjoyment and law to the way that law must go beyond itself as a *logos* that sees the world from a perspective rather than as a totality. Rather than fixity, this chapter underscores how contingency is vital to understanding the institutionalisation of law and its *logos*.

The fourth chapter delves deeper into the established questions of legal knowledge by examining the structure of jurisprudence as a *Wissenschaft* or interpretative science in the work of Max Weber. This discussion shows how the gap inherent to Weber's distinction of charismatic and rational authority reveals what type of satisfaction is possible through jurisprudence as a vocation. By critically discussing the limits of rational authority, this chapter moves the view of rational authority beyond an elementary reading of Weber and towards the concept of jurisprudence as *Wissenschaft* that is a science of rational limits.

Moving to a more acute assessment of the 'promise' of knowledge in the wake of jurisprudence as a *Wissenschaft*, the fifth chapter unravels the analytic of knowledge that makes legal training difficult in a university discourse. Taking the

1 As Lacan tells us in *Seminar XX*, there is no *jouissance* of the law, only the law of *jouissance*.

Wissenschaft of jurisprudence seriously as a vocation, this chapter examines the desire to enjoy knowledge that is constitutive of the university discourse imposed by the modern law school, as it increasingly becomes the only entry into the legal profession. The discussion takes aim at the nihilism of technical knowledge of the rules and how this, in itself, appears sufficient but remains fantasmatic: you can never know enough about legal knowledge.

The sixth chapter marks the end of the methodological discussion and the opening of the cultural case studies in this volume. As a text at these interstices, the discussion turns to perhaps the most culturally volatile force in the jurisprudence of justice today: restorative justice in cases of sexual assault. The discussion examines how the non-legal or para-legal process of restorative justice seeks to normalise the humanist gesture of elevating emotion as an end in itself – but at what price? The changing face of the legal profession and legal processes envisaged by restorative justice is a brave new, criminological world where law becomes the victimisation of the perpetrator and their prey. It is shown how the critical question hinges on the formulation of enjoyment at the heart of alternative dispute resolution debates that motivate the restorative justice methods.

Moving to a closer examination of the perception of transgression at the heart of alternative dispute resolution, the discussion in the seventh chapter then examines the formulation of law and transgression in the psychoanalytic philosophy of Slavoj Žižek and Franz Kafka's micro-story *The Cares of a Family Man*. This chapter is the first of the 'cultural legal case studies' in this book and it elucidates Žižek's unique and counter-intuitive formulation of law as it intersects with Kafka's tale. It also seeks to answer why Kafka's work more generally is attractive to legal philosophy.

The eighth chapter changes pace to focus on what might be termed 'the reverse of the law' or 'the other side of the law'. Through the vantage of Neil Gaiman's gothic young adult novel *Coraline*, this chapter examines questions of how authority is internalised, how fantasies of the commands of the sovereign become the glue of social discourse. This chapter offers a critical analysis of Gaiman's enterprising tale of Lovecraftian beings in alternative realities and familial blackmail. By critically evaluating this in(ter)vention of kinship, it will be shown how the story of *Coraline* develops an alternative to the normative coding of childhood imaginings as fantastical escapism. We shall see how the world of *Coraline* is not reducible to a psychical projection of the girl-child protagonist but is instead a radical move towards trying to bring to light the unnameable distortion that founds kinship and authority.

The ninth chapter ventures a return to the work of Žižek for a further discussion of the tension between the unsettling distortion and the modulation of authority. Using a comparison of the science fiction neo-noir thriller *Minority Report* and the postmodern spy tale *The Recruit*, it will be seen how the Freudian reading of authority revolves around a triptych of paternal figures that secure access to language, enjoyment and reality. However, Žižek's Lacanian return to these Freudian Fathers in *The Ticklish Subject*, *The Fragile Absolute*, *The Puppet and the Dwarf* and *The Parallax View* reveals some grave problems for those ready to enjoy as agents of law in post-modernity. This discourse examines the permutations and patricide of authority that open onto the existential world of 'homo sucker' to see whether Žižek can give some clues as to where authority will turn after the eclipse of prohibition and the colonisation of enjoyment.

The tenth chapter seeks the power of love as a contractual allegory in HBO's supernatural melodrama *True Blood*. This chapter attempts a clarification of the Lacanian concept of enjoyment beyond enjoying: *jouissance*. While *True Blood*'s Sookie Stackhouse might seem to long for the sun, she endlessly devotes herself to what is in the undergrowth of enjoyment of Bon Temps' polite civil society: vampires, werewolves, shape-shifters and more. This chapter aims to unearth the erotics of Sookie's *jouissance* – *jouis-sens*, *jouis-sans* and *j'ouïs-sens* – that allows her, and specifically her alone, access to this undergrowth of the cultural Imaginary. Particular attention will herein be paid to how this *jouissance* gives Sookie 'a time for love' in the vein of what Jacques-Alain Miller calls 'the erotics of time'.[2] Herein, it is hoped that one might imagine Sookie as having something to say back to Miller, the analyst, which emphasises a different type of temporality, another psychical feminine *jouissance*. Sookie's erotics of time will herein be shown to perforate the modes of *jouissance* in a different way than those put forward by the phallic voices within contemporary Lacanian theory such as Miller, Chiesa and Stavrakakis.

Power, nationalism and *jouissance* in China Miéville's speculative fictional novel *The City & The City* form the focus of the eleventh chapter. This chapter critically examines the construction of law in China Miéville's weird detective narrative. The discussion charts the excesses of law's embodiment in Detective Tyador Borlú of the Beszél *policzai* with and against the primordial natural law discourse of the Law of Breach, and carefully examines the ways that this Law interdicts the commons in both parts of the fictional split city Beszél-Ul Qoma. Using the psychoanalytic concept of *jouissance*, this paper unveils some of the modulations of authority presented by the novel's unusual arrangement of politics, common law and natural law.

The final chapter examines the systemic politics of enjoyment created by contractual agreement and licence arrangements for objects that commodify and sell *jouissance* on a massive scale: massively multiplayer online videogames. Taking the exemplary case of science fiction MMO *Eve Online*, this discussion locates the way players move between the socio-legal subtext created by the corporate entity of CCP Games and player interactions. Taking the semiotics of the game and metagame space seriously, this discussion explores the place of *jouissance* in player revolt, the consolidation of political power, and the very contractual obligations imposed by the game itself.

Lastly, I would like to acknowledge the prior publication of some discussions and inspiration for continuing with some debates. The discussion of law's forced

2 J.-A. Miller, 'Introduction to the Erotics of Time', B. P. Fulks (trans.), *Lacanian Ink* 24/25, 2005, p. 13.

choice first appeared in the *Griffith Law Review* 21(2) in 2012. The discussion of *The City & the City* first appeared in *Law, Culture and the Humanities* 9(1) in 2011. I am indebted to my colleagues John Mandalios, William MacNeil, Roshan de Silva Wijeyeratne and Gideon Baker for helping me to refine some of the ideas in this book in the course of informal discussions, seminars and reading groups with the School of Humanities, Griffith Law School, and the Socio-Legal Research Centre at Griffith University. The kaleidoscope of cultural legal topics in this book speaks to the intellectual strength and diversity of those groups during my time at Griffith University from 2004 to 2014.

CHAPTER 1

Reading law with Lacan

When *Le livre noir de la psychanalyse*, edited by Catherine Meyer, appeared in 2005, the world once again heard that the time of Sigmund Freud was over. By eulogising neuroscience and cognitive behaviour therapy's critique of psychoanalysis, the funeral oratory of the volume attempted to write psychoanalysis out of history. But not all were as keen to uphold the fashion of flaying Freud. Against this critique, Slavoj Žižek has asked: haven't we been here before?[1] Throughout the twentieth century, challenges to psychoanalysis, particularly Freud's classical models, came and went with peculiar repetition. Again and again the supposedly dead and outmoded discourse of psychoanalysis was attacked for being methodologically questionable but nonetheless enlivened with immense explanatory power for those who would dare to engage with it. What is so dangerous about psychoanalysis for its critics? Can we locate that which makes psychoanalysis the object of such sustained, repeated, seemingly interminable trashing?

Unlike sciences of the brain, psychoanalysis is a science of the mind. Or, to be more appropriate, it takes aim at the product of a self-conscious animal's failed attempts to find happiness in civilisation. The emphasis of psychoanalysis is on this tension between the organic and the man-made; the ancient trope of the alienation and unhomeliness of humankind allegorised by Homeric verse. Therapy in the psychoanalytic clinic does not aim to make one happy. Instead, the aim is to bring the patient or analysand closer to understanding the reconfiguration of their conscious life by civilisation. To put it somewhat simplistically, symptoms, tics and other parapraxes are just as real for the analysand as the external demands that are empirically verifiable. The challenge of the analytic session is different from case to case. However, it is coming to terms with this torsion of lived life that remains central to the processes of the clinic, despite whether I am a neurotic, pervert or in the grip of a psychosis.

Law was never far from what Freud called 'civilisation', the great motivator of parapraxic blunders. When Freud and his family fled to London at the outbreak

1 S. Žižek, 'Is Psychoanalysis Really Outmoded? Apropos the 150th Anniversary of Freud's Birth', *Journal of European Psychoanalysis* 23, 2006, pp. 3–9.

of the Second World War, his work turned from the intricacies of cases in the psychoanalytic clinic to the case of civilisation and its regime of power at large. In *Civilisation and its Discontents*, Freud traced the powers and promises of Western civilisation with his characteristic scepticism.[2] For the late Freud, civilisation was a force of collective sublimation of the organic aggressiveness of the human animal. Law is central to this process of giving up one's own welfare or self-interest for the benefit of a neighbour who may not feel especially generous but in whom one must entrust one's well-being. Freud questioned whether it was even rational to expect the golden rule of 'love thy neighbour as thy self' to manifest in another person when we ourselves know how uncomfortable or counter-productive such love can be for our own self-interest in pleasure and, ultimately, survival.

It is more than a coincidence that modern legal systems in common-law jurisdictions such as Australia, Canada, the United Kingdom, Hong Kong and the United States of America perform this function of promising happiness and future pleasure at the price of one's own individuality noted by Freud. Rather than having a particular person in mind as my neighbour, the commons of the common law creates and regiments a collectivised image of neighbours whose essential characteristic is assured by the arbitrary authority and enforcement of law. While the discourses of positive and negative liberty engaged the circle of seeking freedom from others, where these others are the condition that measures such freedom, Freud sought a somewhat simpler and more critical questioning of the *nuovo organon* that appeared in the wake of the ever-deferred pleasures of civilisation. Unlike advocates of positive liberty who may elevate law and its rights as tools of progress, Freud's new organ of thought is never quite at ease with 'progress', yet nor is it of a particularly radical political persuasion.

Written in 1929, *Civilisation and its Discontents* was out of step with many of the more fashionable modes of thought of the period. It was even unwelcome for psychoanalytic schools that had become hyper-clinical or scientistic, evolving ever more methods and modes to entreat political and economic support. By the end of the Second World War this puzzling image of psychoanalysis achieved a kind of cultural apogee in Europe and America where psychoanalysts appeared in Hollywood films as savant-experts. The 1945 film *Dead of Night* particularly exemplifies the psychological fiction of the era. In the tale, a ventriloquist called Maxwell (Michael Redgrave) and his dummy become embroiled in a series of murders. By the conclusion of the film, a therapist rushes towards Maxwell's cell while the police guarding him treat him as a crazy man with a puppet. The therapist knows all; knows that the puppet is the puppeteer, that the ventriloquist is dangerously close to losing himself in the identity of the puppet, to have his

2 First published in German under the title *Das Unbehagen in der Kultur*. *Unbehagen* is commonly translated to English as 'discomfort', but for Freud's English translator James Strachey the term 'discontent' was closer to the way that psychoanalysis views our subjective participation in a world beyond the end of our own noses while contorting our bodily selves to serve drives and desires that aren't always our own.

ordinary self ventriloquised through the substitution of his voice with the puppet's. But the therapist is too late, and Maxwell becomes ventriloquised by the voice of the puppet Hugo. The therapist then explains exactly what psychological processes came to pass for Maxwell, in a long, obscure excursus. The emphasis is extremely unpsychoanalytic in that it argues about one identity supplanting another, by insisting on the epistemological rather than empirical issues at hand.

In a curious way, *Dead of Night* appears to echo the logic of the attacks on psychoanalysis since the 1940s. Far from being a death by a thousand cuts, psychoanalysis is ventriloquised by new methods and modes that its own heritage has spawned, participated in or influenced. Psychoanalysis is now always in danger of being a guest in its own house: an odd situation that its own narrative of a decentred *nuovo organon* is all too ready to listen to.

The fate of Maxwell in *Dead of Night* also stands as a metaphor for the subject of law and psychoanalysis. In both discourses, a meta-definition used to describe a topology of relations overdetermines the thin self-interest of the individual. As the famed legal philosopher John Austin argued: without weight, without sanction, the commands of law lack the substance to compel action.[3] And similarly for Freudians like Jacques Lacan who return to Freud's texts rather than dismiss classical theories as detached from the genealogy of contemporary ideas about psychology, the compulsion to repeat an action against one's own self-interest is about the recognition and internalisation of the demand of an authority – to bear the weight of the command for oneself.[4] For both discourses, law has to be believable and not merely authoritative.[5] The *Dead of Night* narrative shows that the identity of Hugo has the power to compel the liquidation of Maxwell's self-interest in his own mind. Whatever the complementary ideas and parallel arguments between law and psychoanalysis, it is important to recognise them as distinct discourses. Therefore, readers of the intersection of these discourses, readers of this book for example, may need to engage in a little brainwashing *à la* Hugo, because reading law psychoanalytically eventually arrives at a legal reading of psychoanalysis.

While psychoanalysis in general is a useful tool for reading law, few analysts have been as embraced by academic legal inquiry as Lacan. Lacan has historically

3 As all good students of legal history know, Austin's positivist jurisprudence defined Western legal philosophy for a century. Many of the developments in legal thought during the twentieth century arose as symbiotic and parasitic reactions to Austinian positivism.

4 There is an underriding distinction here between Hartian positivism, which relies on the self-reference of the legal system to maintain the regime internalised by those subject to law, and the earlier Austinian model, which proposes a more coherent account of the legal subjects thrown into the maw of legal power who do not experience the source of law as anything more than obscure.

5 See in particular William MacNeil's insightful discussion of John Austin with Jane Austen in his *Lex Populi: The Jurisprudence of Popular Culture*, Stanford: Stanford University Press, 2007.

been one of the only analysts to be invited to continue his psychoanalytic discourse in an academic legal frame. Yet despite the popularising work of Slavoj Žižek, Lacan stands as one of the most impenetrable and obscuritanist of all Freudian thinkers. After the linguistic turn in philosophy in the wake of Ludwig Wittgenstein and logical positivists such as A. J. Ayer, obscuritanism has lost favour. Yet as Žižek and others have shown, the obscure can be far more instructive about some existential matters than can the jargon of plain language truths. Classing Lacan as either reflexively Lacanian or outwardly Freudian is one of the naming conventions that attempt to demystify his work. By designating Lacan as Lacanian, there is an attempt to signal a break with Freud, and Lacan's own auto-critique. But Lacan himself admonished any disciples announcing themselves as Lacanian: his proper class was 'Freudian' and by extension so was theirs.

The mystification of Lacan's work is part of the construction of his difficulty for new readers. Against decrying Lacan as simply difficult or incomprehensible we should instead approach him with greater regard for the context and structure of his *oeuvre*. Let us begin by approaching several common distinctions that are made about Lacan's *oeuvre* by biographers, commentators and editors of his life and work. Firstly, we must read Lacan in reverse. Contrary to current academic practices of writing a book or article and then discussing the findings in a seminar, Lacan used his seminars as the main event of his discourse. The documents compiled in the *Écrits* are exegetical-come-symbolic texts that are thick with intertextual connections to the seminars, Freud's body of work, puns, and some unusual medieval sources. Lacan is a thinker whose texts may be best read as hypertext. Secondly, we must read Lacan's seminars as qualifications and attempts to resolve problems, sometimes without success. This means that Lacan's ideas change over time and also that turns to new neologisms such as sinthome, a contraction of 'symptom' and 'Saint Thomas', are not static concepts but are instead active processes connected with the intra-textual temporality or precedent of Lacan's *oeuvre*. Thirdly, we must read Lacan as a re/turn to Freud. Rather than merely reading Lacan as a psychoanalytic critic or Freudian stooge, we instead must be aware of the double-edged quality of much of his reading of Freud. The return to Freud is as much an anchor for Lacan's discourse as it is a departure point. Fourthly, we must recognise the way that the reception of Lacan's ideas in the Anglophone world has primarily centred on the early seminars. These seminars appear in the aftermath of Lacan's doctoral thesis on paranoia in the 1920s and are an attempt to interact with the rise of structuralism.[6] More millennial writing on Lacan, particularly what has followed in the wake of Lacan's rearticulation by the prolific Žižek throughout the 1990s and 2000s, has gone some

6 Lacan's doctoral thesis was catastrophic for its subject, incarcerated actress Marguerite Pantaine. And some have speculated that it may have prolonged her incarceration. Biographer Elisabeth Roudinesco has noted that he 'borrowed' various writings and photographs from Pataine but refused to return them. Whatever the moral indignation, Pataine was incarcerated at the time and the rules of the period could bend to enable Lacan to hold onto these items.

way to deepening the collective Anglophone comprehension of Lacan's Freudian thought. Lastly, scholarship dealing with Lacan since the 1990s has tended to engage his work as a working through of deconstruction and psychoanalysis. This unique blend of ideas entertains both the textual play of deconstruction and reconstruction around an *aporia* with psychoanalytic scepticism. This final distinction presents an often-overlooked feature of psychoanalytic discourse: its rational scepticism with regards to other normative discourses. This scepticism is what makes psychoanalysis an especially attractive mode for critique, and it also enables us to take illusions, humour and irony seriously. The latter has been particularly fruitful for thinkers from Ljubljana, Slovenia, such as Žižek, Alenka Zupančič, Mladen Dolar and Renata Salecl and an international cultural-legal studies movement including William MacNeil, Peter Goodrich, Jeanne Schroeder, Desmond Manderson, Juliet Rogers and Alison Young.

The changing location of Lacan's famous *le Séminaire* offers some insight into why psychoanalysis and law are discourses that can be critically allied to produce new readings of one another. The seminars are generally credited with showcasing Lacan's re/turn to Freud, yet they also demonstrate his growing relevance to the intellectual culture of Paris and tensions with the increasingly narrow definition of what was medical in the middle to late twentieth century.

Lacan began *le Séminaire* as an event at his apartment in Paris in 1951. He then moved the location to the Sainte-Anne hospital from 1952 until the politics of psychoanalytic associations and the medical establishment ended its tenure there in 1963. In 1964 the event moved to the university grounds of the École normale superieur, where it stayed until 1969, at which time it moved to the Sorbonne. The Sorbonne shift is significant for the connection between law and psychoanalysis, as the seminars during this period were hosted by the Law Faculty and held at the Place du Panthéon. The location of *le Séminaire* changed again in 1979 as Lacan's performances became increasingly interrupted by his multi-infarct dementia. This loss of speech left Lacan grasping for words during his late seminars; it was painful for his enamoured audiences to watch, as some of his past analysands report.[7]

The decade of seminars hosted by the Law Faculty of the Sorbonne are notable for their very untraditional topics for both law and psychoanalysis. The inaugural seminar, *Séminaire XVII L'envers de la psychoanalysis*, focuses on matters of social upheavals and quixotic group identification where a collective identity subsumes individual identity in the object of collective fascination yet does not exhibit any regard for the well-being of the collective, e.g. fans at football matches. Topics of the other seminars hosted by the Law Faculty focus on the primacy and artifice of the symbolic order, the relationship of fantasy to temporality, and the space outside the normative order of law – psychoses – and the blunder one must make to stay inside the symbolic order that law epitomises. The latter point,

7 A number of analysands express their anguish at seeing Lacan's speech deterioriate in the documentary film *Jacques Lacan la psychoanalyse réinventée* (2001, ARTE France) co-written by Elisabeth Roudinesco and Elisabeth Kapnist.

while of interest to legal philosophy since Hobbes, has not found an easy fit within doctrinal technicalities, partly due to the nature of teaching law as a university discipline, as is discussed in later chapters.

While there is damning evidence of Lacan's terrible clinical practice, his ideas, particularly around conceiving of fantasy and desire, received attention from the then intellectual master of Paris in the 1960s, Louis Althusser. Whatever the clinical disasters of Lacan's practice, his ideas may not have attracted the attention of the Law Faculty had Althusser not made inroads for Lacan some years earlier. This elevation of Lacan by Althusser has been explored in depth by Elizabeth Roudinesco in her multiple biographies of Lacan. The core argument is that Althusser's ideology-with-a-human-face accords neatly with Lacan's view of fantasy in the seminars of the 1960s. However, by the end of the decade of seminars at the Law Faculty, Lacan's position had further developed beyond the soft socialism of Althusser.

Lacan's teaching did not progress in a straight line. Its many twists and turns were partly spurred by Lacan's auto-critique and, at other times, by the politics of the medical and psychoanalytic establishments. This openness and movement with Lacan's *oeuvre* 'returned in the real' when Lacan died in 1981, as a schism erupted amongst his followers, each claiming to have the authentic message of the master. Few figures engaged in critical discourses today have elicited such powerful responses from their disciples. When Lacan passed away, as many as thirty-four associations appeared, each arguing that they embodied the true spirit of their master.[8] The curious feature in this multiplication of schools and traditions was the frequent absence of a sceptical spirit from the essential claim of authenticity. It had instead been replaced by a rabid belief in and allegiance to interpretation rather than analysis. Proclamations of a 'right way' to read Lacan still ring out today as we saw from the four qualifications above – *mea culpa*.

The politics of psychoanalysis 'outside' the clinic is still multiple, internecine and one of difference today. Sceptics attack literature departments for their use of psychoanalysis, even though its theories have condensed in common language and metaphor, and remain a way in which some writers read themselves. In law and literature there is a niche embracing of psychoanalysis as a way of reading law; it is an alternative path, a fellow traveller that rejects philosophical totalisation or reductive formalism, connecting the philosophy of law to currents in contemporary European thought. In the history of ideas, film studies and literature have tended to prefer the structuralist and post-structuralist Lacan of the 1950s and 1960s, where the Unconscious functions like a language. There are corollaries to themes of the gaze, the imaginary and affect here. In more recent years law and literature researchers have tended to prefer concepts and processes from the middle and late periods of Lacan's work, such as the Real and *jouissance*. This book is

8 For a broader account see E. Roudinesco, *Jacques Lacan: An Outline of a Life and History of a System of Thought*, Oxford: Polity Press, 1999.

part of the law and literature discussion and has an avowed interest in thinking through enjoyment and *jouissance*.

Reading law with Lacan hinges on the logic of the Moebius strip. The twist of this logic is that just when one thinks one is in the middle of demand, one finds oneself needing to address the other side and, in so doing, becomes stuck in this other side. Neither side directly addresses the other. Instead, they are two sides of the same problem. In terms of reading law with Lacan, while we may begin to read law psychoanalytically, it will eventually arrive at the other side of the discourse: a legal reading of psychoanalysis. From the vantage of a traditional form/content distinction, this is a paradox. Yet this binary distinction relies on forcing content to fit the frame, or at least codes the framing as a predatory structure laying in wait to slowly capture and digest randomly selected content. Content is here the life of the frame, yet the frame is given all of the explanatory power. What if, on the contrary, particular content already entertains many different modes of explanation? Rather than utilising psychoanalysis as a universal frame for many different topics, the discussion of enjoyment in this volume is instead engaging enjoyment through its possibility for a psychoanalytic, philosophical and legal reading. Rather than textuality, we have inter-textuality. And is this not also the common construction of legal cases in matters of statutory interpretation where what appear to be random events invite a legal reading to become coherent series of actions before the law …? My aim in this exegesis is thus not to explain away enjoyment but to consider enjoyment as part of the way that we might access the puzzle that is the legal construction of enjoyment in other texts, where we can read 'law' as something that rearticulates the organic and lives the life of a legal imaginary outside the given legal boundaries, a nomological unconscious.

CHAPTER 2

Law's forced choice (to enjoy)

When thinking about how we live with a rule of law, it is often fashionable to propose a myth of a time before the law came to be that retroactively legitimates the present constellation of values and ideas that imagines this prehistory.[1] Questions hang over this prehistory of law like a pall: how could things have been done differently? Would they have resulted in a different order, better or worse laws? What might humans be like without the corrupting luxury of civilisation and its laws? Common to all such questioning is how the open horizon of the future in this time before law becomes historicised as a *necessary* building block towards the rule of law, only to necessitate some future involvement with the law in the present.

Whether it is the social contractarian tradition stretching back to Jean-Jacques Rousseau and earlier, the original position of John Rawls, or the story of proprietary rights of Robert Nozick, the attempt to get behind the existential façade of the rule of law in the present leads these and other thinkers to commit themselves to an 'ontology of the present', their present position from which they project their thought experiments. But what such a move leaves oblique is the way in which the symbolic gesture of enjoying the rule of law in the present, be it through compliance, obligation, duty or rights, must be lived and experienced in the broad range of all too human responses. The attempt to get behind the law is thus intimately bound to the limits of the conditions of the present in which the rule of law is understood. The problem therefore arises that the rule of law exists without an index in history. This categorises our access to the history of the rule of law as intellectually *speculative*.

Such speculative inquiry cannot be restricted to historical and hypothetical scenes, however. Speculation is constitutive play in the way we philosophise about the law. Without speculation the social contract could not be entertained by

1 My thanks go to the reviewers and editors of the *Griffith Law Review* for their feedback and recommendations on an earlier version of this discussion. See D. Hourigan, 'Postmodern Anarchy in the Modern Legal Psyche: Law, Anarchy and Psychoanalytic Philosophy', *Griffith Law Review* 21(2), 2012.

Rousseau, the original position could not be deduced by Rawls, and the possession of proprietary right discussed by Nozick is impossible to construct. Speculation enables us to access the enjoyment in abiding with a rule of law. This is the lynchpin of the Rawlsian and Nozickian positions, for example, wherein the speculation on a time before the law is an attempt to portend a future enjoyment of law, albeit of very different stripes. What such an approach to enjoyment suggests is that enjoying in a rule of law is as much about the enjoyment as it is about the law. What is at stake for speculations on law is therefore pleasure for law, being for law, *enjoyment before law*.

The interplay between these three senses of enjoyment form a speculative sensibility of law as sublime image, real beyond reality, and symbolic exchange. But note here that it is only in the latter, symbolic exchange, that law appears attached to the normative ideal taught in doctrine courses at law schools or published in law reports. The other two senses direct our attention elsewhere, towards an image of the law that ruptures the legal frame and that which remains outside of law and is nonetheless subject to law's attempt to domesticate it as part of legal reality. Rupture of and resistance/dedication to law echoes the anarchic potential of enjoying law. And, moreover, this anarchy is party to the symbolic exchange that maintains the believable veneer of the rule of law by facilitating its internalisation as an image that is gazed upon by legal subjects and the elevation of the banal material reality of the law into a thing that is in the legal subject more than themselves. Yet anarchy itself is a spectre of law, it haunts its formal structure with fantasies of its overturning or dissolution by way of strife, crisis, or constitutional politics.

Traditionally, views on the law and anarchy are split across the general political spectrum from right to left and back again. To the right we find thinkers such as Nozick proposing a type of private-property anarchism where property is mostly stripped of government regulation and becomes its own mechanism of social and legal validation. To enforce such a rule of property one needs a private force or army at ones disposal. Such a mercenary attitude to law enforcement seems contrary to the utopic liberalism that is the thrust of Nozick's arguments.[2] Yet logically played out, this libertarian scenario commits itself to a collapse of jurisdiction and provisional power and creates a state that is just as violent as the really existing state that it is supposed to substitute.

Juxtaposed to the views of the libertarian right are arguments for a return to the commons by the new left. Following Hardt and Negri's *Empire* (2001) and *Multitude* (2005) and works by other Italian political philosophers such as Roberto Esposito and to a lesser extent Giorgio Agamben, this return to the commons portents to provide a new socio-legal link on the basis of shared power in the space of a common municipality or new communism.[3] Where the libertarian

2 R. Nozick, 'The State', in E. Stringham (ed.), *Anarchy and the Law*, Washington D.C.: The Independent Institute, 2007, pp. 193–217.

3 I rely here on discussions with Prof. Timothy C. Campbell (Cornell University) after his keynote at the 2009 *Trans(l)egalité* conference hosted by Griffith University, the

vision collapses jurisdiction and power by confusing the form of property as its substantial content, the new left's new communism repeats and reinvents the very political apparatus that it critiques. In the new commons we do not escape law, but rather law once again becomes a fiction of the shared social world: in no one person do we find the seat of law's power, but projected as a totality together, in their being-with-one-another-in-common, the subjects of the commons function as if the common law exists.[4] In critical terms, the new left's vision of a new communism of the commons highlights an all too familiar deadlock between the shared common experience and the difference between such experience and the subjective perspective upon the rule of law that insists on such egalitarian sharing, rendering the latter a legal fiction that legitimates social order.[5] Such fictions are today the hallmark of any society claiming legal authority, and how a population behaves in accordance with the law or not is perhaps a sign of the psychic problem of believing in or distancing oneself from these fictions.[6]

What neither the libertarian view nor the new left vision provide, however, is a method to analyse the garden of manias, fantasies and other structural psychic phenomena created by the psycho-social relation founding both property and the commons. This is not to propose yet another psychology of the law. Rather, the critical point here is to examine how anarchy is a speculative phenomenon of the structure of the law as an aberration, an artificial but nonetheless objective order.

Psychoanalysis, particularly of the post-Freudian or Lacanian variety, is becoming a more common sight in the contemporary study of law and culture, legal history and legal theory. Unlike philosophies of law, psychoanalysis resists inventing a grand metaphysical totality that secures law's conservatism.[7] Rather, psychoanalysis is a technique for reading, analysing and interrupting the all-too-smooth and arbitrary operation of the law.[8] Because of its fascination with the order of the signifier, Lacanian psychoanalysis is particularly pertinent to this discussion.[9]

Law and Literature Association of Australia and the Law and Society Association of Australia and New Zealand, and also on transcripts from the *Commonalities: Theorizing the Common in Contemporary Italian Thought* conference hosted by Cornell University in 2010.

4 C. Debreuil, *The Right to Water: From Concept to Implementation*, Marseilles: World Water Council, 2006, p. 94; R. Esposito, *Communitas*, T. C. Campbell (trans.), Stanford: Stanford University Press, 2010, pp. 14–16.

5 S. Žižek, *In Defense of Lost Causes*, London: Verso, 2008, pp. 337–338.

6 R. Salecl, *The Tyranny of Choice*, London: Profile Books, 2011, pp. 22–28.

7 P. Goodrich, *Oedipus Lex: Psychoanalysis, History, Law*, Oakland: University of California Press, 1995, pp. 240–247.

8 W. MacNeil, *Lex Populi: The Jurisprudence of Popular Culture*, Stanford: Stanford University Press, 2007, p. 10.

9 P. Goodrich and D. Gray Carlson, 'Introduction' in P. Goodrich and D. Gray Carlson (eds), *Law and the Postmodern Mind*, Ann Arbor: University of Michigan Press, 1998, p. 6; A. Lysy-Stevens, 'Unconscious and Interpretation', *Hurly-Burly* 1, 2009, p. 79; S. Miller, 'Lacan at the Limits of Legal Theory: Law, Desire, and Sovereign Violence', *UMBR(a): Ignorance of the Law*, 2003, pp. 88–89.

According to Jacques Lacan, the fundamental point about any law, whether civil or common, express or construed, is that it is composed of signifiers.[10] At base: the law is a signifier. But what does this mean? Here it is instructive to recall that Lacan's return to the work of Sigmund Freud heralded not only a reinvigoration of psychoanalysis but also a response to deconstruction and what the Anglophony dubbed 'post-structuralism', a vague amalgam of many different continental European schools of thought from the 1960s to the 1990s that includes, among others, the work of Roland Barthes (semiotics), Jean-François Lyotard (aesthetic postmodernism), Gilles Deleuze (immanent postmodernism), Jacques Derrida (deconstruction), Edward Saïd (postcolonial studies), Michel Foucault (historical genealogy) and Julia Kristeva (semiotics and psychoanalysis).[11] This philological point is significant because it provides a context for the way that Lacan emphasises the signifier as shifting, fragmented, metaphoric, metonymic and chained. For Lacan, signifiers exist in a chain of signification wherein a given signifier refers to the other signifiers in the chain to generate its meaning.[12] This network of signification or 'symbolic order' operates through endless differentiation.[13] This is the space in which a name or symbolic title is alienated through the misrecognition of the symbolic order: it never says what something is, only what it is not. What is meaningful is thus always shifting, always a point of difference, always portended by the signifier but never equivalent to the signifier.[14]

The symbolic game of difference signifies the meaning of a sign. But for this game to succeed, the subject of language must submit to this symbolic belief in metaphor whereupon something is something else: Signifier$_1$ is Signifier$_2$.[15] The belief in these symbolic fictions infers a 'body of meaning' or symbolic Other to whom these beliefs are addressed in language.[16] The grammar of signifiers thus rests not in the subject's consensual hallucination but in the submission to a symbolic order that counters subjective needs with symbolic demands.[17]

10 J. Lacan, *Écrits*, B. Fink (trans.), New York: W. W. Norton & Company, 2006, p. 240.

11 This arbitrary amalgamating of thinkers and methods is epitomised by 'Graphesis: Perspectives in Literature and Philosophy', M.-R. Logan (ed.), *Yale French Studies* 52, 1975.

12 J. Lacan, *The Seminar of Jacques Lacan, Book XI: Four Fundamental Concepts of Psychoanalysis*, J.-A. Miller (ed.) and A. Sheridan (trans.), New York: W. W. Norton & Company, 1998, pp. 210–212.

13 Lacan, *op. cit.*, pp. 682–683.

14 A. Zupančič, 'When Surplus Enjoyment Meets Surplus Value', in J. Clemens and R. Grigg (eds), *Jacques Lacan and the Other Side of Psycho-Analysis*, Durham, NC: Duke University Press, 2006, pp. 160–161.

15 J.-A. Miller, 'Interpretation in Reverse', in V. Voruz and B. Wolf (eds), *The Later Lacan: An Introduction*, Albany: State University of New York Press, 2007, p. 7.

16 M. Dolar, *A Voice and Nothing More*, Cambridge, MA: The MIT Press, 2006, pp. 16–17.

17 L. Chiesa, *Subjectivity and Otherness: A Philosophical Reading of Lacan*, Cambridge, MA: The MIT Press, 2007, p. 48.

From the Lacanian position, the subject is in some relation to that which is meaningful or desirable.[18] Such desire is symbolic rather than a natural basis of the human animal. The Other of this symbolic order thus appears to 'know' what the subject wants, irrespective of what the subject intends. This has its echo in the trial process where the sentencing judge signifies the meaning of the charges brought before the court in their sentence. The important point is that without this game of symbolic fictions the judge would be unbelievable; *law would be unbelievable.*[19] Hence the letters of the law, its messages composed of signifiers, 'always' arrive at their destination – their legal sense.[20] If they do not, then the symbolic misrecognition fails and the court ceases to retain its juridico-legal meaning as accepted by those who are subject to, for and by the court.[21] Yet is this collapse of symbolic misrecognition an avenue to think of anarchy in psychoanalytic terms? Or, to rephrase, can the subject desire anarchy?

To answer this question we must turn to the delimiting question of desire: 'What do you want?' *(Che vuoi?)* The form of this question iterates upon the metaphoric structure of meaning wherein $sign_1$ is $sign_2$. But to whom is *'Che vuoi?'* addressed? The big Other of the symbolic order, a symbolic apparition of the order of differences between signifiers who proffers commands and prohibitions. In the symbolic form of the signifier such questions of desire take aim at the Other's satisfaction, to the extent that they are questions reliant upon the belief in the symbolic order and what it renders meaningful.[22]

Because the order of the symbolic is one of difference, all further differences offered in reply to *'Che vuoi?'* amount to the same symbolic lack touched upon by the question of desire. The Other's answer is thus restricted to the identical inverse form of the subject's own question of desire, 'what do you want?'[23] This point is a further renovation of the concept that for a signifier or part of law to become meaningful it must draw the subject into a symbolic space that then reflects meaning – *vis-à-vis* the subject's message – back to the subject.[24] Yet the meaningfulness of this reply requires a minimal difference be established between the subject and the Other. The repetition of the question's symbolic form suggests that the question of desire must rest on something extra, beyond the substantial content of the message.

This something extra in the question of desire *(objet petit á)* can be observed in the basic question that underlies discussions of law and anarchy: addressing

18 Lacan, *op. cit.*, p. 108.

19 S. Žižek, 'Death and the Maiden', in E. Wright and E. Wright (eds), *The Žižek Reader*, London: Blackwell, 1999, p. 219.

20 S. Žižek, *Enjoy your Symptom! Jacques Lacan In Hollywood and Out, Revised Edition*, London: Routledge, 2001, p. 12.

21 *Ibid.*, pp. 16–17.

22 J. Lacan, *The Seminar of Jacques Lacan, Book III: The Psychoses*, J.-A. Miller (ed.) and R. Grigg (trans.), London: Routledge, 1993, p. 48.

23 S. Žižek, *Violence*, London: Profile Books, 2008, p. 74.

24 Lacan, *op. cit.*, pp. 228–229.

the law, the subject asks, 'do you want anarchy?' and the law responds, 'do *you* want anarchy?' The minimal difference here flags the fantasy coordinates that are involved and yet are not part of the empirical symbolic content of the message. Reading the question positively, the question of anarchy propounds the overthrow of law, as though in its reply the law flays itself, sunders its own condition by tempting the subject with its dissolution. In the negative, the question of anarchy is much more orthodox and familiar: the subject admonishes the law and the law tyrannises the subject's questioning. Both thinly fantastic readings demonstrate how a simple adjustment in the fantasmatic coordinates of the message drastically alter the status of law as such and always impute an intention to it.[25]

A further point here is that to unreflective reasoning, the equating of law with anarchy is impossible or 'mad' unless one is willing to suggest a pre-legal space by retroactively establishing a minimal difference between the legal order of today and a past that we only have fantasmatic access to.[26] The view that repealing legal order invites anarchy establishes the fiction that anarchy is always lying in wait. More strongly, if repealing the law is said to lead us back to a non-legal space, we again commit to a fiction that we can somehow escape the law's conditioning of our view of 'not law'.[27] The Lacanian formula for the arrival of the letter in its inverted form thus demonstrates the always-already symbolic nature of anarchy if it is taken in a non-legal sense, that it is always part of the law.

Naïvely we can assume that law in general has some substantial content to it, a legal meaning or purpose and so forth. As noted above, such meanings are sustained by symbolic differences, the law as it is composed by different elements that are all unlike each other but that seem to circulate and function according to an order that no one element of law can be unto itself. These associations are fictions in the strict psychoanalytic sense that they stage an objective fantasy that operates independently of the human subjects who encounter the law, but can only be accessed through the imaginative symbolic capacity of legal subjects. The law is thus not humanistic but rather radically anti-humanitistic; it does not negate the humanity of legal subjects so much as such humanity will only matter to the law if it can be 'named' by a signifier common to its signification as law. This naming does not describe anything, but instead delineates what is named from other elements in the symbolic network of legal meanings and legal fictions.

The position of the law is not merely expressed across statute, case law and common law *stare decisis* but is also posited as thinkable in very particular ways. There are two common approaches to law's thetic positing. The first is a construal wherein law is a quilting of substantial legal and para-legal fragments that function as a type of normalised disorder or anarchy that is given normative value

25 This discussion targets the speculative construction of anarchy by the law's own operations. Other authors have attempted to examine how the ethos of anarchy inflects this question of desire, including Victor Yarros, Henry David Thoreau and David Miller.

26 J. Lacan, *Le Séminaire, livre XIX: ... ou pire*, Paris: Seuil, 2011, p. 70.

27 I have discussed this previously in D. Hourigan, 'Breach! The Law's *Jouissance* in *The City & The City*', *Law, Culture and the Humanities* 9, 2013, pp. 10–12.

by the quilting of purpose that is, in strict clinical terms, a 'delusional metaphor' for what the law is and does.[28] The second view, in what we might term a kind of jurisprudential modernism, rejects para-legal materials or metaphors of purpose in favour of what is literally 'there' in the formal writ of the law itself. This fidelity to the law-as-signifier maintains the Otherness of the law that prohibits disorder or anarchy entirely; anarchy is out of the question, unthinkable, there are only the law and what the law says. In both instances what can be ascertained is a certain psychic economy of access to the law.

If the law is thus posited as either normalised anarchy or the symbolic order, what does this tell us about its relation to anarchy? In its vulgar definition as the absence of order or a type of mayhem, anarchy stands out as an antithetical negation of both positions mentioned above. For the purposive construal that quilts together the symbolic fragments of law, politics and culture, anarchic mayhem is a mischief that the law protects against by incarnating powers, jurisdictions and the difference between the two: power comes from jurisdictions, jurisdictions come from the purpose of having law, the incarnate powers of legal subjects such as rights and duties thus ward off anarchic mayhem from this legal reality. Anarchy is here an imagined, fuzzy totality that is law's other: it is everything that does not inhere to this delusional order of purposive construal. Conversely for the second more literal position, anarchic mayhem is a diffuse phenomenon among many phenomena that occur outside the law. The law operates to protect us from this dark continent of grotesque things that obey no law. Both of these positions attempt to distance anarchy from law although they go about it in mutually exclusive ways: the purposive position centres on the empowerment of the legal subject, while the literalist position has the law maintain order contra the anarchic 'outside' of law. The definition of anarchy by either position is vague. Anarchy may be outside law, but this then begs the question if it is therefore a rejection of law and imbued with some purpose that partakes in legal reality.

Defined in its strong meaning, anarchy is the rejection of law. This emphasises the thrust of anarchy as the antithesis of law, it is law's negation but also ultimately without substance in the absence of a legal order to reject. This suggests at least speculatively that legal order constitutes/is constituted by its relation to anarchy. For the purposive and literalist positions this appears equally valid: both must tarry with the negative image of law proposed by anarchy. The law must always tarry with its negation by anarchy insofar as it is a remainder of law that stands for what law is not. This negation of law is constitutive of law's existence and intelligibility because it facilitates, as Derrida, and Hegel before him, knew, the delimiting of a thesis.

The constant mediation and negotiation of anarchy by the law is perhaps only possible insofar as the law exhibits a reflective dimension that makes it aware of its conditions and limits. Yet the incarnate purposive position elaborates a synthesis

28 B. Fink, *A Clinical Introduction to Lacanian Psychoanalysis*, London: Harvard University Press, 1997, p. 107.

that posits and then rediscovers anarchy. To argue from the purposive position against anarchy, the law is generated by its negation of anarchy through attending to some purpose. Here the law retroactively posits anarchy as some mischief to be remedied by something that is avowedly part of this anarchic pre-legal space. The law is not distinct from anarchy but rather reacts to it parasitically. Purposive construal's reactive process founds the law before it on anarchic mischief, meaning that the law is not distinct to anarchy but is instead to be read as a normalised disorder, a type of 'pre-order' that attempts to regulate all other disorders; a radical anarchy as the rule. The opposition between law and anarchy thus becomes a kind of empty gesture that assures the symbolic efficacy of the rule of law by obscuring its radical disorderliness.

The dialectic of law and anarchy for the purposive position's radical treatment of anarchy does not, however, assist a literalist reasoning that is instead mired in the elaboration of endless differentiation, endless negations of what is and is not in the law. The literal position remains trapped in the fantasy that there is something substantive to be taken away from the rule of law. While this seems empirically or sociologically sound, i.e. the law has a calculable impact on how people can live their lives, it misses that for the rule of law to be effective it cannot remain a merely external force but must be internalised by its subjects so that they know what the limits are. The wager of 'ignorance of the law is no excuse' suggests that those ruled by law would do better to acquire legal knowledge than to remain ignorant of it. Yet it is most unlikely that law schools could cope with entire populations gracing their halls. The literalist position thus silently reinforces what Marxism calls 'class struggle'; those with access to enter law school are rewarded with legal knowledge. In the absence of attending law school, the knowledge to be somehow gained through social osmosis or other indirect means smacks of a modernism that suggests that law is somehow a deep structure or mathematics of society, blind to class war. Such law has trouble moving from formal to substantive changes because the law stands as a repressive commodity only able to be bargained with by those with enough knowledge-capital. Legal knowledge is thus an interminable problem for the moral conscience – i.e. notions of fairness, reasonableness, social utility, equity, unconscionability, etc. – of law for the literalist position.

What changes between the vantage of the purposive and the literal view is not the law but rather the perspective on the law, how the law is apprehended by and involves the nomological psyche of the judge or other legal subject. For law to function as a synthetic construct the anarchy that is normalised as legal order must lose its anarchic tinge. It does this through the well-known arbitrary gesture of enforcing its order with negotiations that will always have an end point. Arbitration and construction offer an important glimpse of the negation of anarchy by law disappearing from view: we all know there is law and that which is not law, but the point is that when we talk about the law this mediation between the legal and the para-legal vanishes. This vanishing is not an elision in the same way that literalist reasoning portrays the law as endless negations of the anarchic thing-without-law to be constantly arranged and specified. Rather, the purposive reasoning presents an extremely different view of the law with a purpose.

In proper dialectical fashion then it must be asked what negates this new thesis of law? Where exactly is anarchy in this arrangement and what are the negations that operate as invitations to anarchy therein? The first point to return to is that the law here is a normalised anarchy. This effectively means that any approach to anarchy in other than its normalised form as the law is not beyond the borders of the law but at its very core. If anarchy is not the law, incomprehensible to the law, but is at the same time part of the law, it is otherwise to be known as a symptom of the law. Anarchy today is a symptom of the law. The task of law is thus to enjoy in this symptom in a legal way, to give it legal meaning and legal definition, to make socio-legal sense of it.

Demands for anarchy as no law are thus thoroughly legal demands insofar as they reinstate the order of law by inviting its negation. Calls for anarchy in this way are not absolutely free in the sense of philosophical idealism but are instead tyrannies to yet another universal legal ordering. This is the modern twist to the dialectic of the law: once you know the dialectical form of law, you cannot go back.

From the above, it is supposed that anarchy today must handle a fundamental epistemological problem: once you know the law, you cannot go back. There is no metalanguage for anarchy theorists to rely upon in postmodern jurisprudence. The species of anarchy that is ruled by the market is of a species of anarchist thought that fits with a modern rather than postmodern frame. The useful psychoanalytic insight here is that the law is all too capable of disrupting itself as though its order is in fact a disorder.

This is an admittedly speculative critique of the law, but it is at the same time an important avenue to explore because it renders visible a range of complex structural issues for modern legal knowledge. Anarchy in the present is not outside the law. Radically normalised, anarchy is 'the law', and the repression that forgets this in modern literalist reasoning risks repressing this traumatic encounter with disorder at the heart of the modern Australian legal system.

CHAPTER 3

Law and contingency

In the previous chapter we observed the way in which anarchy is outside itself as law. This raises a deeper philosophical issue as to the way in which law is not universal but forever attending to particular matters from within and without. Actions that people take, promises that entities make, possibilities for unconscionable catastrophe, and inequitable travesty are all themes of areas of life where law promulgates its discourse. What makes law more than just a tool, however, is that it is a radically normalised anarchy of sorts, and that this exterior of law is constantly changing while remaining part of the most intimate of legal concerns: the logical cohesion of law in the face of contingency. The immanent changes spawned by liberal societies and representative democracies, such as new statutes, amendments, and social identities for example, create a persistent contingency for legal meaning and the coherency of lawful enjoyment or enjoyment of law. Yet far from shying away from this contingency or treating it as a dangerous thing that must be curtailed, modern law continues to embrace this chaos with doctrines such as precedent. Contingency is necessary for common law developing in the course of historical time and yet even statutes must attend to some historical moment through their intended meaning from the legislature. What then is this contingency, this moment that materialises law?

Turning to current debates about contingency, we can see that it is not only an existential issue of law interacting with the lives of people. The way that existence comes forth to be enjoyed in the first place remains the prize for those willing to think through what makes the existence of any stripe persist in the legal frame. This ontological emergence of existence is the deeper philosophical foundation of law as a social and political force that contorts, produces and distorts enjoyment. More particularly, law reform commissions and law schools are forms of what the ancient Greeks termed '*logos*': sites of gathering together to study and discuss in a rational manner. Talking about the existence of law is not merely nomological: it is about the ontological contingency at the heart of law's emergence and operation in existence as part of *logos*.

Recent upheavals in modern thought have made *logos* a problematic concept, however. Quentin Meillassoux's discussion of contingency has been a paramount force in destabilising the assured stability of ratiocination that technical discourses such as law abide by. In this chapter we will seek to examine the contingency upon which law rests by engaging with an ongoing debate between Meillassoux and psychoanalytic philosopher Slavoj Žižek. Particular attention will be paid to some logics of causation, particularly Meillassoux's weighty critique of correlationalism.

Much contemporary legal philosophy has dealt with problems of existence *vis-à-vis* law, the ontology of legal forms and fictions, and so on. However, little work has attended to the properly philosophical discourse of contingency and chaos that has pervaded Western philosophy more broadly since the turn of the twenty-first century. This chapter is a diversion into these issues so as to try and ascertain some speculative basis for the discussion of jurisprudence as a *Wissenschaft* in the next chapter.

Meillassoux's philosophical discussion of Chaos in the polemic *After Finitude* has invigorated the discussion of the necessity of contingency when contemplating existence in its essential status: as Being.[1] Meillassoux's examination of the chaotic necessity of contingency is an attempt to think through that most ancient of philosophical questions: why is there something rather than nothing? Yet where Meillassoux's argument arrives by the close of *After Finitude* is, for commentators such as Žižek, a return to some unorthodox readings of Hegel and Schelling.

The cutting, speculative critique of *logos* as an arbitrary totality based upon the withdrawal from Chaos by Meillassoux is examined at length by Žižek in Appendix B of Adrian Johnston's *Badiou, Žižek, and Political Transformations*. Žižek's argument herein raises some interesting questions about not only the hermeneutics and marginalia of Meillassoux's interpretations of thinkers such as Kant and Hegel, but also, and more importantly, the mode of philosophical speculation itself. To understand this link between Meillassoux's elaboration of Chaos and Žižek's appended critical comments, three basic features will be made clear in the following discussion: the Chaos argued for by Meillassoux makes the case for an atemporal chaotic contingency that (un)grounds any possible *logos*; the movement from Chaos to the *logos* of Being is read by Žižek to be a 'mad act' of withdrawal from the maddening endless night of Chaos; and Žižek frames this shift from the (un)grounding of Chaos to the *logos* of Being in its earlier Schellingian variation wherein this supposes a philosophical subject (a being who can speculate retroactively on the mad act of withdrawal from Chaos) who obsessively returns to the moment of contingency in the analysis of *logos*. We have already seen how this Schellingian logic operates in the structure of law as radically normalised anarchy that has withdrawn from itself yet endlessly returns to the contingency that spawned it in the central notion of the rule of law.

While the first two points outlined above are exegetical, the obsessional subject presented by Žižek's critical view of Meillassoux reveals the dangerous potential

1 Existence in its totality of existing as such. European philosophy after Heidegger often takes this thesis as the basis for all things; there is nothing that does not have existence as an aspect beyond nothingness itself. Logically speaking, Being obliterates difference. Meillassoux's project makes space for difference anew.

for Meillassoux's (and Žižek's) analysis to be appropriated by the political interpretations of post-secular philosophy. This possibility to be appropriated by one's theoretical opponents is a point that Johnston's *Badiou, Žižek, and Political Transformations* labours over at length, but what is useful to note here is that Johnston vouches for a kind of forcing *(forçage)* that moves from theory to practice, from the contingent necessity of a subject to the contingent possibility for an act; from jurisprudence to a decision. And yet, as we shall see, such a move is plotted on an obsessional course by Meillassoux's reading of contingency. Before we can arrive at such an elaboration, however, it is first necessary to turn to the basis of Meillassoux's 'contingency': the mad act of withdrawal from Chaos in Meillassoux's speculative realist approach to *logos*.

In *After Finitude*, Meillassoux's examination of contingency reveals a chaos that is both primordial and hyper-realised: the thinking subject becomes 'the purely intelligible chaos that underlies every aspect [of phenomena]'.[2] The confrontation with the possibility of contradiction opens onto a chaos that is terrifyingly ever-present. However, such an ontological Chaos is not present without being. Indeed, one gets the feeling that Meillassoux's reading of (the illusion of second order) contradiction suggests that *being is chaotic*; inducing an anxiety that drives the philosophical subject towards a speculative reasoning. And herein philosophical, although non-metaphysical, speculation is embraced by Meillassoux as the path to understanding the foundations of the reason that recognises existence apart from the conditions of the thing-in-itself and its dogmatic given-ness in Kant's transcendental apperception.

What makes Meillassoux's *After Finitude* such an important work is that it turns the all too regular philosophical reasoning of existence on its head. The reading of Chaos endorsed by Meillassoux exhibits an unusual sensitivity to non-being, a sensitivity that colours much of the discussion in the latter part of the volume. Herein it is important to note that, at times, this reading enters into an elaborative mode with such analytical precision that is hard to not view it as a form of minimalism: 'The necessity of the contingency of the entity imposes the necessary existence of the contingent entity.'[3] Such a mode of elaboration enables the discussion of Chaos in *After Finitude* to bring forward an ambit limited to the strict bounds of the task at hand. Chaos, however, seems to permeate Meillassoux's svelte analysis with a speculative pulse.

One can observe this rhythm of Chaos in Meillassoux's stated commitment to 'a *logos* of contingency, which is to say, a reason emancipated from the principle of reason – a *speculative form of the rational* that would no longer be a *metaphysical reason*.'[4] The *logos* of which Meillassoux speaks is not one that iterates the gathering together of facts that a study of something implies. Rather, this *logos* is a contingent

2 Q. Meillassoux, *After Finitude: An Essay on the Necessity of Contingency*, R. Brassier (trans.), London: Continuum, 2008, p. 83.

3 *Ibid.*, p. 76.

4 *Ibid.*, p. 77.

kernel of force that draws out speculative threads of inquiry. Chaos is herein bound up with a scathing critique of what Meillassoux perceives as strong and weak correlationalisms, modes of philosophical (post-Kantian) inquiry that bind existence (determinism) and inexistence (possibility) to the transcendental apperception of the subject. The problem with correlationalism, according to Meillassoux, is that it is a way of reasoning that only remains valid so long as 'facts' discovered by science about the universe remain within the horizon of the subject; that is, the conditions of the Kantian transcendental.[5] Ancestral statements about the beginning of the universe, the origins of life, and so forth, are not amenable to this correlationalist position because they are events outside the supposed self-perception of the subject-in-the-world-perceived; they stand prior to any perceiving subject as such. Meillassoux is thus forced to return to the formulation of being that can manage the chaotic necessity of these statements of ancestrality and origin.

The return to the instantiation of subject-as-being in *After Finitude* is framed in the opening chapter as a discovery that 'the time of science temporalizes and spatializes the emergence of living bodies; that is to say, *the emergence of the conditions for the taking place of the transcendental*.'[6] Meillassoux pivots on this problem to reveal the paradox at hand: how a being can manifest 'being's anteriority to manifestation'.[7] The core of this paradox rests on the correlation between being and manifestation, and it is common to Western philosophy as far back as Descartes' *Meditations on First Philosophy*, in which the solution is to appeal to a transcendental entity (God) to secure the truthfulness of the world manifested to the senses. What Meillassoux offers us is a way to disengage the being and manifestation by marking the pre-conditions of being as 'a *hyper-Chaos*, for which nothing is, or would seem to be, impossible, not even unthinkable'.[8] Rather than pursuing Descartes' assurances through a dogmatic metaphysics, Meillassoux here pushes the question of being to the very limit of its conceivability in time: 'this is not a Heraclitean time, since it is not the eternal law of becoming, but rather the eternal and lawless possible becoming of every law. It is a Time capable of destroying even becoming itself by bringing forth, perhaps forever, fixity, stasis, and death.'[9] Despite the nihilistic overtures offered by Meillassoux, such a view moves us from a view of scientific facts as things limited by language, to facticity itself as an absolute by returning to the pre-conditions of being as a fact: the fact that something exists.

But should we even be surprised that Meillassoux moves through an argument that empties the pre-conditions of being of temporality only to arrive at the absolute? For was it not Hegel, whom Meillassoux casts as a *premier* correlationalist, who showed the emptiness of the absolute … What the Chaos conceived of by

5 *Ibid.*, pp. 80–81.
6 *Ibid.*, p. 25.
7 *Ibid.*, p. 26.
8 *Ibid.*, p. 64.
9 *Ibid.*

Meillassoux shows is simply the speculative endorsement of the absolute. But rather than place this absolute within being, as a dogmatic metaphysics of 'sufficient reason' might attempt to do, Meillassoux places the absolute as the primordial Chaos at the site of every possible elaboration of a *logos* as such.

Given the primordiality of Chaos, how are we to then approach Meillassoux's suggestion that 'the speculative releases us from the phenomenal stability of empirical constants by elevating us to the purely intelligible chaos that underlies every aspect of it'?[10] Here the Chaos of *After Finitude* is the primordial necessary abyss that opens thinking to *logos* and forms 'a transcendental ground of unity'[11] that is eternal possibility. But this moment of contingency, of eternal possibility, is not an *a priori* necessity. The accentuation of contingency is herein an event (with the full weight Badiou gives to the term); it is 'something that finally happens' irrespective of and irreducible to 'all pre-registered possiblities'.[12]

What at once seems chaotic in its infinite openness is thus rendered by Meillassoux as a necessary contingency, a necessity of contingency where the event of *logos* emerges. Herein Meillassoux does not wish to slide into a metaphysical view that puts Chaos in the intangible reach of a *meta*-physics. Rather, Chaos is experienced as the ancestral thing – to use his term *'arche-fossil'* – that appears in every moment of conditional representation to call forth the event of *logos* that founds the contingency of these conditions.[13] And, connected to this, Meillassoux charges non-metaphysical speculation with the task of recognising the diachronicity of Chaos in mathematics insofar as the absolute discourse of the latter 'cannot be reduced to a correlate of thought'[14] and operates diachronically, across time and always with the necessity of contingent existence.

Meillassoux's elaboration of the necessity of contingency through the precarious position of being that allows for Chaos to suddenly erupt at *any* moment is of perspicuous interest to Žižek in his appendix response to Johnston's *Badiou, Žižek, and Political Transformations: The Cadence of Change*. Ostensibly, Žižek appears to raise the issue of contingency *vis-à-vis* Meillassoux's analysis in response to Johnston's examination of the distortion and contingency of the Lacanian Act as it is iterated by Badiou and Žižek.[15] Briefly, Johnston's discussion aims at the ways that Žižek's early work construes the Lacanian Act in corollary with the Badiouian event, 'the process of promoting a picture of change emphasizing miraculous moments when the seemingly impossible inexplicably becomes an

10 *Ibid.*, p. 83.
11 Kant in *ibid.*, p. 106.
12 *Ibid.*, p. 108.
13 *Ibid.*, p. 111.
14 *Ibid.*, p. 117.
15 See in particular Chapter 4 'From the Spectacular Act to the Vanishing Act: The Politics of Lacanian Theory' in A. Johnston, *Badiou, Žižek, and Political Transformations: The Cadence of Change*, Evanston, IL: Northwestern University Press, 2009, pp. 127–160.

actualized possibility',[16] and then shifts to a reading of the act that moves away from its Lacanian inflection and towards 'a kind of carpe-diem shift of tactics from patient theoretical assessment to lightning-fast offensives'.[17] Johnston's threading together of Žižek's various positions as regards 'the act' produces a variety of other interesting results, but what is of interest to us here is that Žižek, in his appendix response, takes aim at how the gap between theory and action is radically inherent within being itself as the, and here he turns to Meillassoux's phrasing, 'principle of an *auto-limitation* or *auto-normalization of the omnipotence of chaos*'.[18]

When Žižek takes up Meillassoux's analysis of contingency and Chaos, he does so with an eye to Hegel's *Logic*. Specifically, Žižek is interested in the way that Meillassoux commits to a view of Hegel as a metaphysician that performatively contradicts his deployment of Hegelian methods: 'it was precisely Hegel who deployed the "metaphysical", the "critical", and the "speculative" as the three basic stances of thought toward reality … [and] designates his own position as that of "absolute knowledge".'[19] It should be noted here that it is a familiar hallmark of commentary on Žižek's work to describe his vision of Hegel as heterodox. Yet when one examines the opening of Hegel's *Logic*, one begins to notice just how canny Žižek's reading of Meillassoux is: 'we have the process of Becoming, which is the thoroughly contingent process of generating the multiplicity of Somethings. The "spurious infinity" of Somethings and Something-Others is chaos at its purest, with no necessity whatsoever underlying or regulating it.'[20] Žižek's reference to Chaos in the context above is a direct comment on Meillassoux's linking of necessity and contingency: that even if being is necessary, at its core is something radically negative where the thing-in-itself is 'nothing other than the radically contingent character of our frame of reality'.[21]

While extremely rich, Žižek's reading of the Chaos that drives contingency is not limited to his engagement with Meillassoux. In the extensive foreword to *The Abyss of Freedom/Ages of the World*, Žižek already demonstrated his understanding of the being's necessary contingency with reference to Schelling: 'either it remains still, then there is no life and it is itself as nothing, or it *wants* itself, then it becomes an other, something not the same as itself, *sui dissimile*. It admittedly wants itself as such, but precisely this is impossible in an *immediate* way; in the very wanting itself it already becomes an other and distorts itself.'[22] For Žižek and Schelling, as much as for Meillassoux, when there is something rather than nothing, what *is* presents itself always as something extra, 'in a certain respect

16 A. Johnston, *Badiou, Žižek, and Political Transformations: The Cadence of Change*, Evanston, IL: Northwestern University Press, 2009, p. 167.

17 *Ibid.*, p. 167.

18 Meillassoux in *ibid.*, p. 225.

19 Žižek in *ibid.*

20 Žižek in *ibid.*, p. 226.

21 Žižek in *ibid.*, p. 226.

22 Schelling in S. Žižek and F. W. J. von Schelling, *The Abyss of Freedom/Ages of the World*, Michigan: University of Michigan Press, 1997, p. 40.

something contingent'.[23] Contingency thus comes from the radical otherness not of being but of being-in-itself, because Being is not in diametric opposition to Nothing as an alterity but is always *sui dissimile* when it is itself, because it is predicated upon alterity as such.

Žižek's comments on Meillassoux's project in the aforementioned volume by Johnston give us a moment for pause when examining contingency in this way. Žižek openly states his view that Meillassoux engages with the 'naïve but urgent question of the status of "ancestrality": how can transcendental philosophy account for statements about natural processes which took place prior to the rice of humanity on the Earth, from the beginning of our universe to fossils from the early stages of life on the Earth?'[24] The problem of transcendental philosophy's finitude – that always puts the interrelation between humans and reality as the site of being; they only exist through their correlation – is handled with great finesse by Meillassoux. Yet Žižek's initial agreement with Meillassoux's deduction of the formal-structural reasons for 'the recent rise of irrational religious orientations within [post-secular] philosophy'[25] turns into a disagreement about Meillassoux's reading of Hegel in the guise of 'standard opinion'. Žižek redirects Meillassoux's reversal of the ontological proof of God ('it is the very radical contingency of Being which allows us to make a jump from notion to reality, that is, to prove that some entity necessarily HAS to exist'[26]) to follow a reading of Hegel that shows how 'Hegel can pass to the existence of "something and not nothing" precisely because his starting point is the pure contingency of Being.'[27]

This redirection of Meillassoux's argument eventually arrives at a critical conclusion. For Žižek, Hegelian contradiction eludes Meillassoux: 'Where Meillassoux falls short is in reading this atemporality [of self-identity] in an all too "immediate" way: he fails to grasp how, for Hegel, "contradiction" is not opposed to identity, but is its very core [...] the tautological coincidence of form and content.'[28] Here Žižek targets the onto-genetic coupling of Being and Nothing wherein the form of Being holds Nothing as the content of Being as a form in the first place, the 'first formal-notional determination'.[29]

This critical point of Žižek's is important because it underscores the arbitrary tautology of *logos*. Where Meillassoux directs our attention to the way that a truly speculative *logos* experiences Chaos as the contingent moment of being-in-itself, in the very ground of Being as the "first formal-notional determination,"[30] it can be seen that the contingency of *logos* is contained in the totality of Becoming as it oscillates endlessly between Being and Nothing, form and content. This

23 Schelling in *ibid.*, p. 40.
24 Žižek in Johnston, *op. cit.*, p. 214.
25 Žižek in *ibid.*, p. 215.
26 Žižek in *ibid.*, p. 217.
27 Žižek in *ibid.*
28 Žižek in *ibid.*
29 Žižek in *ibid.*
30 Žižek in *ibid.*

movement is missed if we merely treat Meillassoux's argument at the level of discourse alone. As Žižek shows, it is in the tautological moment of the emergence of *logos* as such (what Badiou might call 'the count') that contradiction is in the very self-identity of *logos* as a Notion.

Žižek's encounters with the Chaos belying Meillassoux's vision of contingency persist in the interstices between the *Jenaer Realphilosophie* of Hegel and the *Die Weltalter* of Schelling.[31] The vestiges of these two *oeuvres* are especially prominent in an essay by Žižek called *The Abyss of Freedom*, which accompanies a 1997 translation of the second draft of Schelling's *Die Weltalter*. Here, in the opening discussion of the interaction of Ground and Existence, Žižek comes upon the concept that locates Chaos in both Hegel and Schelling: madness. No mere psychologism, Žižek's analysis attempts to pinpoint the way that the normal run of our immediate natural surrounds *(Umwelt)* is always-already thrown off balance by the incommensurability (in principle) of Ground's maddening impenetrability and the transparent 'rational' determinism of Existence. What is at stake here is not the given-ness of things, but the hampering of Ground's preontological status, 'it only "is" *sous rature*, in the mode of its own withdrawal'.[32] Thus any being in particular (up to and including God), for Žižek's reading of Schelling, is rendered contingent on the basis that its full self-identity is thwarted by the withdrawal of Ground from the ontology of Being (Existence) because it lacks 'any proper ontological consistency'.[33] Here madness enters as the 'violent gesture of contraction that negates every being outside itself'.[34] But it is precisely at this point of madness that Žižek draws together Schelling and Hegel with the view of Descartes favoured by Meillassoux:

> Was this withdrawal into self [from natural surroundings into their humanisation] not accomplished by Descartes as his universal doubt and reduction to cogito, which, as Derrida pointed out in his 'Cogito and the History of Madness,' also involves a passage through the moment of radical madness?[35]

The danger is thus to think of the hyper-Chaos of Meillassoux apart from this earlier Schellingian–Hegelian iteration as radical madness, where in fact there is a close corollary in their respective speculative analytics.[36]

Žižek pursues this moment of madness through the *Jenaer Realphilosophie* of Hegel to a point that is noticeably similar to Meillassoux's encounters with the

31 It is curious how Žižek's more recent engagements with the discourse between Meillassoux and Hegel, most notably *Less than Nothing*, insist on a more 'mature' Hegel than his Jaener period. It is as though Hegel writ large is at issue in Meillassoux's discourse on contingency for Žižek.

32 Žižek in *ibid.*, p. 6.

33 Žižek in *ibid.*

34 Žižek in *ibid.*, p. 8.

35 Žižek in *ibid.*

36 See in particular Žižek's analysis of the *vel* through radical madness in *ibid.*, pp. 40–42.

chaotic necessity of contingency. As Žižek states, 'the subject is no longer the Light of Reason opposed to the nontransparent, impenetrable Stuff (of Nature, Tradition ...); his very kernel, the gestures that opens up the space for the Light of Logos, is absolute negativity *qua* "night of the world."'[37] What concerns Žižek here is not the fall into madness as a regression into the chaotic abyss of Ground's inconsistency (as *Abgrund*), but how the subject emerges from the abyss of madness into 'normalcy'.

This locus of Chaos in Žižek operates in a manner that matches Meillassoux's speculative mode. In Meillassoux the question of how to make sense of ancestral statements beyond the finite horizon of the subject's normalcy (Kantian finitude) locates its mad 'principle of unreason' in the realism of Ground's preontological status: Schellingian Ground as characterised by Žižek is, for Meillassoux, the Chaos that belies contingency. The Hegelian confrontation with madness achieves this in terms of the subject while Schelling conceives of such radical contingency in terms of the unity of Ground (Chaos) and Existence (Being) in the world.

Here, following Žižek's reading of Hegel and Schelling, we are in a better position to understand Meillassoux's emphasis on the absolute statements of mathematics as ontological Truth – a categorical Truth of the necessity of contingency; that the *logos* of Being could, at any moment, disintegrate. The Žižekian key to tracing the figuring of contingency in Meillassoux is thus not to begin from ontology but to ask after the incommensurability of the self-identity of the Absolute, its oscillation, fuelled by the necessity of contingency, between Being and Nothing (Chaos). The absolute statements of mathematics inhere at this moment where *logos* 'forms' itself through the withdrawal from Nothing, *ex nihilio*. The madness of chaotic nothingness is here parleyed through the 'mad act' of forcing a closure on Being, constituting it as a totality *(logos)* whose chaotic content (Nothing) hampers the totalisation of *logos* through a minimal difference. This minimal difference resides in the self-deferral of Nothing that brings forth Being.

At this point it is crucial to emphasise that although Ground and Existence are not identical, this does not make them co-dependent or correlated. Rather, they operate in a manner that allows one and the same cause to produce opposite effects. The 'mad act' of contingently withdrawing from the madness of Chaos is to shift out of the excessivity of Chaos and not to instate a type of cosmic balance between Ground and Existence.[38] Compositely, the contingency that grounds the instantiation of every *logos* reveals the insufficiency of Being to promise, but fail to achieve, a state of totality. The logic of this may read: a being is not given but rather is not no-thing. Parting ways with Schelling's effort to unify Ground and Existence, Žižek similarly underscores how 'the codependence of two antagonistic forces does not reside in the fact that one force needs the other as the only ground against which it can assert itself.'[39] Thus, with Žižek, it can be shown that the

37 Žižek in *ibid.*, p. 9.

38 This parallels the motion of anarchy withdrawing from itself to form law.

39 Žižek in *op. cit.*, p. 20.

contingency of the assertion of the absolute *logos* touches upon a realism that does not bind what exists to a delusory primacy.

Yet one must ask if all this ado about chaos renders Being indifferent? Certainly, the 'mad act' that breaks with the chaos of Nothing to instate the *logos* of Being suggests that the possibilities for the psyche of the subject remain at a remove from the un-certitude (contingency) of necessity. Both Žižek's reading of madness and Meillassoux's rendering of Chaos thus confront us with the question of whether philosophy itself manifests here because of a speculative gap in the self-identity of Being that emerges as a consequence of the mad withdrawal from Chaos. Specifically, and without reducing Schelling's insights to a mere vulgarisation of existential nothingness, is the task of attending to this Chaos that precedes the ontological instantiation of *logos* making a state of anxiety palpable? At any moment *logos* may collapse into the chaos of Nothing, its necessity resting on the contingency of Being as such; a partial remainder of Nothing withdrawn from atemporal Chaos. The withdrawal from Nothing that un-grounds Existence (Being) facilitates the freedom of the subject. But when this freedom freely attends to its necessity for fear of over-determination (the sublime object of ideology derided by both Meillassoux and Žižek), we find ourselves encountering the question of Being-in-itself that takes aim at its un-grounding. The philosophical 'putting into question' can quickly turn to nostalgic fantasy here if we reject the mad act of withdrawing from Nothing as a necessarily contingent act. Hence the properly philosophical subject that is put into question by Schelling and Hegel *avec* Žižek is always out of joint, restless and anxious for its persistence in *form* (the un-grounded Being generated by the 'mad act' of withdrawal) rather than content (the chaotic Nothing underpinning the contingent assertion of every *logos*).

Although we might contend from the above discussion that the contingent withdrawal from Chaos/Nothing is necessary for the manifestation of any *logos* as such, the properly philosophical encounter with this withdrawal appears to arise at the very moment of a contingent gap emerging in the extant state of *logos*. This presents, quite literally, a terrain of possibilities by exposing *logos* to its arbitrary foundation. Yet the *logos* of Being elucidated by Meillassoux, according to Žižek, seems to indicate that this *logos* encodes Chaos as an impenetrable symptom: the mad withdrawal from Chaos that has no *logos* to its movement.

The retroactive sequence that marks the mad act of withdrawing from the madness of Chaos is here enciphered in *logos*. But herein it is the status of the contingent act of withdrawal as a cipher, an enigmatic moment unremittingly resistant to the interpretations of *logos*, that suggests that this contingency arises as the first formal-notional determination of *logos* (Being). To follow Žižek's reading and quotation of Schelling: 'in the primordial *vel*, the subject has to decide between "nothing" and "something", but always irreducibly in the sense of "something extra, something additional, something foreign/put on, in a certain respect something contingent."'[40] And what is the name for such a formation of

40 Žižek in *ibid.*, p. 40.

contingency in *logos* as a cipher (on the side of *logos*, an element irreducible to *logos*) but 'the symptom' – a term noticeably absent from Meillassoux's discourse in *After Finitude*.

Certainly, we might consider this symptomal character of contingency is what makes the normalcy of *logos* go awry in the sense that every attempt at formal-notional determination rests on a 'mad act' of an arbitrary violent gesture: not being nothing. Yet *a propos* of Meillassoux (and Schelling), the contingency of this persistence in *logos* also suggests that contingency is a troubling, maddening element that puts the human subject awry. The subject supposed by Meillassoux's speculative non-metaphysical philosophy herein must come to terms with the symptom of their own mad arising/grounding in Existence – not in the limited subjectivist view of some New Age construction of natural wisdom, but instead in the infinitely demanding atemporal depth of Chaos in which even our natural surroundings are necessarily contingent and prone to giving way.

This infinite demand is an effect of the contingent withdrawal from Chaos. But we should avoid here resorting to a pseudo-therapeutic attitude that assuages the anxious danger of lapsing into chaotic madness by carrying on 'business as usual' in *logos*. Meillassoux's analysis in *After Finitude* is keenly aware that to commit to such an elision of Chaos dooms the subject to a vicious circle of fetishistic obsession that situates knowledge as a promised but ultimately unachievable totality.[41] Here, then, we might see Žižek and Meillassoux effectively vouching for the task of analysis proper to be the separation of elements that *logos* would otherwise hold together in the aftermath of the first formal-notional determination of Being to the end of elucidating the 'mad act' grounding this *logos*.[42]

Such an analysis of the contingency of the symptom (of existence) invites an opportunity to think through the subject of Meillassoux's philosophical, non-metaphysical speculation as 'non-All'. The rejection of totality in Meillassoux's analysis breaks apart totality from *logos*, the space between which is chaotic: an unfolding of partial objects in an endless night. The speculative subject of the contingent withdrawal from Chaos is thus confronted with their void-status.[43] Herein the subject is rendered as 'void' by the ontological Void of Chaos; the site of speculative analysis becomes the enigmatic ground of Being. The symptom highlighted by contingency in this way is therefore the very existence of the subject as such; the subject as a formal construct of minimal difference between *logos* of Existence and some enigmatic, impenetrable, imperfect, contingent Ground. It is only on virtue of this incompleteness of Existence–Ground that the mad act of withdrawal from Chaos can be recognised retroactively as the 'necessity of

41 It is particularly interesting to note that Meillassoux (*op. cit.*, pp. 10–13) returns to the old epistemological distinction between the primary and secondary qualities of objects to criticise such a move.

42 S. Žižek, *The Parallax View*, Cambridge, MA: The MIT Press, 2006, p. 299.

43 This same movement is how law is confronted with its own Void-subject in the previous chapter.

contingency'. Herein the subject is non-All, never quite elucidated by the totalisation of *logos*, always a partial void.

Such a view of Chaos and Being can be seen in the cyberpunk fictionalisations of virtual reality. In these literary speculations, authors such as William Gibson draw out the affective materiality of the contingency of being-in-the-abyss but also go further than Meillassoux by examining the extension in a chaotic Void. In his early works Gibson provides us with an interesting example of how the 'mad act' of withdrawal allows the subject to be non-All and yet prone to the contingent effects of *logos*. In the acclaimed *Neuromancer* (1982), *Count Zero* (1984) and *Mona Lisa Overdrive* (1988), Gibson develops a topological vision of cyberspace as an empty plane populated with geometrical objects that represent hordes of data. One enters cyberspace through electrodes placed about the head that are attached to a 'deck,' or interface, allowing access to and navigation around the matrix of cyberspace. The spatiality of Gibson's cyberspace is itself empty, a kind of Void-Nothing whose depth is characterised by the relative quality of the representations of geometrical data *(logos)* to one another and the user's intellect (analogical to Meillassoux's 'speculative realism') that may, at any moment, shift, turn, collapse, and so forth. Embodiment remains a necessary evil of this technological interaction in Gibson's narrative vision. For example, the subject can still experience vertigo but feels an uncanny absence of resistance when hastening through this Void. Gibson's cyberspace cowboys 'feel' the Void-Nothing of cyberspace, the Void impresses sensations seemingly from within the 'sense' of *logos*. 'Sense' is thus rendered categorical and formless in itself, a type of non-metaphysical *chora* in the way it opens the possibility for these sensations felt in the Void to be incommensurable with the disembodied rationale of navigating cyberspace.

What is curious about Gibson's narration of the Void is how, upon entering cyberspace, a character will lose their sense of actual embodiment because the domain of virtual reality (all *logos* is, in the view of Meillassoux and Žižek-*vis*-Schelling, put on, fake, virtual, etc.) is far more replete with immediacy, however chaotic. The senses that absorb the 'natural surroundings' of the *Umwelt* intrude on the virtual field of possibility; the feel of using the deck to navigate cyberspace, for example, tends to only report sensations pertinent for the intentions in cyberspace, the phenomenology of this Void. With immediacy on the side of the virtual, the actual is overcome by the reality of the virtual/*logos*. That is to say, where there is no active subjectivity the Void remains in its virtuality to hide the necessary contingency of the body.

Something within Sense but greater than a sense itself informs the cowboys' intelligence to navigate the space: fantasy. The fantasmatic here unifies the experience of the world encountered through consciousness in the Void of Gibson's cyberspace because the Void is replete with an irrational immediacy coextensive with the 'effervescent punctuality' of consciousness. The Void/Chaos appears in the most fleeting of instances as it withdraws and speculative fantasy sublates the 'gap' in its wake. However, as Meillassoux and Žižek show, the subject cannot transcend this paradoxical 'empty' permanence of the Void/Chaos but only the withdrawal, the contingency of Sense.

Elsewhere Žižek suggests that it is the 'reality of the virtual' that is at stake in the Void, its transcendental empiricism. This empiricism is transcendental in the sense of the 'a priori conditions of possibility of our experience of constituted reality', or, as Gibson accents with the presence of an electroencephalogram (EEG) on each deck to measure brain activity: you can really die in cyberspace; *logos* can really annihilate you.[44] Such a view understands the Void/Chaos as the formlessness from which the subject-as-a-being emerges, and is distinct insofar as it lacks the oceanic feeling of being amongst a multitude of like beings. But given Žižek's comments on Meillassoux's analysis, what Gibson's narrative portrayal shows on the contrary is that Chaos is not that which receives the existing thing in its death, the collapse of our mad withdrawal from it, but that which endows the *logos* of Being with an unreflective and even narcissistic 'thereness'. Herein the withdrawal from Chaos provides temporality only to make it recurrent and without end, although in itself it is *a priori* to the mediation of the grounding of any *logos*.

The persistence of a subject in Gibson's Void/Chaos rests upon the mad act of the withdrawal from this Void. But what is ultimately contingent, what is most precarious, is the counting of this Void-subject in Existence as a gap inherent to the foundation of *logos*, the very point where any *logos* can be arbitrarily grounded. Gibson's phenomenology of the Void-Nothing reveals that the death of the subject is only possible through the disappearance of its registration in *logos*, but that such a death is always part of *logos* where the chaotic Ground unhinges the arbitration of the formal-notional determination of Being.

Given that the symptom upon which the subject persists is the movement from Chaos/Nothing to Being/Existence, it is possible to read the practice of philosophy, including legal philosophy, as an obsessive returning to *logos* given that the necessity of contingency (un)grounds Being. Such obsession can be defined as a burdensome and uncontrollable compulsion to repeat an idea, emotion or thought; and is not the compulsion to repeat contingency in recognising the infinite contingencies of all possible *logoi* precisely such an obsessive move that renders visible the illusion of *logos*' logical necessity (being-as-form) that facilitates its ritualisation in post-secular philosophy? Although obsession is often considered pathological, such a definition is only possible if the obsession obstructs the free-will of the subject in a prohibitive and disquieting way, and a survey of current media may indicate some misuse of the term to define a generic passionate attachment. What we are locating here is the way that Meillassoux's and Žižek's attempts to think in terms of contingency rely upon an obsessive modality wherein the contingent void-subject, whose symptomal existence is defined as the mad act of withdrawal from Chaos, is driven towards *logos* as a totality despite its

44 S. Žižek, *Organs Without Bodies: On Deleuze and Consequences*, London: Routledge, 2004, p. 4.

primordial un-grounding. Such a view opens their work to this appropriation as ritual with little defence against it.[45]

It was Freud who already noted the modalities of such obsessionality. The way *logos* is a fake, put on and contingent, is exactly the way Freud, and later Žižek, account for Being in its ontology. Three types of obsession emerge in Freud's work: obsessional neurosis, erotic-obsessiveness and narcissistic-obsession.[46] In the former, obsessional neurosis, the transference between the person and others is forged through a diverse range of references to the compulsively repeated object.[47] This transference need not be limited to human beings, but always retains a structure that futilely attempts to defer the object of obsession because it is a neurosis.[48] One might easily observe this psychodynamic process in any conservative view's distaste for elaborate upheaval and change which itself is inevitable, as one may glean as a possible response to Meillassoux's and Žižek's readings of contingency. That is not to say that all conservative responses to contingency are neurotic, but rather that the anti-natural structure presented by Meillassoux, especially, functions by way of an obsessive repetition of contingency as an object that it is possible to think about despite our immersion in *logos*.

The second obsessive mode defined by Freud, the erotic-obsessive, has similar neurotic operations to the form obsessional neurotic, but exhibits a form of rebellion that demands recognition from other people and objects as they appear to the perception of the obsessional subject.[49] Pertaining to the conception of *Eros* from Hellenic antiquity (Plato), the erotics of this type of obsessive are part of Life itself.[50] This means that the dependency on the constructions of *logos* is interior to the obsessive's consciousness and explicitly refutes its philosophical analysis as an exhibitionistic phenomenon since the chance for *logos* to extinguish the contingency of Existence transcends the perception of this Existence.[51] Oddly, one need only watch a Hollywood film about serial killers, such as *The Silence of the Lambs*, *Along Came a Spider* or *Se7en*, to observe the psychodynamics of this type. In these three films in particular, the serial-killer characters have an intense consciousness ritualisation of murder that discharges its energy through private ritualistic practices, i.e. hidden shrines, macabre and playful murder scenarios, etc. For our purposes here we are interested in the way that the contingency of grounding Existence as a *logos* (an erotics) means that every being's encounter

45 Johnston (*op. cit.*, p. 166) has made some acute, though pessimistic, observations on the potential for this in Žižek's work in particular.

46 See especially 'Libidinal Types' in S. Freud, *On Sexuality: Three Essays on the Theory of Sexuality and Other Writings*, J. Strachey (trans.), London: Penguin Books, 1991, pp. 361–365.

47 *Ibid.*, p. 382.

48 S. Freud, *New Introductory Lectures on Psychoanalysis*, J. Strachey (trans.), London: Penguin Books, 1991, p. 200.

49 Freud, *op. cit.*, p. 363.

50 Freud, *op. cit.*, p. 201.

51 *Ibid.*, p. 44.

with their enigmatic withdrawal from Chaos can be privately ritualised in their unique and singular 'mad act' – every night we go to sleep we die, and every morning when we wake we are reborn. One can easily envisage a post-secular discourse (loathed by both Meillassoux and Žižek) taking up precisely such a reading of contingency wherein the analysis ceases separating what, in *logos*, remains together and treats contingency as an essential category of Existence.

The final type of obsession in Freud's schema is narcissistic-obsession. Whereas the obsessional neurotic can find support for their rebellion against Kantian orthodoxy in any manner of things in *logos*, including other people, politics, science, religion, and so on, and the erotic-obsessive seeks out the virulent strains of the mad act of their contingent emergence in *logos*, the narcissistic-obsessive relies on a purely cultural network of support. For Freud, this type of obsession pursues the arts and humanities for their well-documented open and interpretative functions.[52] As the phrasing implies, this type of obsessive person again inflects their demand for the recognition of their rebellion against an ideal authority within their own psyche. A reading of Meillassoux's view of contingency goes awry in this mode because it is all too easily brought under this rubric to explain an atemporal, ahistorical fixation with particular cultural objects, i.e. the historicist reduction of Meillassoux's argument to its historical, Heraclitean, time – precisely the reading of Chaos that Meillassoux explicitly rejects.[53]

According to the Freudian view, obsession shares its neurotic disposition with phobias and some forms of narcissism, all of which are species of transference neuroses (structures focused on the links forged by *logos*).[54] Admittedly, this view facilitates a reading of obsession through a character typology that economises the storage and discharge of psychical energy or libido. But what it shows above is the way that a reading of contingency that begins from the contingent act of withdrawal from Chaos can take many forms and entails a contradiction of rebellion and recognition; and this may, on occasion, lead to self-torment or the torturing of the object that is being obsessed over.[55]

What is interesting herein is that Meillassoux's critique of post-Kantian philosophy is precisely that it tortures the finitude of the subject. This obsesssion entraps the subject in a correlationism (strong or weak) that creates the illusion of an indexicality between what is and its necessity to be. Both Žižek and Meillassoux are critical of this illusory index, and it is the profound idea in response to this illusion – that it is: contingency is necessary – that will assure philosophical speculation of its future.

As can be seen from the above, the position of Chaos in the terrain of the Ground of Being is given several very interesting twists by the analyses of Meillassoux and Žižek. But beyond this being merely a scholarly curiousity, it is important to note

52 Freud, *op. cit.*, p. 363.
53 Meillassoux, *op. cit.*, p. 64.
54 Freud, *op. cit.*, p. 190.
55 *Ibid.*, p. 132.

that such a revisioning of contingency as the Ground of *logos* provides the political cache to act (rather than merely act-out *logos*) insofar as every over-determination that characterises the totalities of *logoi* is prone to collapse. Yet such a collapse is not given in Being. Rather, it is the mad act of the auto-withdrawal from Chaos that renders the persistence of the subject in Existence as a symptom that cannot not be and yet cannot not stop being written off by *logos* as void. This speculative reading of ontology intimately connects with the task of philosophical analysis and presents a subject of philosophical and non-metaphysical speculation that demands endless necessary contingency. It is by engaging with this radical madness of the withdrawal from Chaos that Meillassoux is able to carve a new path for contingency. Herein, Žižek's critical comments that Meillassoux's work misreads Hegel is a matter for further scholarship but, all the more philosophically, it is Žižek's engagement with this withdrawal from Chaos *vis-à-vis* Schelling that shows us the importance of accounting for the Existence of Being in its illogical and 'mad' dimensions. Meillassoux and Žižek are justified in their resistance to the totalisations of any *logos*, particularly that of post-secular philosophy, given this necessary contingency of Being. And, hopefully, we will see further debate about the links between Meillassoux's speculative realism and its 'other' Idealist heritage.

CHAPTER 4

Capitalist subjectivity and the *Wissenschaft* of jurisprudence

Max Weber's vocation lectures have made a significant impact on sociological and organisational thinking in the twentieth century. At the outset of the twenty-first century, however, Weber's distinction between prophets and priests of science *(Wissenschaft)* has become an introductory lesson on authority and perhaps even nostalgia for emphasising a difference in authorial attitude. Yet is there still something important to be recovered from Weber, something to explain the salient longevity of his theory? To access the domain of such saliency, the analysis below traces Weber's reading of jurisprudence as a *Wissenschaft* and reads its fascination with the limits of its rational authority against the grain.

To begin, let us turn to the two forms of authority that emanate from Weber's analysis of the inner calling to *Wissenschaft* in the lecture '*Wissenschaft als Beruf*' ('Science as a Vocation'), first delivered in 1918 at Munich University.[1] The first form of authority discussed by Weber is charismatic authority. This authority draws people to it for the sensation of externalised, objective belief that it brings; a public statement of truth that burdens the subject to enjoy in and testify to this truth-statement. Legal-*cum*-rational authority forms the second prong of Weber's analysis. In his lecture, Weber is at lengths to redeem *Wissenschaft* from the internecine rejection of it as boring, mechanical or uninspired. Weber's distinction between these two modes of authority is not a mere convenience. Rather, they are an attempt to analytically depict accountability and moral duty in *Wissenschaft*. Weber's portrayal of jurisprudence as a part of *Wissenschaft*'s rational authorial disclosure in the world is particularly instructive in revealing a socio-legal link: a psychic connection between the law and the hearts and minds of its subjects.

To discuss this link between the understanding of jurisprudence as *Wissenschaft* and the people subject to it in law schools, professional practice and beyond, this exegesis will explore the Freudian topography of Weber's view of *Wissenschaft* to the end of returning us to the Weberian insights into law awry and anew. In

1 Weber uses the term *Wissenschaft* to designate science in general or the rigorous systematic approach to inquiry into the world that eschews dilettantism, i.e. mathematics as a science, poetry as a science, jurisprudence as a science, etc.

particular, the subtexts of capitalism, Romanticism and rational disenchantment of Weber's discussion will be alloyed with the new kind of subjectivity that has emerged under capital's social discourse reported by psychoanalysts since the 1970s but that has been overlooked by some inter-disciplinary uses of psychoanalytic theory in cultural legal studies.[2] Not to dismiss these earlier uses of psychoanalysis out of hand, this chapter makes particular use of the theories of Lacan and current proponents of Lacan's Freudian anti-philosophy. While the discussion will touch on knowledge production under *Wissenschaft*, it does so with an eye to the psychological faith in this knowledge and the intimate epistemological construction of this knowledge in the wake of current renderings of rigorous systematic inquiry by *Wissenschaft*. As we shall see, where Weber talks about the inner calling to *Wissenschaft* in the legal-*cum*-rational authority, it is clear that the epistemological veracity of the knowledge exchanged between law and its subjects is maintained by a deeply intimate censorship and sublation *(Aufhebung)* of the desire of the teacher, the giver of laws.

Weber's vocation lectures are an important part of his *oeuvre*. The lecture 'Science as a Vocation' raises a voice against scientific determinism in ethical, social, aesthetic, legal and political matters. Weber's main concern is how the '*inward* calling for science' generates an antipathy with moral sentiments or value judgements: 'And whoever lacks the capacity to put on blinders, so to speak, and to come up to the idea that the fate of his soul depends upon whether or not he makes the correct conjecture at this passage of this manuscript may as well stay away from science.'[3] Science *(Wissenschaft)*, for Weber, is impersonal, but that remains part of its charm. The scientific calling requires a passion for alienation, poetically phrased by Weber as 'thousands of years must pass before you enter into life and thousands more wait in silence.'[4]

The opening remarks to the lecture position the passion for science away from an organic or fated notion of vocational calling; a perception engrained into Western civilisations since at least the time of Plato, who writes of Socrates' divine visitations that call for philosophy. In its stead Weber promotes shades of scientific interests from the reflections necessary to advance calculations and experimental endeavour (Weber calls this having an 'idea' about your work), to the irrigorous dilettantes interested in scientific inquiry but hamstrung to exploit their findings because of a lack of procedure, and onto the modern risk-obsessed capitalist subject whose scientific work is a bargain struck with the chance rather than the assurance for an idea to occur. Weber remains churlish about naïve

2 The influence of Romanticism on the Frankfurt School of Critical Theory, of which Weber is counted among their number, is discussed by Susan Buck-Morss' influential *Origin of Negative Dialectics*. A useful outline of Romanticism can be found in Freidrich Beiser's *The Romantic Imperative*.

3 M. Weber, 'Science as a Vocation', in H. H. Gerth and C. Wright Mills (trans. and eds), *From Max Weber: Essays in Sociology*, New York: Oxford University Press, 1946, pp. 134–156 & 134.

4 *Ibid.*

visions of mathematicians as merely calculators closeted at their desks, preferring instead to argue that the calling to science, like any calling, is artistic at base and requires both mania and inspiration. Are jurisprudes not also depicted as similarly bloodless academics rather than the law-inspired maniacs and fetishists of the letter of the law that we are? Weber's discourse on *Wissenschaft* thus points us to the question of jurisprudence-as-*Wissenschaft* where its pursuit is both inspired and manic.

The channelling of mania and inspiration by the scientific worker devoted to *Wissenschaft* constitutes 'personality' for Weber, or what we might otherwise term status or respectability. Weber distinguishes such personality from narcissistic self-involvement in his cutting dismissal of those out to 'experience life' as merely seeking sensations – the weight of his prose and echoing the Platonic discourse on mania that suggests that such sensationalists are confused about the good to be sought in science.[5] In this way, personality is distinct from modern ideas of celebrity or media communication of scientific work for Weber.[6]

Moreover, Weber argues that the experience of the world and construction of personality rely on the way of life or ontology of the society in which they appear. Citing a comparison between 'civilised man' and 'savage man', Weber directs our attention to how, unless one is a physicist, the forces of motion exerted on a moving vehicle are taken as given rather than understood in modern societies. In the modern world, for Weber, increased 'intellectualization and rationalization' have led to no necessary improvement in 'general knowledge of the conditions under which one lives'.[7] 'The savage,' Weber argues comparatively, 'knows incomparably more about his tools.'[8] Weber's discussion thus maintains a certain Romantic impulse, if not of the time before civilisation and its social contract, then at least of the illusion of mass social progress promised by science in the same movement that it must be taken seriously as a vocation and motivator of social change.

Indeed, Weber's lecture reflects a Romantic lament about the rational disenchantment of the world. The critique of intellectualisation in Weber's lecture rests on this motion of disenchantment. Citing Tolstoi's ruminations on modern life, Weber argues that the world is disenchanted because 'for civilized man death has no meaning'.[9] The disenchantment of the world thus fits with the impersonal scientific endeavour that is nonetheless inspired and driven. The problem for Weber is that *Wissenschaft* has taken on an artificial construction in modern civilizations that is disconnected from the everyday experience of the world; or, as Weber puts

5 *Ibid.*, p. 138.

6 For a helpful depiction of contemporary celebrity see R. Salecl, *The Tyranny of Choice*, London: Profile Books, 2010, pp. 49–54.

7 Weber, *op. cit.*, p. 138.

8 *Ibid.*

9 *Ibid.*, p. 139.

it, 'during the period of the rise of the exact sciences one expected a great deal more . . . to show the path to God.'[10]

Weber explicitly touches upon jurisprudence as an example of the intellectual disenchantment of the world in his 'Science as a Vocation' lecture. Of jurisprudence Weber says:

> It establishes what is valid according to the rules of juristic thought, which is partly bound by logically compelling and partly by conventionally given schemata. Juridical thought holds when certain legal rules and certain methods of interpretations are recognized as binding. Whether there should be law and whether one should establish just these rules – such questions jurisprudence does not answer. It can only state: If one wishes this result, according to the norms of our legal thought, this legal rule is the appropriate means of attaining it.[11]

Jurisprudence thus has an intellectual inwardness according to Weber. That is to say, jurisprudence is reflective, jurisprudes are inspired and driven, jurisprudence is a vocation insofar as it is a science *(Wissenshaft)* or effort of reason and intellect, and jurists may arrive at an idea, from time to time, about where laws are heading. And, with Weber, jurisprudence is part of the disenchantment of the world as it withdraws from lived experience in favour of the law as a rational body of knowledge.

The lures of the sciences in the disenchanted world are reasons of control over (most) things, methods and strategies to acquire (most) things, and clarity of reasoning and conviction, for Weber.[12] It is clear from Weber's discussion that it is the self-accountability of the scientific worker that is paramount. His three lures of science are limited by their third term and it is the peculiar feature of this moral conscience that is internal to the rational individual who attends science as a vocation and will be the focus of our later discussion.

The popular allegories of Weber's critique of science as a vocation are charismatic and rational forms of authority. These are radically different positions more akin to the difference between prophets and priests. Of such charismatic prophets Weber is insistent upon their accountability: 'speak where criticism is possible'.[13] For the academic priesthood on the other hand, Weber argues that it would be irresponsible to confront students expecting knowledge with the intention of a demagogue.[14] At issue for the priest/teacher above and beyond technical questions of facts and facticity is their own moral conscience when the elimination of private sympathies from the facts taught fails.[15] These allegories of authority are

10 *Ibid.*, p. 141.
11 *Ibid.*, p. 144.
12 *Ibid.*, p. 148.
13 *Ibid.*, p. 147.
14 *Ibid.*
15 *Ibid.*

the focal point of a comparison between academic rigour and political convictions in the later part of the lecture, perhaps reflective of Weber's private experience of the rise of nationalism and its impacts on the university environment of his native Germany. Further, Weber's discussion of charismatic and rational authority operates under the conditions of disenchantment, not in intellectual abstraction. Yet all too often in popular university textbooks, the disenchantment of the world and its Romantic *Sturm und Drang* is cleaved from the understanding of these forms of authority.[16] The importance of these authorities for Weber is that they serve to bind people to *Wissenschaft* through the acceptance and internalisation of a social link.

But what of this social link today? It is widely accepted that there is a marked cultural shift from the early twentieth century to the early twenty-first century in most parts of the world, developing or otherwise. Much of this is explained as globalisation or mobility, but what of the constitutive forms of authority, charismatic and rational, that make this world believable? Capitalism is the premiere socio-economic system, politics and morality that contributes a significant understanding to how the world works today. Yet although it is Eurocentric in its general conception, capitalism has managed to adapt to a variety of different geo-political regions where some cultural customs contest the historical nihilism of capitalist exchange.[17]

While there is, has been and may yet be a plurality of capitalisms, i.e. Western liberal democratic, Eastern authoritarian, Eurasian plutocracy, Indian post-nationalist, corporate white Anglo-Saxon protestant (WASP) and so forth, the term 'capitalism' and its meaning remains slippery. It is still fashionable to announce capitalism at the first sign of economic exchange in which everything has a price irrespective of the material constitution of the object priced as such; such is the power of commodification in the construction of capitalism. But the edifice of capitalism is much more than mere economic exchange. For capitalism to prosper it needs to be believable, it needs to proffer a normative social link of sorts or else its moral agents may reject it as a social system. Given the shift in perspective between Weber's time and our own – one is tempted to call it a move from neurosis to perversion – how is the disenchantment of the world attended to in the categories of Weber insofar as they present the image of an individual person in contract with science and civilisation more broadly?

16 *Sturm und Drang* is conventionally translated as 'storm and stress' but may be better understood for its affects and content as 'storm and noise' or 'storm and strife'.

17 For an exploration of this historical amnesia as a condition of capitalism's Eurocentric theorising, see any number of postmodern philosophers and deconstructionists inspired by Marx including Jean-Luc Nancy, Giorgio Vattimo, Paul Virilio, Jean Baudrillard, etc. One wonders if this tradition has reached its apogee with Quentin Meillassoux's notion of hyper Chaos, which has been critiqued by Adrian Johnston for its strong dissolution of lived life – see A. Johnston, 'The World Before Worlds: Quentin Meillassoux and Alain Badiou's Anti-Kantian Transcendentalism', *Contemporary French Civilization*, 33(1), 2009.

It is the contention here that Weber's argument, while seemingly sociological, is in fact strongly psychoanalytic and this facilitates a way to read Weber anew today. The accounting for capitalism and its social link has been a serious concern for psychoanalytic literature. Yet Weber's account is curious because it turns on questions of criticism, charisma, reason, and submitting oneself to authority. It may be said that at base Weber's argument is about the attraction towards believing in someone or knowing something about oneself. The mistake according to Weber is to not see the politics in knowledge, for instance the necessary investments of a teacher in the material taught and how this regulates their private sentiments.

However, Weber does not gesture so much to political economy as to an economy of satisfactions. The inner calling to science *(Wissenschaft)* as a vocation is precisely a matter of such satisfaction. Weber links vocational calling to mania and inspiration, be it in the arts or the sciences, that are ideas more attuned to one's private and singular experience of desire than to employment or institutional issues. Weber also identifies the relationship between the individual, their psychic disposition and the occupation of science in general as a kind of big Other who assures the individual of their expectations about lived experience but is not limited to any individual in particular. As discussed above, Weber even goes so far as to argue that those seeking experience as sensation are in error about what is really important. For Weber, the question is not to be the sensationalists' ipsetic motto 'what do I want?' but more so the vocational mantra 'what am I called to?' or 'what does the Other want of me?' The psychoanalytic emphasis in Weber is therefore grounded in the interstices between the social world, the Otherness of authority, the fantasmatic coordination of desire that creates an authority proper to its political domain and the inner-life of the individual human subject who hears or shuns the calling of science as a vocation.

Arguably, the contention of *Wissenschaft* that Weber has in mind is knowledge of what is real where such knowledge is free from the political views of the teacher. The Freudian question here is where are such views – or at least the psychic investment in such views – then displaced to if the views are not expressed in the teaching of a science such as jurisprudence? Far from being reductive, psychoanalysis recognises that there may be a plurality of positions that an individual may take with regard to retiring their private politics from the field of teaching, including sublimation, disavowal, rejection, foreclosure, conscious negation, deferral and many others.[18]

At face value Weber's arguments in the 'Science as a Vocation' lecture appear to indicate that the teaching of science is a 'higher' civilised form, not merely distinct from the prophecy of political values but also driven and inspired beyond belief. To this extent Weber's view has curious points of connection with the Freudian

18 It is important to note that each of these psychoanalytic concepts has temporal depth. For example, Russell Grigg (1998) has examined the three temporal modes of foreclosure: *Verdrangung, Verleugnung* and *Verwerfung*; the act of repression, the affect of repression, the repression of language.

notion of the sublimation of the drives. Simply defined, drive *(Trieb)* is the gravity or pull of need. Drive is an unseen force that we feel pulling at our waking life or in our dreams. In its more complex framing, drive lacks an object of satisfaction; it is 'need' in this strict/strong sense.

Moreover, we may conceptualise drive in line with Lacan's rereading of Freud as a circulation of silent force around a core of emptiness. The effects of this circulation are particular to the singular expression of the individual person and warp the otherwise ordinary objective universe on the basis of the satisfactions it may offer, transforming ordinary epistemological relations into something that is a psychological need. In fact, for Freud and Freudians like Lacan, an objective universe is defined by the satisfaction such objectivity promises; it is always already caught up in the effects of drive.

The Freudian tact with which to approach Weber's prohibition against the satisfaction of need in politics for the priest of science (e.g. a teacher) does not annul the need. Instead, it only redirects the need into a recognised and reasonable cultural form. This has two logical impacts for Weber's argument. The first effect is that the ordinary cultural form is elevated to the level of dignity. For example, the mundane form of 'a job' becomes in itself more than itself; the job is not merely a means but a feature that defines the individual who works that job. The second effect is that drive is sent back to where it came from. Sublimation means that there is an *a priori* or primary repression of drive, and in the wake of this repression the sublime elevation of the ordinary form takes place. In the topographies of Freudian psychological philosophy, the agent of prohibition is the person against themselves; the ego is split between the need for satisfaction and the repression of this demand's rational form.

In terms of Weber's argument, the splitting *(Spaltung)* of the teacher's ego from their role as a teacher of *Wissenschaft* presents a formal condition for the moral conscience that bears down on the teacher. In psychoanalysis, the ego is an empty space that gives we mere humans time to reflect on our needs and desires, deciding what to enjoy, what will satisfy us, and what will not bring satisfaction or what is forbidden from being satisfied. In the splitting of the ego by the demands of reality in infancy, the separated part of the ego returns over and above itself. At the level of the ego the fragment is destroyed and replaced by the fantasies of the subject about itself – we no longer merely enjoy satisfaction but we also think about how to get it when it's not there – and through this sublation *(Aufhebung)* it returns at a higher level as the agent of moral conscience or super-ego.[19]

From a psychoanalytic perspective Weber presents us with a tragic figure of the teacher called to science.[20] On the one hand they are destined for *Wissenschaft*,

19 The division is thus: sublimation elevates the individual's need outside itself in a quasi-transcendental manner, whereas sublation fashions an inner censorship masquerading as what is reasonable.

20 The teacher as some protagonist whose strength to adapt to civilization is also their undoing insofar as it may lead to neurotic differences, nervous tics, anxieties about

called to it for the satisfaction of some inspiration, some mania of furious activity. On the other hand this inspiration and mania is sublimated and sublated into acceptable forms where the teacher is to suspend their politics and the demagogue is opened to criticism. The calling to *Wissenschaft* as a vocation becomes the undoing of the one who is called, as part of the inspiration becomes moral conscience. The ensuing mathematics of guilt about how much or how little private political morality enters into what is taught is viewed by Weber as a question of the individual within a society, a self with an Other. Yet it is this Other that calls the individual to a vocation and at the same time stymies the satisfaction of the individual with matters of conscience.

To go further into this problem, let us return to Weber's view of *Wissenschaft* and its disclosure by a priest of science: a teacher. It is clear from Weber's lecture that the knowledge of the teacher is not imaginary or a circular representation but instead aims for knowledge of the real above and beyond the teacher's utility of pleasure. The precise meaning of this 'real' is a matter of some debate. On the one hand, modern post-positivist knowledge, the kind produced through rigorous testing and analysis, is written about particular things in a particular way so as to be accepted by a linguistic community who can make 'sense' of the studies. On the other hand, the separation of perspective from an element of knowledge is frankly absurd: there must always be some mind to do the 'knowing'. The vestiges of such a sense of first-person perspective were the philosophical mainstay of much nineteenth- and twentieth-century philosophy from Fichte to Heidegger and Levinas.[21] Yet it was Freud in the nineteenth century and psychoanalysts from there on – rather than phenomenologists like Levinas – who recognised that reason was not the master of its own house.[22]

For Freud, knowledge about oneself is always incomplete; there is always some level of censorship involved in waking life. When we are asleep, however, this censorship is lifted and the 'mad' play of the dream state ensues. The lesson of Freud's seminal work *The Interpretation of Dreams* is that there is a fundamental gap between the manifest material of our dreams and the latent meaning we attribute to our dreams. The difference, argues Freud, is not put forward by conscious self-censorship but rather by irrational wishes and desires that make such censorship useful to mental functioning, i.e. we can avoid being overwhelmed by the infinite relativity of all things by focusing on what is directly connected within

performance or promotion, perverse rituals of entertainment over education, etc. That which is supposed to bring pleasure and satisfaction in fact brings its opposite.

21 This lineage of phenomenology is very much 'on the nose' for some involved with the speculative turn in contemporary philosophy such as Quentin Meillassoux.

22 In *The Science of Rights* Fichte famously studied the self-positing I of apperception where the logical deduction of subjectivity from such an I is thwarted by its necessary trust in its own positing. This puts Fichte closer to speculative realists like Meillassoux and Freudians like Lacan than is often given credence. See J. G. Fichte, *Foundations of Natural Right*, F. Neuhouser (ed.) and M. Baur (trans.), Cambridge: Cambridge University Press, 2000.

a given situation.[23] For Freud and more recent thinkers like Žižek, manners and etiquette are ways of obliquely satisfying drive with social desire and language games.[24]

For Weber, the social desires and language games of the vocational scientist – the one who hears the call of *Wissenschaft* – rely on the distinction between the priest and the prophet. For the priest, legal and rational authority is maintained by formality and damming up irrational desires. The prophet, on the other hand, maintains charismatic authority, which is more unstable than rational authority and carries greater sway with group psychology, argues Weber. Rational authority can but look on at the popularity of charismatic authority. Yet it is the instability of the latter that makes it prone to criticism. As noted above, however, rational authorities, like a teacher or an adjudicator, do not abide such criticism for Weber. The strange twist that Weber gives rational authority, well worn by psychoanalysts and social theorists in the early twentieth century, is that this lack of open contestability renders rational authority as a highly intimate phenomenon; I must censor myself, I must be reasonable enough, to maintain the veneer of rational authority. The mainstay of charismatic authority, however, is the publicity of belief.

The difference between charisma and reason for Weber thus mirrors the difference between dreams and waking life for Freud. Charismatic authority is irrational yet it is also public. This mirrors the insight from Freud that one's dreams are not really one's own but are a conflux of the 'residues of the day', a poetic phrase that means both the empirical interactions and the cultural epoch received in waking life. Rational authority, like the super-ego of censorship, is an intensely private relation which is set up through the formal strictures of legality and process. In practical terms the difference inheres where charismatic authority displays a parade of ego, voice and action, whereas rational authority interrupts the wild play of the ego to reveal something beyond the pleasure of speaking: knowledge.

The knowledge sought by rational authority in Weber has the peculiar aspect of being desubjectified. This does not render knowledge universal and general applying to all things some of the time[25] but rather singular and particular, applying now and then, respective of the angle of the light, the alignment of various elements, and so forth. Although he is speaking in general conceptual terms, Weber's rational authority is deeply expressive of a singular relation between the call to *Wissenschaft* – this call of the Other – and the coordination of the desire to know that is unique to each individual called to *Wissenschaft*. Unlike the binary oppositions of 'us and them' promoted by charismatic authority, rational authority separates the moral fantasies of the individual from knowledge and subsequently alienates the subject on the side of knowledge rather than subjectivity. The

23 S. Freud, *The Interpretation of Dreams*, Harmondsworth: Penguin Books, 1958, pp. 431–438.

24 S. Žižek, *Tarrying with the Negative*, Durham, NC: Duke University Press, 1993, p. 197.

25 Such a view of occasionalism was famously critiqued by Spinoza as a use of God as an ideological filler for what was inexplicable rather than a calling to study relations more fully.

great struggle of the rational authority is thus how to present knowledge without reducing it to a historicism or the presentism of politics. Rational authority seeks to show what is real insofar as it is not a representation, nor a thing to be reduced to cognitive conditioning, nor a relic of a time in history – all of which entertain moments of self-defeating auto-critique. Beyond these reductions, rational authority seeks where the object of knowledge persists beyond human sensation or 'seeing is believing'.

Weber's lecture offers few clues as to the definition of this knowledge of the real for *Wissenschaft*. Nonetheless he insists that knowledge is the focal point of the calling to *Wissenschaft*. A similar insistence appears in the work of Jacques Lacan. And like the knowledge of the real in Weber, the enigmatic real of Lacan is a notoriously difficult concept to consider, especially if one is more at home with representation and history where all is considered representable or historicised. The real examined by Lacan's work is unnameable and yet knows too much, is unrepresentable and yet thoroughly symbolic, is devoid of meaning and yet sublimely overwhelming. Knowledge of such a real is what science aims for according to Lacan.[26] Such knowledge is neither politically symbolic nor wild and imaginary but instead objective with regard to the subject's point of view.

This attempt to account for knowledge of the real simultaneously occurs with a 'new' kind of subjectivity in Lacan's seminars. Unlike the 'modern' analysand analysed by Freud, Lacan finds a growth of a subjectivity that commodifies itself rather than settles for the dissatisfaction of not having what it wants. The question for such a subject is not 'what will bring me satisfiaction?' but 'what is satisfaction?'[27]

It is well known how trying and difficult living in modern civilisations can be. In his *Civilization and its Discontents* Freud noted the peculiar propensity for people to suffer for some ambiguous good rather than substantial pleasure. Duncan Kennedy similarly noted in his 'Law School as Training for Hierarchy' how the hierarchy of the legal profession engendered by law schools and perhaps earlier by the legalism and knavery of society itself twists a human subject who is already contorted by civilisation. Where for Freud the masochism and narcissism of the civilised person composed a classically tragic figure undone by the civilisation that promises them happiness, and for Kennedy legal hierarchy maintains a web of illusory promises of status while propagating a certain blindness with regards to one's all too human constitution, Lacan's analysis goes further to suggest that the restlessness of the capitalist subject is not indicative of an external force but rather of treating a part of oneself as a commodity for exchange.

Lacan's refinement of the analysand or patient of the psychoanalytic clinic to an auto-phagic subject of capitalism still has purchase in current cultural criticism

26 J. Lacan, *The Seminar of Jacques Lacan, Book XX: On Feminine Sexuality, the Limits of Love and Knowledge, 1972–1973*, J.-A. Miller (ed.) and B. Fink (trans.), London: W. W. Norton & Company, 1998, pp. 127–128.

27 *Ibid.*, pp. 139–141. The logical consequence is that this capitalist subjectivity is necessarily philosophical: lawyers and law students are already down with jurisprudence; it is the knowledge of the law that is their burden.

and analysis. Moreover, the connection with the model of rational authority proposed by Weber in this discussion entails that this self-consuming individual is a *legal* subject of sorts. While there may be some essential differences between law and culture, our area of concern here is the intersection where the legal and the cultural meet in rational authority.

Let us return to Weber's description of jurisprudence for a moment to clarify the situation. Jurisprudence, says Weber,

> Establishes what is valid according to the rules of juristic thought, which is partly bound by logically compelling and partly by conventionally given schemata. Juridical thought holds when certain legal rules and certain methods of interpretations are recognized as binding. Whether there should be law and whether one should establish just these rules – such questions jurisprudence does not answer. It can only state: If one wishes this result, according to the norms of our legal thought, this legal rule is the appropriate means of attaining it.[28]

The description of jurisprudence here is as *Wissenschaft*, a science of the law. Unlike the mere application of the rules to the facts, jurisprudence seeks a critical distance between criteria of validity and convention. The novel twist that Weber gives jurisprudence is not to say that it is inspired or manic, it most certainly is those things, but rather that in its constitutive moment of constructing the law as a rational authority, it commits to the intimate censorship of the adjudicator and the external or 'extimate' censorship of the person for law.

Subjectivity in law, for Weber, rests in its reasonableness as a rational authority. The normative test of the 'reasonable person' in English common law legal systems reflects this super-egoic requirement of reason; not as intelligence or intellect but as the ability to censor oneself to either the para-legal cultural mores of a situation or the laws of which one may or may not be ignorant.

Tests of causation are particularly instructive of this extimate knowledge of the reasonable person. In *Royall v R* (1991) 100 ALR 669 McHugh J. discussed the reasonable foresight of consequences as the test favoured by authorities, particularly in comparison with other tests including operating and substantial causes, natural consequences and *novus actus interveniens*. McHugh J. further suggested that such causation, reasonably foreseeable or otherwise, 'cannot be separated from moral culpability' in criminal cases.[29] The work of Weber, Freud and Lacan provides a way to view this operation of the law as a demand on the subject. This demand is not merely a construction of a criminal code or body of common law but it is more acutely an emphasis on civilisation and the regulation of drive, demanding the price of legal knowledge be the repression, sublimation/sublation

28 *Ibid.*, p. 144.
29 *Royall v R* at 43.

of private moral interest. One is always already bound up with the rational ideal of the law even before guilt is proven.

The legal definition of recklessness is perhaps a more instructive example of construction of the ideal of rational authority through an individual's internalisation of knowledge of the law. In *Victorian Bar Inc. v CEM QC* [2006] VCAT 1417 recklessness was succinctly summed up as 'knowing an act may breach a rule and intending to take that risk'. If there is not a bona fide belief in the breach beforehand, then there is no recklessness. Knowledge and the rational deduction of a breach thus hinge on the sufficient apprehension of rules insofar as they are not the rules of a particular person but the rules of an Other who demands the reasonableness of the individual. If the individual does not adequately submit to the order of the Other but instead tries to perversely 'game' a transgression, knowing something is prohibited but doing it anyway, then the issue becomes about the desire of the Other in the person accused of the transgression. Rather than a positive element inscribed onto the *tabula rasa* of an individual's mind, what we have here is a position where the individual is not a self in isolation. Instead, they are in a particular relation with a psychic authority who does not know what the individual thinks but demands that they only know (not believe). Therein the only rule is to not transgress the limits imposed by this rational order while part of the discourse. The question is thus what satisfaction does the individual get for adhering to the desire of the Other?

Recent work by Renata Salecl has gone some way to working through the question of this satisfaction. In her monograph *The Tyranny of Choice*, Salecl discusses the way that choices make us anxious and can lead to vicarious decision making. Salecl recounts a debate with a graduate law student about the choice of identity:

> one student who stridently insisted that in postmodern times he feels totally free to play with many identities even link[ing] his obedience of rules to different choices that he makes every day with regard to his identity. How he obeys social prohibitions depends, for example, on which identity he is temporarily taking on. In the morning, on his way to the law office where he works, he obeys the sign at the edge of a park that says 'Do not trespass'. In the afternoon, when he's wearing jeans and free from job obligations, he's less inclined to obey. And in the evening, in his free time, he feels free to take on many different identities on the internet: he participates in a Muslim forum pretending to be a Muslim; sometimes he frequents gay internet sites pretending that he is gay; occasionally he presents himself as a woman or a foreigner.[30]

Salecl's overview carries within it some curious markers about the fluidity of the graduate law student's identity. The student shifts his regard for the trespass prohibition not through some empirical change to the prohibition but instead

30 R. Salecl, *The Tyranny of Choice*, London: Profile Books, 2011, p. 45.

through his discursive position, his particular relation with psychic authority. The underlying theme, however, is that the student, always already, may choose to what degree he heeds the prohibition.

Salecl argues that it is the ideology of choice which has 'taught us that we can control our own emotions and always make rational choices' and we may add to this that what is attractive about this ideology is that it promises some rational satisfaction for its rational order.[31] It is not simply that the student is free to choose his identity, but rather that the knowledge of the rule of trespass requires the sublimation of other energies in accordance with the rule. The student *enjoys* this satisfaction through his symbolic identity that, in this case, is his job at the law office. Salecl's example serves to show that the farther the student's symbolic identity is from the institutional form of law, the greater his antagonism with the prohibition becomes. The rational fabric of the law as *Wissenschaft* is here palpably different to something such as discipline. Unlike the disciplinary power promoted by the early work of Foucault, law-as-*Wissenschaft* does not work with what is already there but instead goes on for ever. The student cannot destroy *Wissenschaft* but only keep it, at best, at an antagonistic distance.

The logical consequence is that this student's subjectivity is necessarily philosophical. It is not simply that the student is free to choose his identity, but rather that the knowledge of the rule of trespass requires the sublimation of other energies in accordance with the rule. Therefore the truly subversive alternative to this underlying antagonism is to over-identify with the law and thereby suspend the question of subjectivity altogether. One could imagine this student in Salecl's example attempting to ascertain the substance of the trespass prohibition. Here it is not the case that the student is being sculpted by his law job, his time off, or his proclivity for fictionalising himself on the Internet as certain social constructivists may have one believe. Rather, in over-identification there is nothing but the symbolic identity of the student irrespective of who he subjectively feels himself to be. The subversion of law is thus in the suspension of jurisprudence insofar as the latter is *Wissenschaft*, enabling the lawyer some sense of where the law is heading.

Our discussion thus far raises the question of why Weber put reason and law into a single form of rationality. As the examples of the student and case law demonstrate, there is a keen difference between the subjective sense of a rule and the extimate knowledge of one's position as regards legal knowledge. Given the law is arbitrary, utilising prohibition, techniques of control, systems of adjudication, and measures what is legal by its own rules, there is something distinctly idealistic rather than rational about its operation. In fact, in the post-Kantian moral universe that many inhabit in the West, there is a pressure to rethink the law as rational. Although many legal proceedings may begin from a place of arbitrary power, the jurisprudence of deciding whether the facts fit the legal criteria is a matter of symbolic power, a matter of language and knowledge.

31 *Ibid.*, p. 78.

For Weber similarly, the legal-*cum*-rational form of authority resides in its relation to *Wissenschaft*. Rather than screening off charismatic authority, rationality herein becomes a façade for the void behind the law. Charismatic authority is not a position for authority to default to should law or reason fail. Instead, the structure of charismatic authority is a distinct form that, Weber says, must open itself to criticism. Legal-*cum*-rational authority conversely demands trust. There is nothing beyond legal-*cum*-rational authority to secure its claim to power where such power needs a reason to be claimed. For example, recall here Weber's rigorous analysis of a teacher and the sublation of their political satisfaction in service to the disclosure of knowledge in *Wissenschaft*. The satisfaction of the teacher does not disappear but rather returns in the 'higher' form of *Wissenschaft* as a calling. There is 'nothing' outside the legal-*cum*-rational authority of the teacher to supplement their politics because this outside is constitutive of the teacher; everything that counts to the rational order is inside this domain. To phrase this anew: the sublation of the teacher destroys their political satisfaction, replacing it with extimate knowledge that relies on the discourse provided by *Wissenschaft*.

Weber's 'Science as a Vocation' lecture provides a rich ground to question and critique the structure of authority and the subjection of both teachers and students. Further, the insights into rational authority presented by Weber suggest that the attempt to distance one's own morality, politics and so forth from rational deduction is a complex matter with a psychic topography. This topography depicts an inspired, energised and dynamic individual at once caught between the inner calling to *Wissenschaft* and the extimate knowledge required by a discourse based upon rational authority.

It is not so easy to dismiss Weber's reading of rational authority by claiming that the law is anything but rational. As some critics have put it, the law is what the judge ate for breakfast (Jerome Frank). Yet there is a psychoanalytic subtext in Weber's lecture that shows that at the very height of its irrationality, rational structures give an opportunity to sublimate this distressing irrationality and redirect its energy into a 'higher' promise of rational order. This is the Romantic tragedy of the law: what it builds up through reason and the promise of the rule of law serves at the same time to bring about unhappiness and a need to sublimate or sublate the rational repression of the human animal. It is this tragedy of the law, of jurisprudence as a 'legal science' *(Rechtswissenschaft)*, which gives body to the moral duty of law beyond the utility of pleasure for any one individual.

The psychological investment in the knowledge produced by legal-*cum*-rational authority is of the utmost importance to understanding what draws us to the law. Were it not for the tragedy of the law, one may wish to depict the career jurist as a 'rosy jurisprude' who hears the calling of *Wissenschaft* as a vocation. Yet as the discussion above showed, the drive to know in a disenchanted world, the world preferred by legal positivism, offers a chance to delve the unfathomable depths of real knowledge and occasionally glean an idea of where the law is heading and not merely what it is saying in the present.

Although the law can be baroque at times, relying heavily on ornamentation and ritual with only seeming aesthetic relevance, the jurisprudence it invites remains nonetheless tantalising for its rational origins. The brilliant insight of Freud was that in order to survive the imposition of rational systems and competition with other people, humans have had to learn to not only repress but also sublimate and sublate aggression. This dynamic process creates not only the Unconscious but also a conscience coloured by guilt and love. Lacan's later review of Freud within the limited confines of what was discussed above, suggests that Freud describes in this movement how we as humans are capable of shifting from animals possessed of reason (Aristotle's *zoon logon ekon*) to subjects of a political Cause, a calling to *Wissenschaft* as a vocation, to jurisprudence-as-*Wissenschaft*.

The future of the calling to jurisprudence, not merely the rational acquisition of a law degree or a law job but as *Wissenschaft*, is difficult to see. Weber, Freud and Lacan offer some solace that the turmoil of legal rationality is what brings satisfaction to the individuals involved in the form of a promise of some future satisfaction. Whether or not that satisfaction is delivered is moot; it is the structure of the promise that binds us all to the law as a rational authority.

CHAPTER 5

The master and knowledge after nihilism

While legal knowledge is constitutive of law as a vocation or legal science, the role that university knowledge-production plays in the modern law school remains pivotal to the political economy of the legal profession. In the past, clerkships assured an alternative stream of incoming labour for the lower branches of the legal profession such as solicitors and law clerks. With the demise of these 'commons' access to the law profession today, however, it is law schools at universities that are the primary, soon to be the only, pathway for new lawyers and therein for laws to be produced, revised, or retired. This is a fascinating thing because unlike other modes of traditional mastery – the master and protégé – the university discourse disperses doubt or 'unknowing what you already believe' as its basic gesture of the power relations between teacher and student. Rather than turn to a techno-bureaucratic discourse of university law school administration, I wish to instead examine the ideological quilting points of the discourse of knowledge-production in the university: the master and knowledge. Specifically, what I am dealing with here are the conditions of knowledge under which different types of new lawyers arise. This discussion hinges on the ways that a university discourse produces subject-positions at the level of the signifier, of language. How university students speak puts a certain coordination of desire (for knowledge) into action and this is my focus. This moves the discussion from Weber on jurisprudence as *Wissenschaft* to the generation of such knowledge by the university discourse itself.

Like his liege Jacques Lacan, Slavoj Žižek links philosophy, and inherently legal philosophy, with the discourse of the master.[1] Framed in this way, legal philosophy is an attempt at mastery through the development of grand systems that produce totalising explanations, i.e different schools of thought in legal philosophy each enjoy a narrative voice that becomes 'the narrative voice' of its persuasion. As Lacan told us in 1969 against this over-determination of total explanation, the discourse of the master locates the constantly desiring subject as the one able to escape (although *not always* escaping) from the awe of the master's 'pure

1 J. Lacan, *Écrits*, B. Fink (trans.), New York: W. W. Norton & Company, 2006, p. 671.

prestige'.[2] This contrary subject is Cartesian to the extent that they do not believe in the grandeur of the master and instead find themselves persistently doubting their own doubts about the prestige of the master.[3] Herein every attempt at totalisation by the master results in failure because the subject 'doing the dirty work' constitutes the remainder of the discourse. In an echo of Hegel: what the master wants done is obtained by their loyal subjects. In *Seminar XVII* Lacan shows such a framing as the reverse of psychoanalysis, and this may well suggest an inherent tension in the work of Žižek given that his engagement with philosophy consistently relies on a Lacanian, psychoanalytic, framing.[4]

Žižek's resistance against the master's discourse, and therein philosophy, takes on a specific structure in the university's discourse and this will be the focus of our discussion to come. As a Lacanian commonplace, the university's discourse is derivative of the master's discourse. In the university's discourse, knowledge is the over-determining factor, present in modernity as 'the hegemony of science' wherein the notion of science, rather than a figure, becomes the master. However, this over-determination finds a point of resistance in the argument for mastery itself. As Lacan notes, 'The slave knows many things, but what he knows even better still is what the master wants, even if the master does not know it himself, which is the usual case, for otherwise he would not be a master. The slave knows what it is, and that's what his function as slave is.'[5] In the same way, Žižek speaks of the ideological shibboleth of modern science; that the purported neutrality of scientific knowledge is in fact ideologically loaded.[6]

Žižek utilises the master's and university's discourses in his attempt to elaborate on a disjuncture between the Victorian culture contemporary of Freud and the *fin-de-siècle* of the twentieth century.[7] In this way Žižek is able to designate Freud's analysis of civilization in *Civilization and its Discontents*,[8] a discussion of the master's discourse, the era when capitalism firmly entrenched itself and spawned a series of social alternatives under charismatic leaders, including

2 J. Lacan, *The Seminar of Jacques Lacan Book XVII: The Other Side of Psychoanalysis*, R. Grigg (trans.), New York: W. W. Norton & Company, 2007, p. 32.

3 This effectively undermines what Žižek, alongside critics of theory such as Knapp and Michaels ('Against Theory' in *The Norton Anthology of Theory & Criticism, 2nd edition*, V. B. Leitch (ed.), London: W. W. Norton & Company, 2010), identify as the belief before belief – the basic assurance of my 'normal' functioning in the symbolic universe.

4 Lacan *op. cit.*, p. 144.

5 *Ibid.*, p. 32.

6 S. Žižek, 'Introduction: Cogito as a Shibboleth', in S. Žižek (ed.), *Cogito and the Unconscious*, Durham, NC: Duke University Press, 1998, p. 3.

7 S. Žižek, 'In His Bold Gaze My Ruin is Writ Large', in S. Žižek (ed.), *Everything You Always Wanted to Know About Lacan (But Were Afraid to Ask Hitchcock)*, London: Verso, 1992, pp. 136 & 140–143.

8 S. Freud, *Civilisation and its Discontents*, J. Strachey (ed. and trans.), New York: W. W. Norton & Company, 2010, pp. 39–41.

socialism under Lenin and Stalin.[9] It has been noted by Žižek's Lacanian critics such as Yannis Stavrakakis, Ian Parker, and others[10] that he does not produce an alternative to today's advanced capitalism because he is not interested in historicising Freud. And it is in this refusal of historicism that Žižek finds himself engaged in the discourse of the university, where one can shift endlessly between perspectives and focus on the *a priori* conditions of knowledge, a kind of mastery without the ideological quilting sustained by a charismatic leader.

If the master's discourse marks the era of Freud for Žižek, it is the discourse of the university that distinguishes the twenty-first century. Knowledge mitigates the university's discourse in opposition to desire, promising itself as neutral knowledge free of vested ideological agendas or pathological interests.[11] This subsequently produces a subject barred from knowledge in its totality. Such a totality of knowledge is even hidden from knowledge itself as it constantly works to discover more. In Žižek's materialism this appears as the point where the subject is a blind spot inherent in their own perspective. Here we find Žižek's reading of Lacan with modern science: it is impossible to explain everything, but knowledge is prized above all else and so everything must be revealed.[12] Yet what is the cost of this elevation of the value of knowledge?

If we turn to the master's discourse for a moment, we find that the master holds sway as the agent and is opposed to knowledge. A master must have his subjects, his others, believe he is a master – his believability sustaining him as the big Other. As soon as the master's position is questioned, belief is lost and the master's authority undermined, so it is necessary for the master to maintain the ideal image of himself as a kind of decoy – the burden of responsibility.[13] The master believes the position he imagines for himself, realises the constitutive exception that affords him supreme authority. That is to say, the God-given right for a king to rule is an impossible relation between the empty place produced by a grand ineffable Other (God) and the king's duty to be king. The reason why a position of privilege exists is thus cast as a mystery that the unprivileged cannot resolve because they believe this mystery to be self-evident – the king is king because he is

9 S. Žižek, 'A Plea for a Return to *Différance* (with a Minor *Pro Domo Sua*)', *Critical Inquiry* 32/2, 2006, p. 311; Žižek, *op. cit.*, pp. 8–9.

10 Y. Stavrakakis, 'The Lure of Antigone: Aporias of an Ethics of the Political', in G. Boucher, J. Glynos and M. Sharpe (eds.), *Traversing the Fantasy: Critical Responses to Slavoj Žižek*, Aldershot: Ashgate, 2005; I. Parker, *Slavoj Žižek: A Critical Introduction*, London: Pluto Press, 2004; J. Glynos, 'Radical Democratic Ethos, or, What is an Authentic Political Act?', *Contemporary Political Theory* 2, 2003, pp. 199–201; T. Foster, *The Souls of Cyberfolk: Posthumanism as Vernacular Theory*, Minneapolis: University of Minnesota Press, 2005, p. 92.

11 S. Žižek, *Iraq: The Borrowed Kettle*, London: Verso, 2004, p. 14.

12 S. Žižek, *The Plague of Fantasies*, London: Verso, 1997, p. 160.

13 This is formulated as the Lord and Bondsman dialectic by Hegel in the *Phenomenology of Spirit*.

the king. Without belief one may choose to obey the king because he is wise and just, but to do so is 'the crime of *lèse-majesté*'.[14]

At this juncture we can also observe how the ideological power of knowledge is linked to the Unconscious. The production of scientific knowledge progresses in its ideology-free state insofar as it remains unaware of its inherent knowledge bias; those who do not know are ostracised to the realm of the *un*-conscious. Those who are conscious of knowledge, who know, are welcomed into the fold of the discourse where one can become a vessel of sharing knowledge, but only inasmuch as they know only what they can as individuals and not the totality of 'knowledges'. Herein the privilege of the university discourse is to be expendable to the discourse; the mastery of knowledge always slips away from the subject, allowing the constant space to learn. Mastery and forgetfulness are here revealed as the impossible truth of the discourse: the promise of power in the form of mastery and the danger of never knowing all knowledge. These two sides of impossibility designate the condition of the subject whereby they are always in process and not a fixed reservoir of knowledge. This culminates in the ethical construction of duty, where the revelation of everything must continue despite any desires to the contrary – desire being created at the very moment we are set with an injunction 'to know'.

According to Stavrakakis, Žižek's Lacanian analyses show the socio-political conceptual effects of this transition from the fascination with the image of the master to the quest for scientific truth or 'knowledge of the real' in the university discourse. By 'conceptual effects' we are here inferring 'what is at stake in Žižek's argument is not only the possibility of resisting, but also of undermining or displacing the existing socio-symbolic network'.[15] Žižek does not wish to return to the imaginary master, but rather sets the scene for another transition co-ordinated by the conditions of the university's discourse. Because the fantasmatic promise of the master-*qua*-Other is barred in the university's discourse, the master loses the mystique inculcated by this promise of being believable as a master standing in for the Other. Žižek thus looks to move through a formal negativity of sorts wherein no mystery can abide because scientific truth is undetermined by ideological fantasies to a frame where concrete experience is contingently symbolised and/or evaluated.[16] In his response to Stavrakakis, Žižek qualifies this latter movement as one borne out by 'an "impossible" gesture of pure expenditure [that] can change the very coordinates of what is strategically possible within a historical constellation'.[17] It follows from this qualification that the production of knowledge in the indeterminateness of the university's discourse emerges from a negative space which can be transformed by an excessive redefining of 'the rules and contours

14 S. Žižek, *For They Know Not What They Do: Enjoyment as a Political Factor*, London: Verso, 1991, p. 235.
15 Stavrakakis, *op. cit.*, p. 171.
16 *Ibid.*, p. 177.
17 S. Žižek, 'What Some Would Call …: A Response to Yannis Stavrakakis' *Umbr(a): Ignorance of the Law*, 2003, p. 133.

of the existing order' rather than a solution generated by the prevailing order of knowledge production.[18]

The critical value of the above to this discussion of Žižek's critical engagement is that it demonstrates how the shift from a discourse creating a majestic master of all to a discourse crafting an expendable subject supposed-to-know is a triumph of the mystifying force of imagination that scientific knowledge is supposed to overcome.[19] Where in the master's discourse we have a master whose existence legitimates and binds our social existence, the discourse of the university gives us no such assurance that the social order is justifiable in itself. Here Žižek is in agreement with Herbert Marcuse and the early Frankfurt School that the desublimation of objects invested with suprasensible value into neutral knowledge to be known by all is, in effect, a repressive mechanism.[20] The claimed neutrality of knowledge removes the limit of civil sociality/engagement rather than bringing us closer to a more fulfilling life flourishing in self-development, opening us to ferocious insatiable desires for ever more knowledge which we will obtain at any price.[21] Notwithstanding this argument's frequently iterated Lacanian coordinates, the casting of this kind of knowledge-directed hedonism as the cultural milieu of the developed world is typical of the social, political and cultural critiques to have emerged from Žižek and other Slovenian intellectuals such as Mladen Dolar, Renata Salecl, and Alenka Zupančič in recent decades.[22]

Following this school of thought, it is the discord created by this contradiction of a subject enjoying their knowledge only to be needing to know in simultaneously less satiating and increasingly intense ways that is the key to unlocking the prevailing strictures for the domain of the Imaginary.[23] The psychoanalytic Imaginary extends through Žižek's critical discourse, the three distinct modes elaborated by the early structuralist Lacan. First as an imaginary image or fantasy decoy keeping the subject from the truth; in the instance of the university's discourse, where the knowledge of the subject supposed to know is reduced to a subjective shadow of vested interests.[24] Second as an imaginary symbol or archetype

18 *Ibid.*, p. 133.

19 S. Žižek, *The Parallax View*, Cambridge, MA: The MIT Press, 2006.

20 S. Buck-Morss, *Origin of Negative Dialectics: Theodor W. Adorno, Walter Benjamin, and the Frankfurt School*, New York: The Free Press, 1979, pp. 103 & 173; H. Marcuse, *One-Dimensional Man*, London: Sphere Books Ltd, 1972, pp. 57–58.

21 S. Žižek, 'The Politics of *Jouissance*', *Lacanian Ink* 24/25, 2005, p. 130.

22 S. Žižek, *Tarrying with the Negative: Kant, Hegel, and the Critique of Ideology*, Durham, NC: Duke University Press, 1993; M. Dolar, *A Voice and Nothing More*, Cambridge, MA: The MIT Press, 2006; R. Salecl, *On Anxiety*, London: Routledge, 2004; R. Salecl, *The Spoils of Freedom: Psychoanalysis and Feminism After the Fall of Socialism*, London: Routledge, 1994; A. Zupančič, *Ethics of the Real: Kant, Lacan*, London: Verso, 2000.

23 P. Dews and P. Osborne, 'Lacan in Slovenia: An Interview with Slavoj Žižek and Renata Salecl', *Radical Philosophy* 58, 1991, p. 31.

24 Lacan, *op. cit.*, p. 73; Žižek, *Tarrying with the Negative: Kant, Hegel, and the Critique of Ideology, op. cit.*, pp. 89–90.

that conditions all possibilities for the subject to share their knowledge or know anything, i.e. talent.[25] And, third, as a real fantasy staging an imaginary scenario in the place of the horrifying truth constructing the impermeable neutrality of knowledge in the place of subjective destitution, so the subject languishes in their enjoyment of knowing and alienates themselves from human engagement.[26] Herein the production of ever more intensive ways of enjoying ourselves logically proceeds from the tyranny of knowledge. But this intensity is absurd, typified by objects that attempt to give us something that is actually nothing, things devoid of all pathological content. When the modern scientific approach removes the element of mystery from the object, it takes away this promise. Without the fantasmatic promise the object is objectively destitute. What we are deprived of here is the rule of fantasy whereby the object we desire seems to enlist our fascination by promising something a little bit extra, beyond its mere objective characteristics. The objects of perception can only exist insofar as it conforms to our fantasy-frame, 'the subject can never occupy the neutral place which would allow him or her to exclude completely the hallucinatory fantasmatic reality', because fantasy offers reality a cogency and therein a placement of the subject despite the inadequacy of what one can know.[27] This primordial position of fantasy facilitates the dialectic of presence and absence wherein some absence or gap in knowledge can only be noted on the basis of something having previously been present. Thus fantasy serves to cover any gaps that appear, due to the uncritical nature of existence by virtue of its being a presupposition as such.

If we examine this entrapment of the Imaginary closely we find the minimal difference appears to dissipate the decoy (fantasised object), and yet this coincides with the real fantasy scenario. The scene is thus set for the epistemological status of the subject – as a rational intellectual being – to detain them from the ontological dimension containing the true object-cause of their desire.[28] Boredom ensues because the subject is trapped in the ontic sphere of ordinary objects. Without recourse to an ontological ordering of the world a manic nihilism permeates the subject's sense of awe, restricting our capacity to enjoy the Imaginary as a theatre for fantasising.[29] To keep awe at bay, nihilism elevates axioms of technological progress to challenge the world of fervent production, instant gratification and immediate contact.[30] At base, the fecundity of a world of ordinary 'technical'

25 Lacan, *ibid.*, p. 79; S. Žižek, *The Sublime Object of Ideology*, London: Verso, 1989, pp. 105–107.

26 Lacan, *ibid.*, p. 80; Žižek, *The Puppet and the Dwarf: The Perverse Core of Christianity*, *op. cit.*, p. 129.

27 Žižek, *Tarrying with the Negative: Kant, Hegel, and the Critique of Ideology*, *op. cit.*, p. 89.

28 *Ibid.*, pp. 196–197.

29 S. Žižek, 'The Real of Sexual Difference' in *Interrogating the Real*, R. Butler & S. Stephens (eds), London: Continuum, 2005, p. 348.

30 M. Heidegger, 'The Question Concerning Technology', in *Basic Writings: from Being and Time (1927) to The Task of Thinking (1964)*, D. F. Krell (ed.), San Francisco: HarperCollins Publishers, 1993, pp. 320–321.

objects is its immediacy; it is a world ready to attend our beckoning, not an alternative social vision.[31] A return to the Imaginary from our passion for the Real is a regression in the eyes of Žižek because we lose the ability to differentiate ourselves amongst a cosmos of technical objects.

This ontological crisis provides Žižek's discussions of scientific-technological innovation and politics with a bastion of critical insight. Advances in biogenetics, particularly the mapping of the human genome, affirm the presence of this dangerous nihilism; 'by reducing man to just another natural object whose properties can be manipulated' we lose the very situation of nature which biogenetic research investigates.[32] To Žižek's mind this brings us closer to an understanding of Fukuyama's thesis. If humanity gives history its enduring value, history ends when scientific innovation and technical rationality have refigured human nature as a transparent object of inquiry reduced to an ordinary ontic object.[33] Human nature must be an opaque 'impenetrable dimension in/of ourselves into which we are born/thrown' to sustain the enigma of each individual's humanity.[34] In this way human nature is more than the ground of desires that can be reduced solely to chemical processes in the brain. By refiguring human nature as a manipulable technical object, it becomes merely another object to be subjected to a scientific regime that cannot perceive its own ideological investment in treating all things as mere undignified objects.[35] Such a process perpetuates the annihilation of the metaphysical subspecies of human nature such as civil sociality, love and care. Herein it becomes clear that metaphysics as 'meta' relies on the ineffability of its object, that something is always beyond our grasp.

The decline of humanity and its ethico-political sub-spheres in this fashion, coupled with the promulgation of a totalising epistemological ideological framework, can lead into an intellectual barbarism. An example of this is Richard Wolin's accusation that Žižek suggests the attacks on the World Trade Center in New York on the 11th of September, 2001, (hereafter 9/11) gave the United States of America what it deserved. Where Žižek states in *Welcome to the Desert of the Real*, his response to 9/11, 'America got what it fantasised about', Wolin suggests Žižek is insinuating '*America got what it had coming*'.[36] Responding to Wolin's criticism, Žižek quotes himself at length to show that he explicitly denies the 'leftist *Schadenfreude*' Wolin accuses him of.[37]

Specifically, Wolin has confused Žižek's discussion of what the US fantasised about with an ethical plea. Elsewhere in this volume Žižek makes his ethical plea

31 M. Heidegger, *The Basic Problems of Phenomenology*, A. Hofstadter (trans.), Indianapolis: Indiana University Press, 1982, pp. 162–166.

32 S. Žižek, *Organs Without Bodies: On Deleuze and Consequences*, London: Routledge, 2004, p. 124.

33 *Ibid.*, pp. 128–129.

34 *Ibid.*, p. 124.

35 Žižek, 'Introduction: Cogito as a Shibboleth', *op. cit.*, pp. 78–79.

36 Žižek, 'A Plea for a Return to Différence (with a Minor Pro Domo Sua)', *op. cit.*, p. 307.

37 *Ibid.*

to defuse the 'moralising mathematics of guilt and horror' invoked by Wolin's criticism, stating 'the only appropriate stance is unconditional solidarity with *all* victims'.[38] This sparring between Žižek and Wolin shows how the collapsing of the real fantasy scenario and the fantasy decoy aspects of the Imaginary blinds the critical gaze from seeing the folly of its critique. Were Wolin to read the notion of fantasy invoked by Žižek as psychoanalytic fantasy and not some epistemological realism about *the way things really are*, as well as observe the coincidence of the real fantasy scenario and objective circumstances producing a nightmare which Žižek ethically marshals against, then Žižek's position ceases to be as easily manipulated and Wolin may need to find a fresh rationale for his criticism – short of reneging it altogether (S. Žižek, *The Universal Exception*, R. Butler and S. Stephens (eds), London: Continuum, 2006, pp. 230–231).

The fundamental problem with Wolin's criticism is a Lacanian–Heideggerian one: the object itself is lost in the very registration of it as a 'functional object'. Žižek's argument disappears in the misrecognition of the functionality of the argument as its dignity – in Heideggerian terms, Žižek's essay has been enframed by the advance of Wolin's ontological forgetfulness or nihilism.[39] This disappearing act situates Žižek's discussion of 9/11 in standing-reserve or, to use Heidegger's term, *Bestand*. By enframing Žižek's discussion within *Bestand*, Wolin sacrifices critical cogency for the opportunity to 'bombastically' read Žižek. Heidegger observes this condition of *Bestand* to be a sense of objectlessness overriding the distinction between objects, gradually levering them all into the category of standing-reserve.[40] In standing-reserve, objects are framed in a passive mode so that they may be ready-to-hand without being present as such. A critical problem arises at this point because *Bestand* is a process of challenging existence, the world as it is, with nihilistic annihilation. Therein *Bestand* affects both interpretations and interactions with the objects around us. It is conceptual as well as pragmatic. Seen through Žižek's critical gaze, this destructive nihilism attempts to cut off the self from investment in a world of objects where we externalise our identity and organise our lives.[41] This is the forgetfulness that so concerned Heidegger when he examined questions of technological progress, and Wolin's critique also appears to succumb to this regression.

This invocation of Heidegger draws on something within the horizon of Žižek's theorising: in its philosophical dimension his theorising of knowledge, science and technology explicitly relies on a Heideggerian analysis.[42] In this spirit of

38 S. Žižek, *Welcome to the Desert of the Real: Five Essays on September 11 and Related Dates*, London: Verso, 2002, p. 51.

39 More recently in *In Defense of Lost Causes*, London: Verso, 2008, pp. 304–333, Žižek has responded to this same *problematique* emerging in Stavrakakis' work *The Lacanian Left*, Edinburgh: Edinburgh University Press, 2007.

40 Heidegger, *op. cit.*, p. 229; Heidegger, *op. cit.*, p. 324.

41 Žižek, *Organs Without Bodies: On Deleuze and Consequences', op. cit.*, pp. 32–36.

42 For example see S. Žižek, *The Ticklish Subject: The Absent Centre of Political Ontology*, London: Verso, 1999, pp. 12–13.

critique his analyses attend to the division of the everyday ontic world of objects and the ontological horizon of meaning, divided by the very existence of the subject.[43] While the phenomenology of Heidegger and the psychoanalysis of Lacan do display an agreement that the subject is split and creates this split, simply by being a subject, each attends to this in quite different ways.[44] Žižek treads a jagged path between these two figures, favouring Lacanian psychoanalysis. This can be observed in his discussions of the modern scientific subject as simultaneously the pure thinking substance of the Cartesian cogito and the Lacanian split-subject.[45]

For Žižek the Cartesian cogito emerges in psychoanalysis as the barred subject of desire, in so much as the cogito is a transparent self that always has something as its object.[46] Yet for Lacan the cogito itself appears as a stain on the perception of its object so that we can imagine seeing ourselves through the gaze of the object.[47] When the ontic world is eroded it becomes apparent that the cogito is still there even though it is deprived of all its positive content, appearing as 'the I of pure self-consciousness'.[48] We may say then that at a zero level the self is a minimal difference, a negative weight. In terms of consciousness Žižek sets forth this Rumsfeldian unknown known as the Lacanian subject of desire.

For Žižek the subject (*qua* cogito) may only manifest itself at the point where the support of the symbolic universe is suspended, where knowledge disappears.[49] If the subject did attempt to fill their lack with knowledge, they achieve what Lacan calls 'knowledge in the Real'. Conceiving knowledge in this way problematically reads the real fantasy of neutral knowledge as the truth of knowledge, its excess. This totalisation freezes the mists of the impermeable kernel of knowledge that exceed what can be known, the very desire to learn that postpones a totalitarianism of knowledge.[50] Such a filling out of the cogito in the university's discourse collapses the discourse into mysticism because the empty place on virtue of which knowledge can be shared by many is filled by one. But this constituting of unity, a unified knowledge, represses the presence of contingency in the symbolic universe constituted by knowledge. Thus we enter a regression from learning to indoctrination, from the process of constant corroboration to blinding ourselves to the reality that it is knowledge's indeterminateness that sustains its validity. Even more importantly, by repressing this indeterminateness in the Symbolic we find its return in the Real where we no longer have the reign of a Symbolic Order and therein no verification of knowledge, only belief.[51] The slippage of

43 *Ibid.*, pp. 13–16.
44 Heidegger, *op. cit.*, pp. 47–49; Lacan, *op. cit.*, pp. 201–205.
45 Žižek, *The Plague of Fantasies, op. cit.*, p. 12.
46 Žižek, *Tarrying with the Negative: Kant, Hegel, and the Critique of Ideology, op. cit.*, p. 42.
47 Lacan, *op. cit.*, pp. 78–80.
48 Žižek, *op. cit.*, p. 38.
49 *Ibid.*, p. 42.
50 *Ibid.*, p. 36.
51 Q. Meillassoux, *After Finitude: An Essay on the Necessity of Contingency*, R. Brassier (trans.), London: Continuum, pp. 110–111.

knowledge allows knowledge to be an effective social lubricant at the same time that it subverts a total mastery of knowledge which would be its mystical undoing (S. Žižek, 'From "Passionate Attachments" to Dis-Identification', *Umbr(a)* 1, 1998, pp. 78–79).

The freezing of the university's discourse through the totalisation of knowledge gestures again toward the role of the Imaginary in Žižek's (1989) critical thought. The Imaginary creates a 'freeze', a temporal loop that repeats over and over again. When knowledge fantastically fills out the subject, explaining away their desires, the tension with our own mortality dissipates into a myth of eternity. And it is here that Žižek can enter into a psychoanalytic discussion of the human condition, precisely because this infinity carries the symptom of being a subject. To put it another way, the knowledge the subject uses to fill out their subjective destitution is a cipher that abstracts the subject from the domain of enjoyment, reducing the self to an egotistic manipulator.[52] By placing the world at hand into a passive mode, 'standing-reserve' succeeds in endowing the subject with a fetishist's delight for further technological domination because it promises fulfilment while the very mode of the subject as a minimal difference bars the subject from actual fulfilment.

Žižek follows Benjamin and Freud in presenting the fetishist appeal of technology as 'the sex-appeal of the inorganic'.[53] But Žižek's critical gaze delineates this reading into two strands: the Marxist modernism of Benjamin, and the psychoanalytic criticism of Freud. In both modes the fetish is covering over a gap, in the process globalising this suture (the fetishist's lie) in the dominant category of the mode of critique, i.e. a social critique categorically over-determines the category of 'the social', thus reducing all phenomena to their manifestation in the idealised realm of the Social. According to Žižek, modernism is fascinated with the Imaginary.[54] Herein Benjamin's critique of technological prosthesis, in the case of nineteenth-century Parisian fashion, considers the outward significance of artificiality played upon by fashion-as-commodity hides the positive social relations that go into the production of the fashion objects, allowing the fashion commodities to magically appear to exist independently.[55] On the other hand, psychoanalytic criticism focuses on the hard kernel of the Lacanian Real resisting integration into the imaginary cosmos of commodities. It is important to note that Žižek articulates the Real in this instance as that which 'always returns to the same place'.[56] Thus in the psychoanalytic framework fetishism hides the lack around which the symbolic universe circulates. But further than this, in the case

52 J.-A. Miller, 'Introduction to the Erotics of Time', B. P. Fulks (trans.), *Lacanian Ink* 24/25, 2005, p. 23.

53 See W. Benjamin, *Charles Baudelaire: A Lyric Poet in the Era of High Capitalism*, H. Zohn (trans.), London: Verso, 1983; Freud, *op. cit.*

54 Žižek, 'In His Bold Gaze My Ruin is Writ Large', *op. cit.*

55 Benjamin, *op. cit.*, pp. 164–166; Foster, *op. cit.*, p. 92.

56 Žižek, *Tarrying with the Negative: Kant, Hegel, and the Critique of Ideology*, *op. cit.*, p. 49.

of modernism the Imaginary register is still structurally sound, a symbolic universe (of commodities) is in full swing. In the psychoanalytic critique we find far less efficient symbolic work, the compulsion to repeat the covering-over of the Real-kernel is explained away by the fetishist acting out their fetish – they repeat without being aware that they are repeating and thus feel unencumbered by this repetition.[57]

Fetishism also persists in the university's discourse where the Real is fetishised as an object of knowledge. While we fearlessly revel in the revealing of the Unknown where 'X really is X', the very method of modern scientific discovery compels us to constantly validate X, lest it cave into a sort of scientific nominalism.[58] To move from the Cartesian subject of modern science to a nominal positive cosmos of New Age archetypes is what Freud observed as the regression into hallucination, not solipsism.[59] Although similarly engaged in instating an imagined reality in the place of the Real, hallucination connects the subject to the world beyond the conscious, while solipsism reduces the world to mere consciousness. The nominalist regression inversely separates from fetishism by tending toward a *sensory* end where the acting out of the fetish is a *motor*-repetition.[60] The repetition of the fetishist is 'beyond the pleasure principle', 'it is striving for a homeostatic balance, and the symbolic order in its blind automatism is always troubling this homeostasis'.[61] Regression is the disintegration of the symbolic order, our assurance of access to some shared universe of communication. Hallucination returns the subject to the sensory emphasis of a nominal modernism, foreclosing on the cut of the symbolic order that castrates the subject thus stealing their homeostasis. Within the structure of the university's discourse this is a regression away from the elevated passion for knowledge (in the Real) to a nihilism founded on a mystical resignation that there is no ground for knowledge to become Wisdom.

The path of regression is often part of Žižek's ideology-critique because both the subject and the big Other of the Symbolic Law are impinged by regression. A regressive understanding forgets that the big Other of the symbolic universe is itself lacking through its dialectical emergence with the symbolic castration of the subject and becomes a monadic entity. Without this inconsistency of the big Other, the only path open to the subject 'would be his radical alienation in the Other'.[62] The inconsistency of the big Other offsets alienating oneself in the known, 'the Other itself "hasn't got it," hasn't got the final answer – that is to say, is in itself blocked, desiring; that there is also desire of the Other'.[63] The lack

57 S. Freud, *Beyond the Pleasure Principle and Other Writings*, J. Reddick (trans.), London: Penguin Books Ltd., 2003, p. 37.

58 S. Žižek, 'Hitchcock's Organs Without Bodies', *Lacanian Ink* 22, 2003, p. 133.

59 S. Freud, *The Interpretation of Dreams*, Harmondsworth: Penguin Books, 1958, pp. 694–696.

60 *Ibid.*, p. 692.

61 Žižek, *The Sublime Object of Ideology*, *op. cit.*, p. 132.

62 *Ibid.*, p. 122.

63 *Ibid.*

in the Other gives the subject a kind of space to breathe, where they can identify their lack with the lack in the Other. Fetishism coordinates this lack, points our desires toward the fetishised object alienated from the ordinary world of objects and alienating the subject from the Other – jealously I assume the Other's desire is my desire.

The globalised lie of fetishism is that such domination over desirable objects is the task of the subject, to compete with the Other for the object (knowledge). For example, without the extensive automation of technology, the subject can only dominate nature through brute force alone, a force that brings mortality to the forefront of the relation with the world.[64] Faced with such Real-finitude, the subject faces a dissolution that is not merely physical but corporeal, the very embodiment of pleasure is threatened by something beyond our control in a moment of tragic realisation. Fetishism takes away this tragic *pathos* with its intense fascination with a particular object which stands in for raw life.

We can see this critique of fetishism and *pathos* in the threat drawn out by human tragedies such as train wrecks, avalanches, earthquakes, and so forth. In these cases of tragedy the threat comes from the rescuers themselves who go into the fray, risking their own lives to save others'. The tragedy of the actual loss of life is supplemented by the potential loss of life, its spectre. Rather than helping us to interpret tragic scenarios, such valorisation of the spectral dimension inflates the trauma of tragedy by desubjectivising our experience of *pathos*. Such a move is contrary to Benjamin's suggestion that exposure to low-level anxieties 'toughens' us to the experience of trauma and tragedy. The Žižekian contention is that we risk losing ourselves in the fantasising of tragedy, only to find ourselves too near the inexplicable horror of trauma – Real-trauma.

Such risk is central to Chuck Palahniuk's short portrait *Bodhisattvas* about Michelle Keating and the dogs she took with her on volunteer aid missions to hurricane-wrecked Honduras in 1998.[65] Talking about another search-and-rescue volunteer she says, 'Harry said, "These people are hungry and they might want to eat your dog." And I was driving home from a meeting with him, I was going, "I don't want to die!" – but I knew I wanted to go.'[66] Keating's knowledge of her own desire to go and help in Honduras brushes up against the ethical limit of political action. Her position is one of universal exception; Keating sends herself despite her conflicted desires and the obvious political option to keep one's distance and send aid (someone else). It is the immediacy of this situation that draws out the ethic of desire from Keating, that she should not give way on her desire. Herein is the lesson of the university's discourse: although we may strive for the mastery of knowledge and be thwarted by the frailty of our own human condition in its exploration of ontic and ontological objects, we must not give in to our desire to

64 Foster, *op. cit.*, p. 92.

65 C. Palahniuk, 'Bodhisattvas' in *Non-Fiction (True Stories)*, London: Vintage, 2004.

66 *Ibid.*, p. 161.

either learn no more or fill in the empty place of mastery we strive for. In short, the ethical injunction of the human condition in post-modernity is 'do not stop!'

With mastery cast as a Pyrrhic victory of perpetual knowledge production and forgetfulness framed as an inescapable aspect of the subject's reticence with the critical value of knowledge, the drive 'to know' appears absurd. Yet such absurdity is ideological *par excellence* because knowledge is now itself ineffable and yet reality is rendered 'straight', without the stains of distortion that are the ideological over-determinations identified by the critique of the master undertaken by the university's discourse. The agony of never knowing enough and the absurdity of pursuing the process itself *ad infinitum* indicate two facets we have so far left unaddressed. When Žižek frames mastery as the substantialisation of knowledge in the Real, he reveals a subject obsessed with possibility.[67] To take up knowledge in the register of the Real is to shun the possibility afforded to the subject in fantasy. The deferral of fantasy in the transition from a subject supposed-to-know to an impossible knowing subject disallows the subject direct access to knowledge, sublimating it through the slippage of knowledge as one ontic idea refers to another.

In his Heidegger-inspired critique of postmodernism, Žižek sets the triumph of everyday ontic objects in two positions. On the one hand we have the objects of our daily lives placed into standing-reserve so they are constantly at hand. The prevalence of multipurpose handheld technologies in urban environments, like mobile phones that can store appointments, emails and music, as well as compose and store video, pictures and phone calls, reinstates this haste of everyday living. It is curious how the more compact and functional our everyday objects become, the faster our way of living becomes. Complementing this pace is the inescapable forgetfulness of the finite knowing subject contained in the very structure of knowledge; new technologies perpetually overturn old systems, old technologies return with new uses, and so on, but always with the subject alienated from this cycle of obsolescence.[68] This situation is functional without having a political cause or *raison d'être* as such.[69]

Although this functioning within a field of energies is reminiscent of the Nietzschean overcoming of mystical idols, it holds a course that is the underbelly of this overcoming. Žižek distinguishes his critique from Heideggerian analysis at this point by identifying this underbelly as a plentiful domain of imaginary decoys, scenarios and archetypes in an effort to compensate for the loss of symbolic structure *à la* Adorno.[70] However, without the efficient ordering of the Symbolic, this nihilism cannot grasp the world anew, and indeed the Imaginary modes themselves are reduced to whatever enjoyment they can bring to the subject – their

67 Žižek, *For They Know Not What They Do: Enjoyment as a Political Factor*, *op. cit.*, p. 242.

68 *Ibid.*, pp. 221–222.

69 Žižek, *The Ticklish Subject: The Absent Centre of Political Ontology*, *op. cit.*, pp. 156–157.

70 S. Žižek, *The Fragile Absolute – Or Why the Christian Legacy is Worth Fighting For*, London: Verso, 2000, p. 41.

functionality. In this way communications technologies intervene in the absence of human contact, yet they do not relate the subject to an other but stand in for the absence of this other.[71] Žižek alludes to such examples to indicate Imaginary-fantasisation running riot without sufficient symbolic efficiency, and therein the need for a reflexive auto-critique of oneself to constrain this fantasising mania of such nihilistic narcissism.[72]

The title of Palahniuk's *Bodhisattvas* gives us some clue as to the core dynamic of such a reflexive critique. Žižek takes up an analysis of the namesake *bodhisattva* to demonstrate the way dwelling in the realm of fantasy, the Imaginary, postpones leaving the fantasy scenario which appears as reality.[73] In Žižek's discussion, the *bodhisattva* of Mahayana Buddhism is defined as an enlightened being of compassion that can enter Nirvana because they are a *bodhisattva*, and yet they simultaneously cannot enter because this movement displays a selfishness which a *bodhisattva* does not have. The *bodhisattva* is in a deadlock. Danto's *Mysticism and Morality* is quoted by Žižek to bring this point to greater effect: 'no one can reach Nirvana: we cannot because we are not *bodhisattvas* and the *bodhisattva* cannot because he is a *bodhisattva*.'[74] The *bodhisattva*'s resolution of their deadlock highlights the '*impossibility* of such an immediate withdrawal of the individual from the world of illusions' by postponing their own bliss until all human beings have reached the same level at which the *bodhisattva* makes the ultimate sacrifice for the salvation of humankind.[75] For the rest of humankind, the *bodhisattva* appears as a reflective element embodying the impossibility of immediate liberation from the 'technological veil of illusions', the fantastic functionality of everyday objects.

This critically reflexive core constitutes a limiting principle that disrupts our daydreaming and introduces a gritty verisimilitude from which we can distinguish the smooth running of fantasy. The epochal turn of the university's discourse distorts reality, making this gritty verisimilitude appear to be the natural state. In lieu of this distortion Žižek raises the critical point that the human condition is comprised of a sense of being alien to our existence; strangeness inheres in the fundamental structure of experiencing oneself as a subject with an identity that is an authentic presentation of who we are yet is in a constant state of fluidity.[76]

If this reflexive critique constitutes a limit, then we are presented with a co-substantial possibility that in the university's discourse the promise of discovering truth stains the neutral scene of the observer with the possibility of what remains

71 Žižek, 'Hitchcock's Organs Without Bodies', *op. cit.*, p. 133.

72 *Ibid.*, p. 125.

73 Žižek, *For They Know Not What They Do: Enjoyment as a Political Factor*, *op. cit.*, pp. 25–26.

74 A. C. Danto, *Mysticism and Morality: Oriental Thought and Moral Philosophy*, London: Basic Books, 1972, p. 26.

75 *Ibid.*

76 Žižek, *The Parallax View*, *op. cit.*, p. 213.

to be known. Žižek refers to the function of medical discourse to demonstrate this ambiguity at the heart of knowledge:

> At the surface level, we are dealing with pure objective knowledge that desubjectivizes the subject-patient, reducing him to an object of research, of diagnosis and treatment; however, beneath it, one can easily discern a worried hystericized subject, obsessed with anxiety, addressing the doctor as his Master and asking for reassurance from him.[77]

The pure possibility offered by fantasy gives us some clue as to how Žižek surveys this promised reassurance as problematic. The role of fantasy is to co-ordinate the desire of the subject, and in the case of this pure possibility it must be postponed indefinitely because our fantasies are always about something quasi-transcendental yet not transcendent – the *objet petit a*. Fantasy keeps the pure possibility at a distance with desire, placing our desire as a screen between us and possibility in itself, i.e. in Palahniuk's short portrait Keating's desire to help people functions as a necessity that helps her deal with the traumatic cost of life in the natural disasters she confronts.[78]

According to Žižek, we gain purchase on a quasi-transcendental mundane possibility ('quasi' to the extent that it is *a priori* and necessary but at the same time able to be overcome) because this pure possibility is lost in the postponement, and herein rendered impossible to attain. Moreover, the fantasised object circles around this place of purity imbuing the world-at-hand, co-ordinated by our fantasies, with the unrealistic expectation of pure satisfaction.[79] Here we have returned to the destruction wrought by the status of knowledge as abstract and universal as it manifests in the concrete in the wake of nihilism. For instance, we may follow Keating's example of human sacrifice as soon as we remove what impedes us from doing so – our self-interest. Yet by removing our self-interested 'pathological' fantasies the world-at-hand takes on a different configuration and the subjective status of human sacrifice becomes a non-pathological normative value. This is an ontological change, because without our fantasies informing us of what we desire, 'how we know what we know', we cannot distinguish between self-interest and disinterest.

The nihilist's conundrum of distinguishing self-interest and disinterest then takes us a step further toward observing the relation to our environment as defined by the structure of symbolic reality, the gaze that situates the viewer and the viewed, and the pervasive object-cause of desire that appears from without, threatening to disrupt the smooth running of our worldly constitution. Following Lacan, Žižek suggests that the gap between the mechanics of the universe and the gazing upon the universe emerges when we obey ('master') the rules of etiquette,

77 Žižek, 'Introduction: Cogito as a Shibboleth', *op. cit.*, pp. 78–79.
78 Žižek, *Organs Without Bodies: On Deleuze and Consequences*, *op. cit.*, pp. 99–101.
79 Žižek, *The Plague of Fantasies*, *op. cit.*, p. 132.

the Symbolic Order, to conceal our intentions from the big Other. We may therefore suppose that the greatest danger to this civil etiquette is for the subject to imagine they know what the Other wants – aping the wishes of the teacher rather than pursuing knowledge itself. For the subject to believe this constitutes a regression into hallucination because the efficient ordering of the Symbolic is torn asunder by fantasisation. Our final point must therefore be that for Žižek's critique knowledge and belief, a criticism of knowledge-production in universities more broadly, must meet in nihilism to avoid a psychotic break or mystical rupture. This allows the university's discourse's fetishisation of knowledge to be spared the crisis of becoming meaningless and, therein, the possibility for new knowledge to be lost. But such a move is still bound to its fetish.

CHAPTER 6

Enjoyment and restorative justice

If jurisprudence is a *Wissenschaft*, then it is possible to formulate the legal beyond the commonplace acknowledgement of law as merely dispute resolution within legal processes. Alternative dispute resolution is the most prominent example of this 'beyond' that relies on an explicitly philosophico-psychological approach to justice. The alternative approaches proffered by the restorative justice programme in alternative dispute resolution challenges the normativity of this philosophico-psychological attachment to justice. Debates around restorative justice practices, particularly those involving child sexual assaults, confront the contingency of enjoyment when it is illegal, taboo and traumatic. Like contemporary cultural legal studies, alternative dispute resolution draws on activities and theoretical concepts from outside law to handle disputes in parallel with, in lieu of, or in opposition to the traditional institutional forms such as the courts.[1] Yet this collation of methods belies the transcendental relativisation of all deliberative actions towards 'dispute' as the core of what is 'legal'; a tic that troubles approaches to restorative justice in particular.

Recent developments in the literature around mediation and negotiation, especially as regards restorative justice processes, have served to highlight some of the most important changes that the rise of mediation brings to legal processes, and the place of lawyers in the future of modern legal practice. In this chapter we begin by examining the context of the debates of restorative justice by establishing two philosophical polarities of understanding conflict in alternative dispute resolution. The discussion then moves to the restorative justice debate between Annie Cossins and Kathleen Daly to examine the special case of activities that bring victims of child sexual assault into conference with the offenders to the normative end of repairing or healing the victim and shaming the offender through an explicit self-acknowledgement of their guilt.[2] These activities are used to focus on

1 B. French, 'Dispute Resolution in Australia – The Movement from Litigation to Mediation', *Australasian Dispute Resolution Journal* 18, 2007, pp. 213–214.

2 B. van Stokkom, 'Moral Emotions in Restorative Justice Conferences: Managing Shame, Designing Empathy', *Theoretical Criminology* 6, 2002, p. 344.

the significant difference that restorative justice presents for the vocation of lawyers, their sense of legal knowledge *(Wissenschaft)*, and the impacts and nominal enjoyment imposed by outcomes of mediation and negotiation.

In tracing the question of mediation and negotiation's impact on the outcomes, institutions and processes of law, it is helpful to first turn to the nature of conflict which grounds the concept of mediation in the modern inheritance of the English common law. Despite significant differences in their constitutional tropes, the United States of America, New Zealand and Australia all have court systems that utilise mediation and are indebted to the English common law system. In its simplest conception the structure of the court is itself adversarial, pitting plaintiff against defendant. Beyond this simple picture lies a contested reality where legal conflicts are social, political and psychic. The question as to the nature of conflict herein rests on whether we ought to view conflict as essential to law, i.e. plaintiff and defendant, sovereign and subject, or if instead we ought to view it as a by-product of the function of the modern legal state, i.e. the liberal culture of rights cultivates conflicts about whose rights have priority.[3] The jurisprudential thrust of this difference opens the way to thinking through if lawyers and their clients are only brought together by and for conflict, and thus the law is succour to this confrontation in a symbiotic and perhaps parasitic way. The question remains, however, as to how we are to conceive of conflict as such.

In the literature on mediation and negotiation there exist many points of view on how we should conceive of conflict. The 'ought' here is indicative of the moral dimension these perspectives entail but do not always acknowledge.[4] At a glance, modern legal states such as Australia prefer to adumbrate their mediation practices with other practices such as applied psychology, demography and legal reform.[5] While these fields provide important conceptual and methodological tools for mediation and negotiation, they remain in the middle ground between two poles of contention.

Ideally, all parties may view the mediation process as fair and equitable. Yet this view of fairness by the disputants must be cultivated as much by the process of mediation as by the disputants themselves, underscoring the intersubjective nature of the process and highlighting the totalising normative impulse of resolution. Tom Tyler, John Braithwaite and others suggest that there are normative

3 W. P. MacNeil, *Novel Judgements: Legal Theory as Fiction*, London: Routledge, 2012, pp. 96–98.

4 See, for example, the different sensitivities to law and morality between R. Birke, 'Neuroscience and Settlement: An Examination of Scientific Innovations and Practical Applications', *Ohio State Journal on Dispute Resolution* 25, 2010, and T. Tyler, 'The Psychology of Disputant Concerns in Mediation', *Negotiation Journal* 14, 1998.

5 L. Arthur, 'Does Case Management Undermine the Rule of Law in the Pursuit of Access to Justice?', *Journal of Judicial Administration* 20, 2010; French, *op. cit.*; K. Richards, 'Police-referred Restorative Justice for Juveniles in Australia', *Trends and Issues in Crime and Criminal Justice* 398, 2010.

criteria that must be met in order for mediation to be acknowledged as both fair and successful.[6] According to Tyler, people are interested in a fair resolution of their dispute as accords with their subjective view of what is fair.[7] While somewhat subjectivist in approach, Tyler's more applied psychological view suggests that process fairness is widely considered as important, and voluntary participation and compliance is more likely if the process is considered to be fair by the participants.[8]

The methodological approach to dispute resolution put forward by Tyler lists several criteria for maintaining or producing a view of the process as fair. These criteria include: the representation of disputants either by direct control over the outcome or by opportunities to present evidence; the ethical appropriateness of parties' behaviour as accords with social expectations of etiquette; the avoidance of dishonesty; and the disputants ought to feel that the resolution reached is consistent with other outcomes for similar issues.[9] These criteria asserted by Tyler respond to the issue of disputant participation within the objective context of negotiation.[10] The core problem identified by Tyler therein is that the subjective expectations of the disputants establish a set of criteria that may not necessarily align with the objective criteria of process fairness and so some enjoyment that is expected is unable to be delivered upon.[11] In keeping with his applied psychological focus, Tyler proposes that the solution for mediators is 'to seek input from the disputants' rather than rely on a mediator's ability to create representative, consistent and ethically appropriate procedures, although these are nonetheless important.[12] Tyler wishes to develop restorative justice approaches that reorient the ineffective punitive measures that are becoming increasingly popular as forms of conditioning wrongdoers.[13]

In distinction to the applied psychological outcomes proposed by Tyler and others, William Felstiner et al. present an argument that examines the transformative effects of the socio-legal context of disputes. Focusing on what they term naming, blaming and claiming, Felstiner et al. argue that, in the sociology of law, the prevailing social forms put the law in a broader socio-legal context cause and are affected by the pre-litigation process of negotiation and naming a perceived

6 J. Braithwaite, 'Restorative Justice and Therapeutic Jurisprudence', *Criminal Law Bulletin* 38, 2002; N. Harris, L. Walgrave and J. Braithwaite, 'Emotional Dynamics in Restorative Conferences', *Theoretical Criminology* 8, 2004; D. Roche, 'Dimensions of Restorative Justice', *Journal of Social Issues* 62, 2006; Tyler, *op. cit.*

7 Tyler, *op. cit.*, p. 367.

8 *Ibid.*

9 *Ibid.*, p. 370.

10 They also echo the way Harris et al. consider emotional dynamics in negotiation practice; see Harris et al., *op. cit.*

11 Tyler, *op. cit.*, p. 372.

12 *Ibid.*

13 *Ibid.*; Braithwaite, *op. cit.*, p. 323.

problem or grievance (blaming).[14] Contrary to the arguments presented by Tyler, for Felstiner et al. what is at stake in disputes is the different perception of 'similarly valued experience' by the participating parties.[15] It is this content of disputes that undergoes transformation through the process of negotiation from mere self-interest to a recognition of a problem in the mind of the agitator.[16] However, Felstiner et al. caution that such a view remains psychologically naïve: 'it is insensitive to the effect of feelings on the attribution of motive and to the consequences of such attributions for the subject's behaviour.'[17] The reinforcement and overlay of private feelings and motives gestured to by Felstiner et al. make up the ideological component of mediation and negotiation practice. Ideology in negotiation is simply defined by Felstiner et al. as 'the individual's sense of entitlement to enjoy certain experiences and be free from others',[18] and the law is a mechanism that maintains and supports this ideological background of negotiation.

The approach presented by Felstiner et al. suggests that the negotiators, lawyers and other mediators themselves transform the parties' interests even before negotiation takes place. They argue that by helping the parties to conceive of their grievances in particular ways, the legal profession retains a transformative power, and its critics 'argue that they "create" at least some of the needs they satisfy'.[19] The point that Felstiner et al. make is that lawyers need not positively transform a dispute; they can also refuse to assist, or provide only a bare minimum of aid, 'thereby arresting the further development of a dispute'.[20] Citing the work of Macaulay, Felstiner et al. further reinforce this by stating: 'Those few [consumers] who do seek legal services will get only what the lawyer sees as appropriate.'[21] In this third position, the nature of conflict in disputes and disputing is viewed as the elaboration and review of shared perspectives between disputants and lawyers and privately held attitudes about the disputants themselves, their fellow disputants, the dispute procedures and the institutions and persons who facilitate the mediation or negotiation.[22]

The nature of conflict for lawyers has many aspects that are multiplied and added to by mediation and negotiation. Put positively, the existing research suggests that lawyers must be many things to many people and adopt a kaleidoscope of views when creating, practising and maintaining ethically appropriate dispute resolution procedures. Yet it is also important to recognise that the position of

14 W. Felstiner, R. Abel and A. Sarat, 'The Emergence and Transformation of Disputes: Naming, Blaming, Claiming …', *Law and Society Review* 15, 1981, pp. 632–633.
15 *Ibid.*, p. 634.
16 *Ibid.*, p. 637.
17 *Ibid.*
18 *Ibid.*, p. 643.
19 *Ibid.*, p. 645.
20 *Ibid.*, p. 646.
21 *Ibid.*, p. 651.
22 *Ibid.*

lawyers is both unique and transformative in mediation and negotiation although it may not directly evoke legal language.

The question still remains, however, as to how we are to distinguish and understand the different ways that disputes are resolved in the courts as against alternative forms of dispute resolution such as restorative justice. Roche argues that we can conceive of restorative justice activities as simply

> a particular method for dealing with crime that brings together an offender, his or her victims, and their respective families and friends to discuss the aftermath of an incident, and the steps that can be taken to repair the harm an offender has done.[23]

There is a debate within the literature on restorative justice between Cossins and Daly that underscores the socio-legal differences produced by dispute resolution obtained through either institutional, conference and/or negotiation forms. Both Cossins and Daly reside somewhere between the positions proscribed by Tyler and Felstiner et al.: they register that ethical appropriateness and fairness on their own are insufficient to account for the experience of victims of child sexual assault in dispute resolution, be it institutionally court based or therapeutically conference based; Cossins favours institutional and legislative reform while Daly argues for more personal, supra-institutional forms. Simply stated, the debate consists of Cossins taking issue with Daly's preference for restorative justice practices because, she argues, such practices are problematic for both the victim and how the legal system handles the offender whose crime is often based on a repetition of acts rather than a single event.[24] Daly has countered that Cossins has misread the limitation of her work to child sex offences as applicable to sexually based offences more broadly on two significant fronts: Cossins used an image of sexual assault based on an adult violation of adult forms of consent that ignore the micro-power relations at work in child sex offences where sometimes the offender is an adolescent rather than an adult, and Cossins overlooks that the restorative justice practices with data currently recorded and archived are limited to the resolution of child sex offences.[25] To clarify the difference between court-based and other therapeutic forms of dispute resolution, this debate will be discussed below.

Daly presciently offered the framing of the Cossins–Daly debate in an earlier article that discussed the mythological vision of triumphant restorative justice or court-based dispute resolution juxtaposed to the empirical and critical understandings of the emerging field of restorative justice and its virtues and

23 Roche, *op. cit.*, p. 217.

24 A. Cossins, 'Restorative Justice and Child Sexual Offences: The Theory and the Practice', *British Journal of Criminology* 48, 2008, p. 370.

25 K. Daly, 'Setting the Record Straight and a Call for Radical Change: A Reply to Annie Cossins on "Restorative Justice and Child Sexual Offences"', *British Journal of Criminology* 48, 2008, pp. 557–562.

vices championed by Daly.[26] Daly elsewhere casts this debate as restorative justice versus legal reform, guided by a view of negotiation as a logical process that ought to resolve a given dispute.[27] Critics of restorative justice who viewed its restoration as soft or unreliable tended to favour more institutional remedies for disputes involving sexual violence. However, such critics, argues Daly,

> neglect to consider the victimizing effects of the formal court process in handling sexual violence cases. Such effects can be inferred from several SAAS measures. Court cases took twice as long to finalize as conference cases, they shifted jurisdiction more often, and victims would have had to attend court an average of six times to learn the outcome of their case.[28]

The result of the institutional processing of disputes involving sexual violence thus tended to be more traumatic and elongated than what restoration invited through conference practices. Daly's criticism highlights that her perspective therein is socio-legal and critical in a manner similar to Felstiner et al.'s deconstruction of the dispute resolution process. Although, as we shall see in her debate with Cossins discussed below, unlike Felstiner et al., Daly advocates for a retreat from the courts altogether, should some mode of adjudication become available within the models of restorative justice itself.[29] Adjudication is the missing link for dispute resolution's measures of fairness and ethical appropriateness and, for Daly at least, a fundamental distinction between it and court-based practices.

The criticism of Daly's work by Cossins carries with it the peculiarities of being focused on sexual violence and aims at the defusing of power relations between the parties involved. Cossins clearly favours measures of legal and institutional reform rather than the supra-institutional practices or para-legal ideal aimed for by Daly. Cossins' argument is that we must prefer institutional methods of resolving sexual violence, particularly the child sex offences analysed by Daly, because the efficacy of restorative justice remains questionable in the absence of 'appropriate standards to limit the reproduction of power relations within restorative justice programmes'.[30] These power relations are the dynamics between the offender and the victim and invoke all manner of psychological and sociological aspects

26 K. Daly, 'Restorative Justice: The Real Story', *Punishment and Society* 4, 2002, pp. 72–73.

27 K. Daly, 'Restorative Justice and Sexual Assault: An Archival Study of Court and Conference Cases', *British Journal of Criminology* 46, 2006, p. 335.

28 *Ibid.*, p. 352.

29 Daly, 'Setting the Record Straight and a Call for Radical Change: A Reply to Annie Cossins on "Restorative Justice and Child Sexual Offences"', *op. cit.*, p. 561.

30 A. Cossins, *op. cit.*, p. 359. Hennessey Hayes also echoes this sentiment in 'Apologies and Accounts in Youth Justice Conferencing: Reinterpreting Research Outcomes', *Contemporary Justice Review* 9, 2006.

of a person, including gender, ethnicity, age, and so forth.[31] Generally, Cossins focuses on instances of an older Anglo-Saxon male offender and a younger Anglo-Saxon female victim brought into conference face-to-face through restorative justice practices.[32] In Cossins' view it is not only that the victim is forced to repeat the traumatic memory of the sexual assault for the purposes of healing or restoration, but that they are also confronted with an offender whose reasons for participating may, in a number of cases, be far more self-serving, contrary to the injunction against reoffending, and thus motivate them to say and do things in the conference that incite further challenges to the dignity of the victim.[33] Thus, Cossins has argued, where restorative justice sets out to give victims a choice 'about how their violation is addressed' in an inclusive way that lets them 'participate in fashioning a penalty' through a supported dialogical encounter with offenders that tells the victims' stories and facilitates offenders' admissions of guilt free of legal linguistic inflection, it in fact produces little consultation with victims and diverts matters from the courts such that the dispute goes unrecorded and fails to clearly encourage either admissions or denials.[34] The comparative difference between an alternative dispute resolution practice such as restorative justice and the institutional processing of offenders by the courts thus appears to favour juridico-legal forms for sufficient outcomes where victims can be protected from appearing before their assailants through legislative mechanisms to be applied by the courts where restorative justice cannot offer any such assurances.[35]

The overview of Cossins' position above touches upon the essential elements of her conclusions. Yet in the context of the previously cited discussion of Daly, and the methodological and epistemological coordinates set by Tyler and Felstiner et al., Cossins' argument is positioned in a problematic space. As already stated, Daly anticipates some of Cossins' criticisms, arguing that there is a difference between the mythical form of restorative justice that is clear cut and the real form of restorative justice that is murky.[36] But further, Daly suggests that the division between court-based dispute resolution and restorative justice practices in fact echoes the

31 See J. Braithwaite, 'Doing Justice Intelligently in Civil Society', *Journal of Social Issues* 62, 2006, for a discussion of sociologically sensitive dispute resolution. See G. Maxwell and H. Hayes, 'Restorative Justice Developments in the Pacific Region: A Comprehensive Survey', *Contemporary Justice Review* 9, 2006, p. 148 on the limits of this sociological focus in situations of systemic power imbalance.

32 Cossins, *op. cit.*, pp. 362–365.

33 *Ibid.*, p. 364.

34 *Ibid.*, pp. 361, 370.

35 Other mechanisms also exist for the handling of juvenile cases such as those focused on by Daly – see Richards, *op. cit.* It should be added that effectively what both processes demand is compulsory empathy; in the specific case of restorative justice for victims of child sexual assault this appears to be one-way from offender to victim. See J. Braithwaite, 'Narrative and "Compulsory Compassion"', *Law and Social Inquiry* 31, 2006.

36 Daly, 'Restorative Justice: The Real Story', *op. cit.*, pp. 72–73.

target of the social psychological critique mounted by the cultural/difference feminist Carol Gilligan:

> (1) Restorative justice is the opposite of retributive justice. (2) Restorative justice uses indigenous justice practices and was the dominant form of pre-modern justice. (3) Restorative justice is a 'care' (or feminine) response to crime in comparison to a 'justice' (or masculine) response. (4) Restorative justice can be expected to produce major changes in people.[37]

While there is not the space here to outline the whole of Gilligan's enterprise, we can establish the connections between the four points made by Daly in light of Gilligan's social psychology and Cossins' critique of Daly. In the first instance, rather than be mutually exclusive, Daly argues that the motivator for both restorative justice and retributive justice is the same and it is instead the salience of any legal process that is a problem.[38] In other words, Cossins has effectively misread Daly's emphasis on adjudication. In the second instance, the criticism of Cossins argues that she has misread the sociology of child sexual assault through adult criteria simply because this is the dominant hegemonic mode of liberalism in the modern legal state; law is for adults, written by adults, and children are counted in the law the way that adults view them, rather than how they view themselves.[39] Cossins' argument treads a fine balance in regards to the third point but it is ultimately unclear from her article if she favoured an ethic of caring for the victims where her criticisms of the reproduction of power relations in the restorative justice dispute resolution practices geared the well-being of victims toward a measure of justice served. This goes to the heart of the fourth point, where Cossins infers that courts can produce major changes in people, while restorative justice lacks sufficient efficacy given the extant literature. Daly, in her reply to Cossins' critique, argues that this confuses the different levels of knowledge between victims' variable experience *within* a court or conference and *between* a court or conference.[40] Moreover, as Cossins cites from Curtis-Fawley and Daly herself, restorative justice 'is better seen as a nominal concept that stands for a set of activities … rather than literally and narrowly being about "restoring"'.[41] This application of Daly's parsing of the myths surrounding restorative justice to the key points of Cossins' conclusions conversely highlights the position of Daly as an empirical skeptic who is measured between both the form of restorative

37 *Ibid.*, p. 56.

38 *Ibid.*, p. 72.

39 The restorative justice literature regularly recognises that indigenous practices are different to modern Western legal systems' approach to restorative justice. See Maxwell and Hayes, *op. cit.*, p. 128; Roche, *op. cit.*, p. 222.

40 Daly, 'Setting the Record Straight and a Call for Radical Change: A Reply to Annie Cossins on "Restorative Justice and Child Sexual Offences"',*op. cit.*, p. 558.

41 Cossins, *op. cit.*, p. 360.

justice activities and the content of its outcomes in the variables of case-by-case dealing.[42]

The depth of Daly's skepticism is evident in her reply to Cossins' critique on several fronts. Interestingly, these points of reply often circulate within areas of interest for modern professional legal practice because they present structural questions about the relationship between parties in a dispute and the special case of child sex offenders and their victims looking for healing restoration, a practical thing no matter how poetic that may sound. Cossins' critique of Daly's evidence was discussed above as the nature of the evidence for restorative justice being limited to child sex offences. In her direct reply to Cossins, Daly pursues three key points with regards to Cossins' construction of victims of sex offences: firstly that positive impacts for the victim necessitate changes for the offender; secondly the success/failure of justice outcomes should not be limited to reoffending; and thirdly that Cossins views the child sex offence as between an adult offender repeatedly offending and a child victim, when Daly is in fact dealing with data from youth sex offences, as that is all that is available.[43] Further, Daly also states that 'although some youth may fit the patterns identified in adult child sexual abuse, they are a minority'.[44] Daly shows that legal reform only creates modest improvements for victims of sex offences, but ultimately agrees with Cossins that more needs to be done in terms of comparative research and socio-legal change.[45]

While there are legislative rules[46] about how the youth child sex offenders focused upon by Daly can be conferenced with, there is nonetheless an emerging wave of change for the role of lawyers in being not only advocates for clients or officers of the court but also facilitators of nominal restorative justice activities. Yet there is also an underlying idea that the professional lawyer may also be able to be written out of the process or confined to an earlier stage of the dispute process such as the trial or settlement negotiation. The victims' feelings of vindication and the manifestation of offenders' feelings of shame stand as the normative end of restorative justice activities in the modern legal state. The role of the lawyer may transform the dispute through the courts or pre-trial negotiation into a matter of restorative justice where the overriding sense of the restoration is supposedly from legal language but nonetheless embraces the stories of the victim with a para-*legal* ear.

42 This variability is strongly supported by H. Strang, L. Sherman, C. Angel, D. Woods, S. Bennett, D. Newbury-Birch and N. Inkpen, 'Victim Evaluations of Face-to-Face Restorative Justice Conferences: A Quasi-Experimental Analysis', *Journal of Social Issues* 62, 2006.

43 Daly, *op. cit.*, p. 562.

44 *Ibid.*, p. 562.

45 *Ibid.*, p. 563.

46 Richards, *op. cit.*

CHAPTER 7

Law, transgression and *The Cares of a Family Man*

In Franz Kafka's *oeuvre*, law somehow insists without properly existing. What is law for Kafka makes his characters, and concomitantly his readers, guilty without knowing what they are guilty of. This guilt clings to life in Kafka's literature, a wound that will not heal and does not let us die. Such a moral-legal trope is most commonly found in Kafka's narratives of bureaucracy in its most 'irrational' aspect and, most pointedly, in 'partial objects' like Odradek in *The Cares of a Family Man*.[1] Kafka phrases the distinction of the object and the partial object as 'One is tempted to believe that the creature once had some sort of intelligible shape and is now only a broken-down remnant. Yet this does not seem to be the case; at least there is no sign of it.'[2] Slavoj Žižek and others have argued that this partial object has a psychoanalytic tenor; it is the Kafkian Thing: either transcendent, forever eluding our grasp (the Law, the Castle), or a ridiculous object into which the subject is metamorphosed and which he can never be rid of, like the insect into which Gregor Samsa is transformed.[3] As such, the Kafkian Thing is engaged through a proto-Lacanian notion of fantasy as an all too human way of curtailing the damaging effects of too much enjoyment. But how then does such a function of fantasy relate to law, and why is the work of Kafka so central to this understanding for Žižek and others?

For theorists sharing Žižek's psychoanalytic persuasion such as Joan Copjec, Russell Grigg and Yannis Stavrakakis, Kafka's importance rests in the way his narratives lay bare the way that belief supports the bureaucratic fantasy that regulates modern social reality. Such a fantasy of bureaucracy, i.e. expert administration without politics, has been given symbolic substance by modern political and legal

1 S. Žižek, 'Odradek as a Political Category', *Lacanian Ink* 24/25, 2005, p. 139. Incidentally, Žižek is one of the first to give the micro-story an extended treatment.

2 F. Kafka, 'The Cares of a Family Man' in *The Complete Short Stories of Franz Kafka*, N. Glatzer (ed.), W. Muir and E. Muir (trans.), London: Vintage, 1999, p. 428.

3 Žižek *op. cit.* See in particular G. Deleuze and F. Guattari, *Kafka: Towards a Minor Literature*, D. Polan (trans.), Minneapolis: University of Minnesota Press, 1986.

institutions, argues Žižek.[4] It is usually said that Kafka has given this institutionalisation of bureaucracy an 'exaggerated', 'fantastic', and/or 'subjectively distorted' expression that thwarts the fate of the individual within it through the 'irrational' universe of his novels.[5] Žižek claims that in saying this we overlook the crucial fact that it is this very 'exaggeration' that articulates the fantasy regulating the libidinal functioning of the 'effective', 'real' bureaucracy itself.[6] 'At the beginning' of the law, there is a certain 'outlaw', a certain reality of violence which coincides with the act itself of the establishment of the reign of the law.[7] The illegitimate violence by which law sustains itself must be concealed at any price, because this concealment is the positive condition of the functioning of law.[8]

This ideological edifice is sustained by an undergrowth of transgressive enjoyment. Žižek argues that law in Kafka "can be sustained only by a sovereign power which reserves for itself the right ... to suspend the rule of law(s) on behalf of the Law itself."[9] Extrapolating from this Kafkian kernel, Žižek envisions a society in which law would no longer sustain itself through its own obscene breach.[10]

'External' obedience to law is thus not submission to external pressure, to so-called non-ideological 'brute force', but obedience to the Command insofar as it is 'incomprehensible', not understood; insofar as it retains a 'traumatic', 'irrational' character: far from hiding its full authority, this traumatic, non-integrated character of law is *a positive condition of it*.[11] This is a fundamental feature of the Freudian superego: an injunction which is experienced as traumatic, 'senseless' – that is, which cannot be integrated into the symbolic universe of the subject.[12] For law to function 'normally', the dependence of law on its process of enunciation or its radically contingent character must be repressed into the unconscious, through the ideological, imaginary experience of the 'meaning' of law, of its foundation in Justice.[13] What is 'repressed', then, is not some obscure origin of law but the very fact that law is not to be accepted as true, only as necessary – the fact that *its authority is without truth*.[14] In his *The Sublime Object of Ideology*, Žižek explains that the necessary structural illusion which drives people to believe that truth can be found in laws describes precisely the mechanism of

4 S. Žižek, *The Sublime Object of Ideology*, London: Verso, 1989, p. 36; S. Žižek, 'The Lesson of Rancière' in J. Rancière, *The Politics of Aesthetics*, G. Rockhill (trans.), London: Continuum, 2004, p. 72.

5 *Ibid.*, p. 36.

6 *Ibid.*

7 S. Žižek, *For They Know Not What They Do: Enjoyment as a Political Factor*, London: Verso, 1991.

8 *Ibid.*

9 S. Žižek, *The Parallax View*, Cambridge, MA: The MIT Press, 2006.

10 *Ibid.*

11 Žižek, *The Sublime Object of Ideology*, *op. cit.*, p. 37.

12 *Ibid.*

13 *Ibid.*

14 *Ibid.*, p. 38.

transference. Such transference is the supposition of a truth, of an idyll meaning behind the stupid, traumatic, inconsistent fact of law.[15] To this end transference names the vicious circle of belief because the reasons why we should believe in law are persuasive only to those who already believe in its necessity.[16]

For such a psychoanalytic purview, people do not decide to break laws. Rather, such action is always mediated by a desire to transgress law's necessity. Such a view of law treats it as a mediator of desire – law demands enjoyment, makes it so the ability or freedom to enjoy becomes the obligation to enjoy. An obligation to enjoy is no joy, however. Law thus takes away the very notion of enjoyment by codifying it as an obligation to enjoy. Psychoanalytic philosophers such as Žižek argue that transference is the process by which we push truth into the law, so we believe that truth somehow resides in the law.[17] It then becomes more difficult to transgress the law because such an action would transgress truth.[18] Žižek writes:

> transference is this supposition of a Truth, of a Meaning behind the stupid, traumatic, inconsistent fact of the Law. In other words, 'transference' names the vicious circle of belief: the reasons why we should believe are persuasive only to those who already believe.[19]

Thus according to Žižek's position performative actions are not enough to displace 'the Real' because these strategies necessarily accept the terrain of 'the Real'.[20] 'Since the very field of such "transgressions" is already taken into account, even engendered, by the hegemonic form,'[21] mere performative resistance is not enough to actually change 'the Real'. It is therefore impossible to do away with 'the Real' while implicitly accepting the ideological foundations upon which it rests.[22]

Žižek and other contemporary critics thus echo the sentiment of Lacan that desire is both encouraged and prohibited by law. In the meta-psychology developed by Lacan, desire can only emerge through a possibility offered by law, not merely because the symbolic universe structures desire but also because law, as the bearing of the symbolic universe upon the subject, functions to prohibit desire. This is the structure of the transgression at the heart of classic psychoanalytic structures such as the Oedipus and castration complexes or structuralist sociological studies such as Levi-Strauss' incest prohibition. 'Post-structuralist' arguments such as those made by Foucault in the *History of Sexuality*, however, tend to conflate these two elements, perceiving desire 'not only as an *effect,* but also as a

15 *Ibid.*
16 *Ibid.*
17 *Ibid.*
18 *Ibid.*
19 *Ibid.*
20 S. Žižek, *The Ticklish Subject: The Absent Centre of Political Ontology*, London: Verso, 1999, p. 264.
21 *Ibid.*
22 *Ibid.*

realization of the law'.[23] This shift is an error for psychoanalytic philosophy for its elevation of performative action over the structure of psychic investment as such.

Against the Foucaultian position, Žižek argues that there is no clear opposition between subjective experience and objective reality: rather there is 'an excess on both sides'.[24] The substance of Žižek's contrasting argument, and that of psychoanalytic criticism more broadly, hinges on the disalienating formulation of desire:

> the advent of Law entails a kind of 'disalienation': in so far as the Other itself appears submitted to the 'absolute condition' of Law, the subject is no more at the mercy of the Other's whim, its desire is no more totally alienated in the Other's desire . . . In contrast to the 'post-structuralist' notion of a law checking, canalizing, alienating, oppressing, 'Oedipianising' some previous 'flux of desire,' Law is here conceived as an agency of 'disalienation' and 'liberation': it opens our access to desire by enabling us to disengage ourselves from the rule of the Other's whim.[25]

Law frees us from the absolute, arbitrary demands of the Other.[26] Žižek is here repeating the origin of law explained by Freud in *Totem and Taboo*: once the horde kills the father, they are no longer subject to his violent, obscene, monopoly of enjoyment.[27] Now authority itself comes under rules: the reign of the band of brothers is a reign of law, of rules regulating access to women, power and the use of violence.[28] Bringing the Freudian analysis to contemporary audiences with a Lacanian twist, Žižek writes:

> One should not identify this Real Thing too hastily with the incestuous object of desire rendered inaccessible by symbolic prohibition; this Thing is rather, *Father himself*, namely, the obscene Father-*jouissance* prior to his murder and subsequent elevation into agency of symbolic authority.[29]

Žižek's point is that the symbolic law is more complex and it also liberates the subject from the unbearable demands of the father, from the father in his obscenity.[30]

Such a view of law distinguishes between an imaginary form of resistance, a 'false transgression' that ultimately serves to maintain and reproduce the law,

23 J. Copjec, 'The Orthopsychic Subject: Film Theory and the Reception of Lacan', *October* 49, 1989, p. 61. See in particular Part Five of M. Foucault, *The History of Sexuality: 1 – The Will to Knowledge*, R. Hurley (trans.), London: Penguin Books, 1978.

24 S. *Žižek The Fright of Real Tears: Krystof Kieślowski between Theory and Post Theory*, London: BFI Publishing, 2001, p. 59.

25 Žižek, *For They Know Not What They Do: Enjoyment as a Political Factor*, *op. cit.*, p. 265.

26 J. Dean, 'Žižek on Law', *Law and Critique* 15(1), 2004, p. 14.

27 *Ibid.*, pp. 14–15.

28 *Ibid.*, p. 15.

29 Žižek, *The Ticklish Subject: The Absent Centre of Political Ontology*, *op. cit.*, p. 314.

30 Dean, *op. cit.*, p. 14.

and 'the effective symbolic rearticulation *via* the intervention of the real of an *act*'.[31] This notion of the act functions as the nodal point of this syntagm and of Žižek's position in general.[32] Stavrakakis has noted how Žižek customarily distinguishes between an imaginary form of resistance, a 'false transgression' that ultimately serves to maintain and reproduce the law, and 'the effective symbolic re-articulation *via* the intervention of the real of an *act*'.[33] Transgression and the law can be related in three ways.[34] The first is that described by Freud, where transgression externalises guilt that is of unconscious origins and relates to the Oedipal situation.[35] The second is that described by Immanuel Kant, embodied by Sophocles' Antigone, where transgression is carried out in the name of the moral law.[36] The third, described by Lacan, is the figure for whom transgression is itself a source of *jouissance*.[37]

The eminently popular analyses of postmodern culture by Žižek further this third category by locating the 'obscene object of postmodernity'as the Lacanian 'Thing'. Such a Thing is the incestuous maternal object, brought into horrible proximity to subject. For Žižek, however, it is this same menacing proximity of the Thing that appears in the modernist Kafka's *The Trial*.[38] Žižek picks out two modernist misreadings of the emptiness at the core of Kafka's bureaucracy portrayed in *The Trial*: (1) as the mark of an 'absent god', (2) as the projection of an inner void into an 'apparition' outside.[39] In *The Trial* the closeness of this presence irrupts in the court in the occurrence of a lewd coupling of a man and a woman at the back of the room, law allowing transgression while seeming to forbid it: Kafka is introducing the punitive superego that is driven by an obscene and anarchic *jouissance*, the inconsistency of which bewilders K., the victim unable to escape law.[40] Žižek claims there is a lack of consistency here between the (symbolic) law and the (real) act of copulation, a 'trespassing of the frontier that separates the vital domain from the judicial domain', investing law with a boundless enjoyment.[41] Žižek states that Kafka's text proclaims that law is 'necessary' but not

31 S. Žižek, 'From "Passionate Attachments" to Dis-Identification', *Umbr(a)* 1, 1998, p. 5.
32 Y. Stavrakakis, 'The Lure of Antigone: Aporias of an Ethics of the Political', in G. Boucher, J. Glynos and M. Sharpe (eds), *Traversing the Fantasy: Critical Responses to Slavoj Žižek*, Aldershot: Ashgate, 2005, pp. 171–182.
33 Y. Stavrakakis, 'On Acts, Pure and Impure', *International Journal of* Žižek *Studies* 4(2), 2010, p. 2.
34 R. Grigg, 'Guilt, the Law and Transgression', *Cardozo Law Review* 24(6), 2003, p. 2379.
35 *Ibid.*
36 *Ibid.*
37 *Ibid.*
38 Žižek, 'The Obscene Object of Postmodernity', *op. cit.*, p. 38.
39 *Ibid.*
40 *Ibid.*
41 *Ibid.*

'true': as K. discovers and pays for with his life, if you cannot invest in law as necessary, you get flooded with *jouissance*.[42]

Žižek is concerned to show the secret transgression that underpins and makes possible the symbolic law. He formulates this concern thus: '"At the beginning" of Law, there is a transgression, a certain reality of violence, which coincides with the very act of the establishment of Law."'[43] Further, Žižek argues that 'they are a satire on legal institutions, an inversion of public Power, yet they are a transgression that consolidates what it transgresses'.[44] But, beyond this, the law itself possesses a certain obscene, unappeasable, superegoic dimension: 'On the one hand, there is Law *qua* symbolic Ego-Ideal, that is, Law in its pacifying function . . . *qua* the intermediary Third that dissolves the impasse of imaginary aggressivity.[45] On the other hand, there is law in its superego dimension, that is, law *qua* "irrational" pressure, the force of culpability, totally incommensurable with our actual responsibility.'[46] Law itself is its own transgression. Žižek says 'the most appropriate form to indicate this curve of the *point de capiton*, of the "negation of negation", in ordinary language is, paradoxically, that of the tautology: "law is law."'[47]

Žižek explains, the problem is that law is not experienced as natural or spontaneous, but imposed.[48] Law involves what Lacan calls the *vel* of alienation, the forced choice between being and meaning. If we choose being, the subject disappears, it eludes us, and falls into non-meaning; if we choose meaning, it survives but disappears into the symbolic universe of the Other. So it is not the case that law is sometimes obeyed and at other times is not; rather, law is *'always-already mediated by the (repression of the) desire to transgress the Law'* and this accounts for guilt.[49] When we obey law, we do so over and against the more primary desire to transgress it, and so 'the more we obey the law, the more we *are* guilty because this obedience, in effect, *is* a defence against sinful desire'.[50] The demand to enjoy appears to transgress the Law of castration (indulge yourself), yet as Žižek points out, this is not always the case; often the very demand to enjoy proves more of

42 *Ibid.*

43 S. Žižek, 'The Limits of the Semiotic Approach to Psychoanalysis' in *Interrogating the Real*, R. Butler and S. Stephens (eds), London: Continuum, 2005, p. 129.

44 S. Žižek, 'Between Symbolic Fiction and Fantasmatic Spectre: Toward a Lacanian Theory of Ideology' in *Interrogating the Real*, R. Butler and S. Stephens (eds), London: Continuum, 2005, p. 254.

45 S. Žižek, 'A Hair of the Dog that Bit You' in *Interrogating the Real*, R. Butler and S. Stephens (eds), London: Continuum, 2005, p. 157.

46 Žižek, *Odradek as a Political Category*, *op. cit.*, p. 146.

47 Žižek, 'Limits of the Semiotic Approach to Psychoanalysis', *op. cit.*, p. 119.

48 S. Žižek, *The Art of the Ridiculous Sublime: On David Lynch's Lost Highway*, Seattle: The Walter Chapin Simpson Center for the Humanities, 2000, p. 142.

49 S. Žižek, *The Fragile Absolute – Or Why the Christian Legacy Is Worth Fighting For*, London: Verso, 2000, p. 142 (original emphasis).

50 *Ibid.*

a prohibition than the prohibition of enjoyment itself. Law is not grounded in Truth, it is impregnated with enjoyment.

Law is not something that we apply to a random empirical content, but the promise of an absent outcome of our acts; we never know if we have really obeyed, or if we have been driven by a hidden pathological motive. Žižek claims that there is a lack of fit between law and obedient performances of it; we are guilty without knowing why. The very notion of a countless law has at its origins founding repression. The symbolic form is never an expression of its content, it doesn't tell you what to do: it tells you that there is work to be done. Žižek argues that the illusion that drives people to believe that truth resides in Law can be described by the mechanism of transference: 'transference is this supposition of a Truth, of a meaning behind the stupid, traumatic, inconsistent fact of the Law. In other words, "transference" names the vicious circle of belief: the reasons why we should believe are persuasive only to those who already believe.'[51]

Dean argues that for Žižek, what is beyond law inheres in law as a kind of faith, as law will always and necessarily be imbricated in violence, transgression and guilt.[52] Žižek's most basic explanation for the investment of meaning in law arises out of his reading of Kafka's *Trial* in conjunction with Pascal.[53] We have to stifle the fact that law is necessary without being true. Žižek attempts to think beyond law through his account of law as being synchronic, and that which is beyond law needs to be thought of as a moment already within law.[54] The moment we come too close to law, its sublime majesty turns into obscene abhorrent monstrosity.[55] This implicit reversal of the traditional theological justification of Evil and disharmony condenses the entire Kantian revolution: what our finite mind perceives as the sublime majesty of the moral law is in itself the monstrosity of a crazy sadistic God. Žižek notes for Lacan also, the greatest transgression, the most traumatic, the most senseless thing is law itself: the 'mad' superegotistical law which inflicts enjoyment.[56] What is at stake in moving beyond law, then, is renouncing its fantastic superego supplement.[57] Law is ambiguous and incomplete.

Žižek argues that in the case of Kafka's *Odradek*, are we not dealing with the reminder/remainder of the failure of the father to accomplish his work of imposing law (castration)? Or are we dealing here, yet again, with the structure of parallax? That is to say, what if the lack and the surplus refer to the same phenomenon, and are simply two perspectives on it?[58] Kafka's Odradek is bound up with the Real. It is the Thing. Odradek loves the symbolic but is constantly ridden with doubt, the

51 Žižek, *The Ticklish Subject: The Absent Centre of Political Ontology*, *op. cit.*, p. 38.
52 Dean, *op. cit.*, p. 4.
53 *Ibid.*, p. 13.
54 *Ibid.*, p. 34.
55 S. Žižek, *The Plague of Fantasies*, London: Verso, 1997, p. 281.
56 S. Žižek, *Welcome to the Desert of the Real: Five Essays on September 11 and Related Dates*, London: Verso, 2002, p. 30.
57 Dean, *op. cit.*, p. 32.
58 Žižek, 'Odradek as a Political Category', *op. cit.*, pp. 149–150.

tool of enjoyment in *jouissance*. Kafka's Odradek is worried about attending to the symbolic. It can't be stopped, it is known for lurking, transgressing, it has no boundary that it doesn't escape. It rejects differentiation. Kafka's Odradek is like too much life, and desire for law is like desire for symbolic structure, regulation, prohibition. Kafka's Odradek prohibits itself through its inherent transgression. The Law creates the other, the obscene, and it is inherently problematic as we are all different and conflicting with each other.

CHAPTER 8

Coraline, or *l'envers de la loi*

Neil Gaiman's *Coraline* is a young adult horror story about a prepubescent girl, an alternative dimension and sinister creatures.[1] It is also a story about the libidinal economy of law and (dis)satisfaction with authority; a parable for the thesis of this volume that is as acutely attuned to the familial as Kafka's *The Cares of a Family Man*. In this chapter we will discuss how *Coraline* is a text that critically reimagines the hothouse of familial kinship. Kinship in this frame is not merely a social link but also a tool of psychic shaping, a cultural site where Western subjects have traditionally learnt to become subjects of paternal law and rules in general. Gaiman's emphasis on the familial opens onto the psychoanalytic reading sketched below.

Because, unlike less skeptical starting points, psychoanalysis resists the temptation to essentialise the identity of a human subject, this chapter will specifically focus on the construction of the possibility to experience the law, to render it material rather than technical. This means that the forthcoming analysis of *Coraline* is interested in a psychic economy that is a political economy of the socio-legality of the law. Here it is not enough to merely point to the writ of the positive law nor the theo-ontological proofs of the natural law, as these are already historical constructions within a horizon of subjective experience. Instead, we must delve into the *infans*, the proto-legal constitution of the subject in the microcosm of civilisation that is the family of the narrative's namesake: Coraline Jones. The value of a reading such as this is that it will examine the often neglected 'coming before the letter of the law' because the *infans* is the one who is outside the law, who constructs the (non)sense of authority ahead of any legal interpellation.

Coraline is a unique tale for Western literature targeted at younger audiences in the way that it contests the notion that the model of the human family is somehow given to humanity by nature as a microcosm of what the medieval philosophers

1 I would like to thank the organisers and participants of two conferences that spurred the ideas in this chapter. They were the Law and Literature Association of Australasia bi-annual conference in 2011 and the Australasian Association of Literature annual conference in 2014.

and theologians called 'the Great Chain of Being'. Gaiman deploys an uneasy apparatus of paternal normativity in *Coraline* that harkens further back to the founding myths of divine violence that sustain the sovereign rule of kinship. As will be discussed, these myths – these old gods – are what give *Coraline* its unique presentation of kinship and familial authority: the family is an invention to protect humanity from old gods.

The twist that *Coraline* gives kinship, its intervening quality, develops an alternative to the normative coding of childhood imaginings as fantastical escapism. Instead of the namesake protagonist Coraline escaping her everyday reality, Gaiman develops a narrative in which Coraline remythologises her world and, specifically, her parents, her figures of *lex*, *sex* and *rex*. This fantasmatic remodelling of Coraline's kinship is marked by a persistent unnamable distortion that eventually becomes embodied by the 'old maternal god' of the story, a spidery maleficent Thing.

These coordinates of the *infans*, kinship and old gods position the world of the narrative protagonist Coraline in a way that is irreducible to a psychical projection or wish fulfillment. Instead, the story takes a radical move towards trying to bring to light the unnamable distortion that founds kinship and authority. Exactly how Gaiman uncovers this distortion will be discussed further, but for now suffice to say that *Coraline* provides a critical femininity that faces down the repressed Thing that endangers the paternal law.

Gaiman's imagining of the terrain of girlhood in works such as *Coraline* popularises a post-feminist view of femininity. Although many of Gaiman's texts and their adaptations into other media such as cinema deal with issues of daughterhood, motherhood, fatherhood, class, power, gender and ethnicity, the overwhelming recognition of Gaiman's work focuses on his innovative story-telling techniques that fuse the art of contemporary fairytales with the traumatic dark encounters of H. P. Lovecraft. The point of focus for this chapter is the story of *Coraline*. Both the book and the film *Coraline* tell the story of a young girl, Coraline Jones, and her encounter with a mysterious other world accessible through a small door in her family's new home. The narrative sets its namesake protagonist on a difficult path to unraveling the enigma of the familial bond and her place within such a bond. More specifically, the question that Gaiman raises in the context of *Coraline* is the question of maternal desire: what does the mother want? Without reducing *Coraline* to an echo of the late Freud's question 'what does woman want?', Gaiman takes his audience through several key thematics of feminist psychoanalysis and post-feminist critique: the formation of gender and identity in the phallocentric economy of paternal authority, the enigma of the Other's desire and the distortion and anamorphosis of the all too human. These themes are important not only to Gaiman's text, but also to broader questions of femininity, sexualities and the faculty of desire itself, for they query the basis of understanding our own embodiment and the possibility for transgression.

While subjective enjoyment is an important device in the story of *Coraline*, it is more difficult to discern the contours of how Gaiman is approaching the mother–daughter relationship. At a glance, Coraline is an oblique examination of the figure of the mother from a daughter's point of view. It is the namesake daughter of *Coraline*, Coraline Jones, who encounters this motherhood in its enigmatic otherness. Therefore the focus of this discussion is how Coraline tarries with the enigma of maternal desire and re-establishes her symbolic position within her family in the wake of a traumatic encounter with an old maternal god. This old god or archaic 'other mother' bears witness to what several psychoanalytically informed analyses of *Coraline* have highlighted as the text's Freudian approach to motherhood: something primal and originary, an otherness that can secure or disappoint Coraline's satisfaction.[2]

Gaiman elaborates this position of motherhood at the outset of *Coraline*. A staple situation found in many contemporary fairytales, the protagonist Coraline is dissatisfied with her domestic arrangement wherein her mother does not cook, her father cooks things she detests and both of her parents apparently ignore her requests for attention. When the family moves to a new home, Coraline finds a small door leading to another world and another family with black-button eyes. As the story progresses we learn that this entire other world is the construction of the 'other mother' who promises to Coraline 'to love you and play with you and feed you and make your life interesting'.[3] But these effusions about future pleasure (what Freud termed 'forepleasure') soon become darker and tinged with sinister maleficence as Coraline realises that the other mother is luring children into her realm and stealing their life-force, leaving them as 'wisps of soul in a cupboard'.[4] When the other mother kidnaps Coraline's real parents, Coraline sets out to rescue both her parents and the trapped souls of the other children whom the other mother lured to their doom. With a lot of ingenuity and the aid of a talking cat, Coraline succeeds in her rescue and saves the day. Yet the defeat of the other mother is never really complete and she remains 'undead' even to the last letter of the story and the last minute of its cinematic adaptation. This is what makes *Coraline* such a terrifying text to a reader seeking symbolic closure – there is none! But more than this, it is a significant moment of denouement for Gaiman's imagining of how Coraline understands herself and her world.

At the outset of the narrative, her parents disturb Coraline's domestic space as they insist on moving to a new house. The symbolic coordinates of Coraline's life are turned inward as she must explore some new space in the wake of the family home now being sundered and replaced: 'I don't want to do those things. I want to explore.'[5] Such exploration avoids the *ennui* of the familiar fragments of domestic life in which 'Coraline had watched all the videos. She was bored with

2 This reading is against the grain of the reduction of the Freudian maternal to the monstrous.

3 N. Gaiman, *Coraline and Other Stories*, London: Bloomsbury Publishing, 2009, p. 42.

4 J. Goss, 'The Mother with the Button Eyes: An Exploration of the Story Construct of the "Other-Mother"', *Papers: Explorations into Children's Literature* 19(1), 2009, p. 69.

5 Gaiman *op. cit.* p. 5.

her toys, and she'd read all her books.'[6] These assurances are telling tropes in a narrative structured around the defamiliarisation of the domestic discourse of paternal power: not only is Coraline in tension with her parents, but also with the re-establishing and cognitive mapping of her surrounds as well. From the outset, Gaiman situates Coraline in a life fraught with fragmentation and strange gaps between these domestic fragments, where anything can and does happen.

When the family arrives at their new home in its spookily mist-filled landscape, Coraline is confronted with a new jurisdiction to map and explore. Roaming the grounds, Coraline attunes herself in her new surrounds and avoids the demands of her mother to help them move into the new house. Avoiding her mother's demands does not appear to have any novel audacity for Coraline, yet the air of childish rebellion with which she confronts her mother's insistences presents the basic figurative position of Coraline's encounter with a kind of nihilism that percolates beneath the fragmentation of her mundane everyday life as the family moves into their new residence.

Coraline is not a nihilistic text. Yet the fragmentation and rearrangement of domestic space does appear to bear out the nihilistic processes of destruction and transformative affirmation. The fragmentation at the outset of Coraline does not presuppose an idyllic totality of life. Rather, the incompleteness of the state prior to the family's departure for their new home is incorporated into the space itself as the changing nature of this space. By the time the story reveals another world, another side of the paternal law, the story cements the suggestion that this new world was always laying in wait to be discovered like some Orientalist fantasy of a dark forgotten continent that is coded as neither prohibition, transgression, criminality nor illegality.

This 'prior space' is of an ambiguous diegetic nature. Such ambiguity is staged in the cinematic adaptation of *Coraline* as a strangely alien and intrusive origin: wiry fingers stuff and thread an effigy of a child, a doll, and send it floating out a window. This scene is shown in the opening credits and is neither analepsis nor prolepsis but rather a kind of Macguffin or formless instance that sets up the unsettling horror of the narrative through its incongruity. These opening credits of the cinematic release of *Coraline* have the effect of a mythical lost scene that appears to be alien to the domestic jurisdiction and its code of paternal law established in the course of the narrative in the first few minutes.

In the novella conversely this unanchoring of certainty is emphasised by the underness and age of things. The narrative reads: 'It was a very old house – it had an attic under the roof and a cellar under the ground and an overgrown garden with huge old trees in it.'[7] Richard Gooding notes that this unsteadiness of the world disclosed by the narrative of the *Coraline* novella coalesces around increasingly menacing and uncanny effects 'intensified by the descent of a "mist that hung like blindness", and the strange behaviour of "the crazy old man upstairs",

6 *Ibid.*
7 *Ibid.*, p. 3.

though at first his talk of mouse circuses can be explained away as the fabrications of a man who enjoys teasing children. Even the characters' names are subtly off-kilter: Coraline's defeats the adults around her, and the elision in Miss Spink's name hints at an identity collapsing in on itself.'[8] There is little doubt that *Coraline* is a text ridden with uncanniness, and it is also important to note that the uncanny is a notably structural phenomenon of psychoanalysis. This means that rather than being merely strange appearances, the uncanny effects of *Coraline* are systemic and the content of narration in the reader's mind.

When I discussed the cinematic adaptation of *Coraline* with a colleague, he pointed out that both he and his daughter found the film terrifying or at the very least disquieting because of the lack of resolution. In an era of Disney productions that conclude with rapturous closure, it is curious to consider what is awry about *Coraline*: the unease of the opening credit sequence, in fact one of many moments of narrative ambiguity, such as a mist-covered landscape outside the house, mysterious other residents, and so on. Yet it is the way that the abstract scene at the opening of the film immediately sets the narrative on a different, less trodden track, which proves most vital for the ambiguity of the film.

Achieving narrative closure seems a false hope of *Coraline*'s domestic fragmentation, as such closure assumes an easily contained totality of narrative temporality where the story has a beginning, middle and end. Instead, *Coraline* presents its audience with something intimately familiar to cultural and critical legal theories of the subject of law: the choice for an accommodation with the unsteady and fragile construction of power (domestic life) but no assurances about such a life, no assurances about the moral compass of justice for all. This double-layering of narrative structure and the diegetic content involving a fragile and fragmenting of domestic life puts Gaiman's work in stylistic parallel with other authors of speculative fiction and magical realism such as Salman Rushdie or Angela Carter, whose *The Bloody Chamber* generates its meanings through local negotiations internal to the narrative.[9] Rather than insisting on a closed notion of Coraline as a subject whose identity is founded in her gender as a biological essentialism, as Catharine MacKinnon and some cultural feminist theorists might suggest, Gaiman's text opens itself to a more psychoanalytic tact in which we must listen to how the character of Coraline positions herself in regards to this narrative ambiguity.

Coraline's kinship position (i.e. daughter) is de-centred within the ambit of the domestic space and paternal order. This is in contrast to other readings of the domestic space, such as Peter King's *Private Dwelling* where the subject becomes a sovereign essence with varying degrees of external attachment from childhood to

8 R. Gooding, '"Something Very Old and Very Slow": Coraline, Uncanniness, and Narrative Form', *Children's Literature Association Quarterly* 33(4), 2008, p. 393.

9 For further elaboration of this point see S. Benson, 'Introduction', in S. Benson (ed.), *Contemporary Fiction and the Fairy Tale*, Detroit: Wayne State University Press, 2008, pp. 1–19.

adulthood.[10] King's reflection on dwelling and the use of housing emphasises the home as an intimate external realisation of the subject's interiority. Such an analytical line seems to broaden and open up the extant variations in housing across nationalities, ethnicities and property laws that give some critics purchase on debunking the typically Western construction of the home presented in *Coraline* as any type of 'normative' standard.

In her feminist interpretation of Martin Heidegger's famous rumination on Hölderlin and the poetics of dwelling, Iris Marion Young critiques such endless ontic variations of housing and dwelling in an attempt to highlight that the 'home' in which the subject dwells is marked by what contemporary European philosophy terms an 'ontological difference'.[11] Although all homes are marked by variation in their manifestation, form and content, what constitutes a 'home' is precisely that it bears out the self-understanding of the subjects who live there. That is to say, far from the dwellers of a home forming the identity of the house, it is the masquerade of the house as an incomplete set of features that always undergo change and modification that bears the burden of truth for an identity or selfhood. In no one single fragment of a home do we find the ontological meaning of the domesticity that makes it unique and more than mere 'stuff'. Instead, to understand the ontological meaning of a home, it must be taken in its *ethos* and the positioning of the beings living therein. Much of King's rumination on the use of housing avoids the charge of essentialising the space of the home, but it is interesting that when he attempts to offer an anthropology of children and adults, he lapses into the trap of positing a subject as a centre. Here King misses that such a centre is only inferred by the appearance of the human being through the ontological consistency of the home as 'a home of someone' as such, i.e. in its meaningful manifestation that becomes the focus of laws governing property.

Psychoanalysis, however, invites us to follow along this path further to note that this masking of the subject lacks a proper totality and operates as a non-all.[12] This Lacanian formula of feminine sexuation (i.e. the paradoxical approach to the real through language) presents two prisms through which to consider Coraline's fragmenting domestic space. On the one hand, there is no phenomenon that is not an object of Coraline's possible experience, leading to the persistent regressive failure to establish a 'home' and therein herself. Indeed, this appears to be where much of the narrative of Coraline spends its time, showing how many improbable and otherworldly things arise in Coraline's experience of her new domestic surrounds, from the other mother with button-eyes to a spidery maleficent Thing and dogs with bats' wings. Effectively, this means that the series of phenomena that

10 P. King, *Private Dwelling: Contemplating the Use of Housing*, London: Routledge, 2004, p. 99.

11 I. M. Young, 'House and Home: Feminist Variations on a Theme', in N. J. Holland and Patricia Huntington (eds), *Feminist Interpretations of Martin Heidegger*, Pennsylvania: The Pennsylvania State University Press, 2001, p. 278.

12 J. Copjec, *Read My Desire*, Cambridge, MA: The MIT Press, 1994, p. 221.

Coraline encounters can go on infinitely. There is no limit to the set that makes up Coraline's 'home', and thus it lacks the definitive judgement of 'Coraline's home'.

On the other hand, this first proposition supposes its antithesis: not-all phenomena are a possible object of experience.[13] This second antithetical proposition reveals the problem my colleague located with *Coraline*, its disquieting irresolution. The narrative of *Coraline* does indeed have a trajectory that brings the tale to a conclusion. But this ending is one that refuses to allow the kinship ties of mother, father and daughter to resume a stable coherency in the minds of the audience. It is not that Coraline's new house is haunted, but that, quite contrarily, the domestic space itself opens up onto another dimension otherwise hidden from regular daily experience by Coraline's assumption that this familial domestic world is a given thing, daily phenomena that are ordinary and normative.

We can observe this inconsistency of the familial structure in *Coraline* in the way that Gaiman's narrative positions the paternal law of the family as a 'set' defence against the unknown. The extent to which the family is set up as a defensive mechanism is initially heralded by the fragmentation of the domestic residence and the uncanny strangeness of the new house and its residents: 'Coraline's family didn't own all of the house, it was too big for that. Instead they owned part of it.'[14] But as the story progresses it becomes clear that the core of the familial bond in the narrative is the relationship between Coraline and her mother.[15] In her relation with her mother, Coraline persists in a state of antagonistic obedience that formulates the maternal authority of her family as one who bars Coraline from numerous pleasurable experiences and yet insists on enjoyment in other forms. In juxtaposition to this figure of the non-all disposition of Coraline's experience of the world and therein the conditions under which she can compose a domestic space, Gaiman presents an otherworldly mother with buttons for eyes and a bountiful abundance of things to feed Coraline's demands for satisfaction and enjoyment, i.e. a vast array of foods, games and other things.

One should be careful here to not commit to the naïve psychoanalytic reading that this other mother is simply a fantasy-projection of Coraline's wish for fulfillment when faced with her real mother's dissatisfying suggestions for fun. Such a line of reasoning suggests that this other world that Coraline encounters is a kind of delusion. But this is clearly not what Gaiman's narrative portrays: the other world is part of the continuum of Coraline's experience. How then do we account for the difference between the 'real' world and this alternative reality in *Coraline*? If we move on from mere description and consider that the fecundity of the alternative reality encountered by Coraline is excessive and almost a kind of forced pleasure, we begin to get a sense of the contours of the distinction: the 'real world' is constituted as non-all, a constantly changing, constantly incomplete

13 *Ibid.*

14 Gaiman, *op. cit.*, p. 3.

15 E. Parsons, N. Sawers and K. McInally, 'The Other Mother: Neil Gaiman's Postfeminist Fairytales', *Children's Literature Association Quarterly* 33(4), 2008, p. 373.

variation that only appears to be full from the position of an 'impossible gaze' that gathers together all the elements of the world in a closed, definitive judgement as a monadic set or whole. Such a totality is a fantasy *par excellence* as it didactically fosters a closure upon the elements that make up that world.

Such a fantasmatic schematism makes the other world that Coraline encounters seem surreal, even more fantastic than the normalising fantasies that maintain the illusory consistency of her 'real world'.[16] From the side of the otherworldly alternative reality however, the 'real world' of the paternal law appears ominously unaware of the horrors and traumatic enjoyment (over-abundance) of pleasurable experiences waiting just beyond its borders. This is literalised in Gaiman's narrative as a door that Coraline climbs through to access the other world and the spirits that inhabit the cupboard in which the other mother imprisons Coraline; an arrangement of ordinary things in Coraline's new domestic residence that are not limited to the symbolic closure that secures the consistency of the paternal law in the 'real world'.

The conclusion of the *Coraline* narrative reveals that this alternative reality is the construction of a maleficent Thing, a dark maternal god who wants Coraline's soul. Once we see this Thing, however, it becomes clear that the everyday life in the 'real world' becomes a nonsense that shields the people living there from ever encountering this Thing. Coraline herself realises this when she becomes wary of the pleasures of the other world and judges its familiarity and satisfactions as the traps they are. It is as though in confronting the antinomy of 'there is no phenomena/satisfactions that are not able to be experienced in contrary to not-all satisfactions are able to be experienced', Coraline is always beginning from the non-all position where every phenomenon or satisfaction is incomplete. This means that it is not just that Coraline does not experience every satisfaction possible between the two worlds, but also that every satisfaction that Coraline experiences is in itself incomplete and drawn from her perspective. We can thus see a way to correct the naïve reading of psychoanalytic projection: it is not that the other world is a pure delusion, but rather that reality becomes palpable through the fantasmatic supplementation of experiences' ontological ambiguity.

The encounter with the maternal Thing of the other world thus discloses to Coraline this important psychoanalytic insight about the persistent ambiguity of domesticity. This facilitates Coraline's movement away from a given erection of reality towards the transformation of reality through her willing engagement and also through the transformation of her willingness through the incompleteness of experience *per se*.[17] Rather than assuming a normative imposition of order from the paternal authority above her, Coraline is able to formulate a critical femininity as a daughter who knows that her daughterhood is both a construction of the familial relation and one possible experience of this relation that invites its subversion.

16 Gooding, *op. cit.*, p. 392.
17 Parsons et. al., *op. cit.*, p. 382.

The unsettling nature of the *Coraline* narrative is thus a matter of the openness of the reader. Discussing the reception of *Coraline*, Gaiman reports, 'Adults [sic] found it really scary and disturbing, and they're not sure it's a good book for kids ... Children [sic] read it as an adventure ... They don't get nightmares, and they don't find it scary.'[18] The curious insight that Gaiman offers here is that the supposedly 'mature' world of adulthood is undone by its trust in a normative order: 'I think ... that kids don't realise how much trouble Coraline is in – she is in big trouble – and adults read it and think, "I know how much trouble you're in."'[19] It is precisely the supposed naïveté of the children that bears witness to the fiction of normative consistency that casts the paternal law as a defence against nightmarish horror. However, the critical feminine position of Coraline herself offers a third vantage from which to consider the problem of readers' responses: the rupture and reconstruction of the knowledge linking the order of experience to its registration in the symbolic order of the paternal law through subjective engagement.

At the conclusion of the narrative, the undead hand of the other mother roaming the real world confronts Coraline. The demise of the hand again repeats this non-all structure of experience: the hand falls down a well that Coraline then seals. This action suggests that it is not the knowledge of the other world as such that is terrifying, but the spectre of such knowledge; the way it fantasmatically fills in the incompleteness of Coraline's experiencing the inconsistency of the paternal law. As Gaiman writes, once the hand of the other mother falls down the well, Coraline fantasises: 'Someone had once told her that if you look up at the sky from the bottom of a mineshaft, even in the brightest daylight, you see a night sky and stars. Coraline wondered if the hand could see stars from where it was.'[20] The burden of Coraline's psychic transformation is thus presented to the reader as their own difficulty with the world's consistency, its fantasmatic orderliness. This position may appear unpopular to some feminist theorists who favour a reading of Coraline as an anachronistic fantasy text with an anachronistic idea of gender.[21] What such a position misses, however, are the structural rather than performative limits to the conditions of what is possible in the narrative of *Coraline*.

The familial relationship of *Coraline* is part of the domestic order of the paternal law and the fantasmatic coordination of its fragments, the incompleteness of its empirical expression. Gaiman's genius has been to recognise the fragmentation of this space as the primordial distortion that activates the defence of the familial bond and narrativises this transformation without relying on a pithy realism that retreats into the naïveté of an epistemological indexing of reality and its forever partial subjective perception. The curious effect of cinema on the retelling of *Coraline* also goes some way to laying bare the implicit and inferred structures

18 G. J. Grant, 'Neil Gaiman Interview', *Indie Bound*, American Book Sellers Association, 2008, http://www.indiebound.org/author-interviews/gaimanneil.

19 *Ibid.*

20 Gaiman, *op. cit.*, p. 108.

21 For such a view see A. Balay, '"They're Closin' Up Girl Land": Female Masculinities in Children's Fantasy', *Femspec* 10(2), 2010.

of the novella. What matters in *Coraline* manifests through a logic of the non-all, the incompleteness of our experience of the world and therein the aporia that the paternal law's normalising fantasies about family, gender, childhood and adulthood attempt to cover over with the arbitrary given-ness of the order of things. *Coraline* is an instructive post-feminist lesson in the importance of understanding how human beings furnish the fragments of their worlds with meaning and how to have the courage to think for oneself in the face of the paternal law's inconsistency. But what then does such a reading of *Coraline* offer to legal theory?

The structure of the paternal law in *Coraline* has thus far been rendered in a philosophico-psychoanalytic fashion. This has facilitated the revealing of the paternal law's function in the textuality of *Coraline* and the treatment of the protagonist Coraline as a character who is subject to, for and by this law. The limitations of such a position are the limitations of the (un)conscious subject itself, its perspective. Unlike theories that foster an abstract view of the law as either a neutral institution or glacial construct of civilisation, *Coraline* offers a vista onto the intensified jurisdiction of the family. This is a jurisdiction where the law is psychic power. For a critical reading of *Coraline*, this pushes the general point that children's and young adult (YA) fiction can be taken seriously as legal texts that display an intimate knowledge of the subjection to law. Law here is not merely its writ, its practice or its code or precedence, but also its believability and its revision, its consistency and its fragmentation, its inclusion and exclusion of that which is subject to the invisible universe of affect and subjectivity.

Many legal theories offer an account of the basis for law, but it is the branch of law and economics that focuses most acutely on the contractual nature of Coraline's familial bond. Law and economics proponents such as Pareto and Coase emphasise the functionality and efficiency of the transactional and contractual nature of the law. But such a theoretical approach to the law is weak in its understanding of the fundamentally irrational and arbitrary basis of the law and its subjects. Law and economics has no place for the unknown laws, the enigmatic suggestion of what is just, the important inefficiencies rendered by the symbolic constitution of a legal subject such as its nervous tics to consent, rights, recognition and equity. In the critical reading above, *Coraline* shows that the purview of law and economics erects an impossible gaze that allows the principles of efficiency, optimisation and maximisation to become the metaphysics of law: law is explained through its efficiency, optimisation and maximisation; not as the law but as an economy 'beyond' the law itself. *Coraline* demonstrates that such a closed set of metaphysical principles misconstrues how a subject *can* enjoy, without feeling they *must* enjoy, their inclusion in law by way of ambivalence or critique, perhaps *the* inefficient means of reasoning through law in a broad range of contexts. Without critique, however, the law would lack a reflexive basis from which to understand itself. Herein it is a small step to wonder if the economising of the law makes the absence of critique and understanding of the sensibility of law a brutish virtue.

But is it not psychoanalysis, especially classical Freudian psychoanalysis, which also proposes an economy of the psyche? To criticise law and economics from the psychoanalytic vantage thus seems masochistic in theoretical terms.[22] Yet here we should pause. As identified above in the figure of Coraline as a feminine subject (of the law), the psychic economy identified by psychoanalysis does not always veer into efficiency. We need only glance over the catalogue of psychoanalytic cases, even in the early work of Freud, Klein or Lacan, to see that psychic economies breed an 'order of the house' that may be self-defeating, subverting the structure that fuels its pleasures as in the acquisition of language where words take the place of things and substantive enjoyment.

What then would it mean to say that the paternal law of *Coraline* has a psychic economy, and, moreover, that Coraline herself figures this economy in the individual and subjective microcosm of her own life in the story? Initially, we can say that *Coraline* demonstrates two points: that the 'real' world is a legal desert that is too easily transgressed and too indifferent in its symbolic treatment of Coraline as a subject of the paternal law; and, secondly, that the 'other' world stages the lost element that has deserted the 'real' world in abudance, enjoyment. In classical Freudian psychoanalysis and the Lacanian clinic of the 1950s such a state of affairs is one possible outcome of subjection to the paternal law known as the Oedipus complex: the child is separated from its binary relationship with the mother through the intervention of a third figure, the father.[23] At the level of metaphor, this process refers to the way in which one is acculturated to the symbolic constellations of law, culture and society, the way one enters the inorganic space of the Symbolic. But more than this, entry into the universe of the Symbolic facilitates a beginning, a positioning of the child as a 'subject' who is 'subject to, for, and by the Symbolic' and therein the paternal law; the subject is given a language, it becomes a thing with voice that is always-already framed within the law sustained in the name of the father, in the name of a supposedly authorial Other.[24] Thus Coraline stands out because the formulation of her subjecthood *vis-à-vis* the paternal law of her parents resolves to see the paucity and bluster of this law.

Of course, one may wonder why it is necessary to begin with language and the other mechanisms sustained by the paternal law in a discussion of authority in a text such as *Coraline*? Slavoj Žižek offers an answer to this question by returning to Freud's various permutations of the parricide myth in *Moses & Monotheism* and *Totem & Taboo*.[25] Here Žižek takes three modalities of the father from this reading of the parricide myth in Freud. The first is the Oedipal father of symbolic injunction, the cruel superego who sets limits in the symbolic universe through an emphatic 'No!' The second mode of the father is the anal Father of the primal horde, a *jouisseur* who has access to all enjoyment and enlists the pathological jealousy of the subject. The third and final mode reveals the figure of symbolic

22 Freud famously considered masochism an economic problem for the libidinal economy of the drives.

23 J. Lacan, *Écrits*, B. Fink (trans.), New York: W. W. Norton & Company, 2006, p. 230.

24 *Ibid.*, p. 344.

25 One should note here that Žižek is following Lacan's review of Freud and not rehearsing Freud.

authority as a father-*logos* of cosmic Order. In this third mode the father is neither the agent imposing cruel symbolic injunctions, nor a *jouisseur* hording all pleasures. The father-*logos* functions as a Real signifier that is the denouement of symbolic unity in the abyss of the Real at the expense of the subjectivity of the subject.[26] The framework of each father supposes a constitution of the subject that predisposes them toward meaningful engagement with social reality and the symbolic universe therein; law, pleasure and power. Here then let us turn to an examination of the three modes of the paternal law to better understand, by way of comparison, the unique psychic economy of *Coraline.*

We will begin with the Oedipal father because his injunction provides the receptive *chora*-like infant *(infans)* with the contours for their ego to emerge within.[27] It is important to note here that the 'ego' is not an epistemic object but rather a posited illusion of unity sustained by the corpus of the symbolic universe rendered in the flesh of the subject. These sinews of the ego are to what the injunctions of the Oedipal father pertain. This father is the agent of prohibition, the one whose mandate is to rigorously apply the restrictive 'No!' Herein the Oedipal father functions as the ego-ideal, the veiled point of ideal identification marred by obscenity. This ego-ideal is obscene because the father's power is arbitrary and non-negotiable, not something to be shared with the subject.[28] Thus the cycle of identification is interwoven with desire because the subject is denied an object central to the ego's gratification, the *gratis* of having their demands met. Desire, in this sense, follows its definition by Lacan as 'neither the appetite for satisfaction, nor the demand for love, but the difference that results from the subtraction of the first from the second'.[29] At the level of topography, this subtraction of satisfaction from the demand for love transmutes desire from 'having' the father to 'being like' the father. Furthermore, the Oedipal father is unified by the meeting of the ego-ideal and the superegoic injunctions in themselves but distances itself from the dissolution of individuality in the Real and instead is entrenched in the Symbolic.[30] Herein the Real as a mitigating force against creative action (free-will/identification) and as a space where the Oedipal father sets the psychical scene for the emergence of creative individualism from subjectivity.[31]

In critical theoretical terms, this shift in how authority legitimates itself is an inversion: we go from humanity as the inaccessible Thing-in-itself to the contrary full-bodied assumption of the Human Thing in all its all too human excess. The Oedipal father is inverted by the anal Father, and the anal Father by the

26 S. Žižek, *The Ticklish Subject: The Absent Centre of Political Ontology*, London: Verso, 1999, pp. 313–322.

27 This follows from Lacan's point that the ego is an illusion of unity. See Lacan, *op cit.*, pp. 75–81.

28 Žižek, *op. cit.*, p. 316

29 Lacan in S. Žižek, *Tarrying with the Negative: Kant, Hegel, and the Critique of Ideology*, Durham, NC: Duke University Press, 1993, p. 121.

30 Žižek, *op. cit.*, p. 313.

31 *Ibid.*

father-*logos*. Often in paranoid fantasy the anal Father is asserted as an agent pre-existing the injunction of some symbolic limit by the order/paternal law of the symbolic universe.[32] To the keen reader of *Coraline*, such an exposition is carried through in both the book and the film wherein the 'other mother' appears as an anal authority who hoards all enjoyments and attempts to recruit Coraline into her world with promises of solving the displeasure and unhappiness of life in the 'real' world. To this end the other mother assumes a position that seems to have the symbolic mandate to guide Coraline in a particular direction by denying her certain displeasures with the promise of full, hegemonic enjoyment. The Otherness of the other mother herein functions as a Macguffin of the symbolic injunction of the paternal law, an ideological interpellation that keeps the forbidden activities of Coraline (i.e. playing in the rain, muddying her clothes) within the 'paternal law' of the other mother. The twist comes when Coraline realises that she is being manipulated by the other mother, that in fact the other mother's paternal law is inconsistent precisely in the moments that it promises Coraline enjoyments forbidden by her parents: Coraline's pleasure in transgressing the law of her 'real parents' is subverted as yet another law, but this time of the other mother who insists that Coraline *must* enjoy. This twist reveals the other mother possessing an entire alternative dimension, another world from where she can spy on the unhappiness of children and entice them to her world, a small world that is composed of only what she needs to convince children to stay and that folds back on itself if you walk too far in one direction, and something a little bit extra, *jouissance*, an excessive enjoyment that rules the other mother like an external authority. There is no Beyond of authorial order and creative individualism for the other mother. The other mother takes on the mantel of the anal Father, the *jouisseur* of the primal horde, not because she possesses a horde but because she is totally consumed by an unholy excess of pleasure, namely *jouissance* and *Schadenfreude*. As an anal Father, the other mother enjoys everything.[33] The other mother's scheming already, in some way, taints anything Coraline touches in the 'other world'.

This scene of the real world versus other world dichotomy provides a way to understand why the paternal law persists alongside the evacuation of enjoyment in *Coraline*. Coraline's boredom with her new residence, her *ennui* with domestic life and the normative paternal law, is only possible if she inheres in a tension between the necessity that the paternal law demands and the freedom to resist or accept the subjection to this necessity. Indeed, there would be no narrative to *Coraline* if not for the ambiguity that Gaiman establishes between the conflux of forces embodied as the character of Coraline and the symbolic registration of Coraline in language that is all too often a misrecognition or mispronunciation. When the other residents mispronounce Coraline's name she becomes agitated, yet such an affect could only emerge if the abstract symbolic space of language

32 Žižek, *op. cit.*, p. 324.
33 *Ibid.*, p. 315.

is also an embodied material thing. Or, more pertinently to the example of the paternal law, when Coraline's parents make their different demands on Coraline it is clear that she responds to these demands with myriad embodied affects from frustration to love and onto dissatisfaction. But here it is clear that the locus of Coraline's affects, the instigator of her (dis)pleasure, is not her interiority but rather the inclusion of her as a subject of the paternal law. For Coraline, as per the *X-Files*, 'the truth is out there'.

The intimate truth of Coraline's subjecthood is external, or 'extimate' as Lacan might suggest, signalling the importance of understanding the inconsistency of the paternal law in the narrative. When it was previously argued that Coraline functioned as a subject of the non-all, this was not mere word play: when Coraline lacks inscription in the paternal law, she literally ceases to exist for that law; that is that Coraline only ever exists partially for the law. It is psychoanalysis in particular that can offer a critical approach to this incarnation of the law and conversely the elision of what precedes the language of law.

CHAPTER 9

Psyche and authority

Questions of authority and satisfaction are paramount to the work of Slavoj Žižek. From the explication of authority and enjoyment in his work from *The Ticklish Subject* in 1999 onwards to *The Parallax View* in 2006, Žižek's discourse has relied on a notion of the human subject as a psychical agency culpable for their discursive engagements (language, practices, etc.) with the prevailing symbolic universe of signified reality.[1] Approaching authority and enjoyment in this context requires that Žižek observe the subject relating to the Father/Other who motivates and motilates this symbolic universe in the three registers established by Lacan: the undetermined Real, the binary oppositions of the Imaginary and the separation of the Symbolic. For law, Žižek's insights are particularly useful because they provide a speculative theory of lived experience of the law. Such speculation enables new socio-legal research, cultural legal studies and shines a light on the soft ideological underbelly of law.

It is not the purpose of this chapter to diagnose authorities' pathologies. Rather, by maintaining the speculative exegesis used thus far, this discussion will draw on a select few exemplar cases in popular and canonical Western culture to makes its case for a critical understanding of enjoying authority: the cinema of *Minority Report* and *The Recruit*, Sophocles' Theban cycle, particularly *Oedipus at Colonus*, and the eponymous *Kinder Surprise*. These examples will serve to unfurl some of the curls in Žižek's psychoanalytic philosophy in tandem with putting forward some observations on what being a 'subject' means for any form of human rights ordained by a psychic authority. Before we can delve into these elaborations, however, it is first necessary to discern the delicate distinction between the Freudian Father and the Lacanian Other within the bounds of Žižek's psychoanalytic philosophy.

This overview of the Other's modalities is qualified by the preliminary observation that Žižek grounds his ideology-critique in the role of the symbolic Other

1 S. Žižek, *Interrogating the Real*, R. Butler and S. Stephens (eds), London: Continuum, 2005, pp. 38–41; S. Žižek, *The Universal Exception*, R. Butler and S. Stephens (eds), London: Continuum, 2006, p. 151.

for contemporary society.[2] This is the Other of psychoanalysis, Lacan's *l'Autre* to whom we address our demands and who recognises us in return as beings answerable to responsibility.[3] As such, the Other stands as the agent of the Order of the symbolic universe that simultaneously reveals and assures the efficacy of our symbolic universe. This symbolic efficacy is introduced through 'the paternal function'. In Žižek's favoured Lacanese, the paternal function is the *'name of the father'*.[4] Hence the ordering of the symbolic universe is enacted, justified and sustained in the name of the Other-*qua*-Father.

It is also important to note that this intercession of symbolic authority occurs where the order of the Symbolic attempts to overwrite the order of the Imaginary. In classical Freudian psychoanalysis and the early Lacanian clinic this is the process through which the Oedipus complex is resolved: the child is separated from its binary relationship with the mother through the intervention of a third figure, the Father.[5] At the level of metaphor this process refers to the way in which one is acculturated to the symbolic constellations of culture and society, the way one enters the Symbolic. But more than this, entry into the universe of the Symbolic facilitates a beginning, a positioning of the child as a 'subject' who is 'subject to, for, and by the Symbolic'; the subject is given a language, it becomes a thing with voice that is always-already framed within the law sustained in the name of the Father.[6]

Of course, one may wonder why it is necessary to begin with language and the other Symbolic mechanisms sustained by the paternal function in a discussion of authority. The answer is that every beginning is nothing short of the tautology revealed during a seminar by Žižek's philosophical and political interlocutor Alain Badiou in the April of 2005. While discussing the subject (of art), Badiou proposed that we begin from the beginning, 'because that is what the Father tells us'.[7] But which Father does Badiou mean? Žižek offers an answer to this question in *The Fragile Absolute*, *The Ticklish Subject* and *The Puppet and the Dwarf* through a return from his Lacanian position to Freud's various permutations of the parricide myth in *Moses & Monotheism* and *Totem & Taboo*.[8] Žižek takes three modalities of the Father from this reading of the parricide myth in Freud. The first is the Oedipal Father of symbolic injunction, the cruel superego who sets limits in the symbolic universe through an emphatic 'No!' The second mode of the Father is the anal Father of the primal horde, a *jouisseur* who has access to all enjoyment and enlists the pathological jealousy of the subject. The third and

2 I. Parker, *Slavoj Žižek: A Critical Introduction*, London: Pluto Press, 2004, pp. 62–64.
3 J. Lacan, *Écrits*, B. Fink (trans.), New York: W. W. Norton & Company, 2006, p. 693.
4 *Ibid.*, p. 230.
5 *Ibid.*
6 *Ibid.*, p. 344.
7 A. Badiou, 'The Subject of Art', *Lacan.com*, 2005, http://www.lacan.com/symptom6_articles/badiou.html.
8 One should note here that Žižek is following Lacan's review of Freud and not rehearsing Freud.

final mode reveals the figure of symbolic authority as a Father-*logos* of cosmic Order. In this third mode the Father is neither the agent imposing cruel symbolic injunctions, nor a *jouisseur* hording all pleasures. The Father-*logos* functions as a Real signifier that is the denouement of symbolic unity in the abyss of the Real at the expense of the subjectivity of the subject.[9] The framework of each Father supposes a constitution of the subject that predisposes them toward meaningful engagement with social reality and the symbolic universe therein.

We will begin with the Oedipal Father because his injunction provides the receptive *chora*-like infant with contours for their ego to emerge within.[10] It is important to note here that the 'ego' is not an epistemic object but rather a posited illusion of unity sustained by the corpus of the symbolic universe rendered in the flesh of the subject. These sinews of the ego are to what the injunctions of the Oedipal Father pertain. This Father is the agent of prohibition, the one whose mandate is to rigorously apply the restrictive 'No!' Herein the Oedipal Father functions as the ego-ideal, the veiled point of ideal identification marred by obscenity. This ego-ideal is obscene because the Father's power is arbitrary and non-negotiable, not something to be shared with the subject.[11] Thus the cycle of identification is interwoven with desire because the subject is denied an object central to the ego's gratification, the *gratis* of having their demands met. Desire, in this sense, follows its definition by Lacan as 'neither the appetite for satisfaction, nor the demand for love, but the difference that results from the subtraction of the first from the second'.[12] At the level of topography, this subtraction of satisfaction from the demand for love transmutes desire from 'having' the Father to 'being like' the Father. Furthermore, the Oedipal Father is unified by the meeting of the ego-ideal and the superegoic injunctions in themselves but distances himself from the dissolution of individuality in the Real and instead is entrenched in the Symbolic.[13] Herein Žižek understands the Real as a mitigating force against creative action (free-will/identification) and as a space where the Oedipal Father sets the psychical scene for the emergence of creative individualism from subjectivity.[14]

This basic tension culminating in the private subjectivity of the subject is played out in the film *Minority Report* (2002) where the chief of the Pre-Crime division, John Anderton (played by Tom Cruise), is accused and pursued for a chain of events *yet to happen* but are to occur *because of his creative individualism*. The finale comes when Anderton is assisted in his escape from his thought-prison.

9 S. Žižek, *The Ticklish Subject: The Absent Centre of Political Ontology*, London: Verso, 1999, pp. 313–322.

10 This follows from Lacan's point that the ego is an illusion of unity (Lacan, *op. cit.*, pp. 75–81).

11 Žižek, *op. cit.*, p. 316.

12 J. Lacan in S. Žižek, *Tarrying with the Negative: Kant, Hegel, and the Critique of Ideology*, Durham, NC: Duke University Press, 1993, p. 121.

13 Žižek, *The Ticklish Subject: The Absent Centre of Political Ontology*, *op. cit.*, p. 313.

14 *Ibid.*

But the point is not that he escapes, it is that someone else assists him because he is immobilised and therefore cannot free himself. At the point where subjective decisions are often associated with freedom, this film twists predetermination in a spectacularly Kantian way, grounding the ethical duty of the subject in the open possibility of creative agency. To phrase this in another way, 'You ought to so you must!' Because you are free to choose, you cannot but choose this path of action.[15] This double negative indicates the absence of a totality that precludes the emergence of freedom and therein the openness of the field of possibility in which duty is asserted as an injunction on this freedom.[16] Yet possibility remains open in light of ethical duty because the Other to whom I am ultimately responsible is able to intervene and disrupt the flow of events. The Oedipal Father is thus the Father of individualism and mobility, bringing attention to the autonomous response to the Other's demands contrary to the rigorous determinism of the 'moralizing mathematics of guilt'.[17]

While this rendering of *Minority Report* concurs with William P. MacNeil's brilliant *Lex Populi* excursus on the 'Law and Economics' present in film, it also exposes the Oedipal underpinnings of continuing with a Kantian notion of 'duty to humanity' in the conditions of possibility that delimit the discourse of Law and Economics wherein humanity becomes the inaccessible Thing-in-Itself *(Ding-an-sich)* founding ethical respect. Where the analysis in *Lex Populi* concludes with a call to deconstruct the antijurisprudence of legal economism while simultaneously reconstructing a positive jurisprudence that finds the 'primacy of the human' in civil liberties, it is also important to recognise that this is a departure from the ethical *cul-de-sac* of Posner and others wherein Law and Economics 'knows the price of everything but the value of nothing'.[18] This shift enacted by MacNeil's discourse must risk individuality itself in the form ordained by the Oedipal injunction of prohibition.

The example of *Minority Report* shows that it is not simply enough to realise that individuals cannot be substituted. Individuality, in its very creative genesis, relies upon the nihilism of perspectivism. The problem of perspective undermines the Kantian alternative to Law and Economics insofar as the consistency of authority in its function as 'prohibitive injunction'. This injunction must avoid either reverting to a naïve positivism that simply interrupts the subjectivity of the subject with a command backed by sanctions (Austin), wherein the law functions as a kind of cognitive behavioural therapy, or repeating the eclipse of prohibition by the injunctions of creative individualism that are unknowable even to the subject until they have come to pass (Hart's rule of recognition), which is the problem of Pre-Crime in *Minority Report*. If a duty to human rights emerges with

15 Žižek, 'The Most Sublime of Hysterics: Hegel with Lacan', *op. cit.*, pp. 42–49.

16 W. P. MacNeil, *Lex Populi: The Jurisprudence of Popular Culture*, Stanford: Stanford University Press, 2007, p. 90.

17 S. Žižek, *Welcome to the Desert of the Real: Five Essays on September 11 and Related Dates*, London: Verso, 2002, p. 51.

18 MacNeil, *op. cit.*, p. 96.

sufficient enough grounds to resist the nihilism of duty-*vis*-prohibition, *mutatis mutandis* the frame of authority will have to shift from the logic of prohibition, with all it implies of mobility and individualism. Yet, were such a shift to single out the primacy of the human as its new focus, the seat of authority can shift from prohibition to the full enjoyment of humanity contrary to creative individualism as it is ordained by the Oedipal Father through prohibitive injunctions.[19]

Analytically speaking, this shift in how authority legitimates itself is an inversion: we go from humanity as the inaccessible Thing-in-itself to the contrary full-bodied assumption of the Human Thing in all its all too human excess. Such an inversion of contraries is a tactic that Žižek deploys again and again, and his study of Freud's mythological Fathers bears this out. The Oedipal Father is inverted by the anal Father, and the anal Father by the Father-*logos*. Often in paranoid fantasy the anal Father is asserted as an agent pre-existing the injunction of some symbolic limit by the order/law of the symbolic universe.[20] An exposition of this is carried through in the film *The Recruit* (2003), starring Al Pacino and Colin Farrell, wherein the Central Intelligence Agency (CIA) appears as the anal Father. Pacino's character Walter Burke 'recruits' James Clayton, played by Farrell, to find a mole within the CIA. To this end Walter assumes a position that seems to have the symbolic mandate to guide James in a particular direction by denying him certain pleasures to the end of unearthing this mole, staining their identification with the CIA. The CIA herein functions as a Macguffin of a symbolic injunction, an ideological interpellation that keeps the seemingly sordid activities of Walter and James legitimate within the confines of the symbolic order. The twist comes when James realises he is being manipulated by Walter, that in fact *James is the mole* and was made thus by Walter's own design. This twist reveals Walter possessing a secret enjoyment of ostensibly unlimited access to meaningful information, a 'boot camp' devoted specifically to breaking James' psyche, and a small army of black-clad mercenaries who pander to Walter's every whim. And maybe something a little bit more, *jouissance*, an excessive enjoyment that rules Walter like an external authority. There is no Beyond of authorial order and creative individualism for Walter, as in the case of Anderton in *Minority Report*: Walter *is* the law's *jouissance*. Walter takes on the mantle of the anal Father, the *jouisseur* of the primal horde, not because he possesses a horde but because he is totally consumed by an unholy excess of pleasure, namely *jouissance* and *Schadenfreude*. As an anal Father, Walter enjoys everything.[21] Anything James touches is already, in some way, tainted by Walter's scheming.

To turn back to the earlier discussion for a moment, this brief examination of *The Recruit* shows that MacNeil's reading of *Minority Report* does not demand

19 Such an argument still does not resolve Arendt's criticism that universal human rights fail those who need them the most – refugees and stateless persons – because there is no state to enforce the rights, since universality erodes all particular differences.

20 Žižek, *The Ticklish Subject: The Absent Centre of Political Ontology*, *op. cit.*, p. 324.

21 *Ibid.*, p. 315.

the resuscitation of Kantian duty in the primacy of the human; it instead cautions against going too far in the other direction, by embodying authorial legitimacy in the *jouissance* of the Thing-in-itself. Herein we might say that the absurd Hollywood plot of *The Recruit* stages a kind of fundamental fantasy that the Oedipal Law cannot admit to itself in *Minority Report*. This fundamental fantasy exposes the *jouissance* of authority not in any particular object but in the transcendental status of the subject as the authorial Other. Walter's black-clad army, extra-judicial boot camp and uncannily unlimited access are every part Walter's status as 'a Master-Subject' as Walter has access to 'subjectivity'. While both James in *The Recruit* and Anderton in *Minority Report* are puppets of others, it is the figure of Walter who stands as a kind of fundamental fantasy to the paranoia that sets in on both James and Anderton. Walter enjoys the fullness of his humanity through its very excessivity, its *jouissance*, the point where the inhuman excess becomes his humanity. This is the danger of privileging the rights in human rights as part of the Human Thing-in-itself: the human rights take on a life of their own as they become the Human Thing. (This fundamental fantasy also appears in Costas Douzinas' *Human Rights and Empire* where the primal scene of the Human Thing is papered over by Foucaultian discussions of sovereignty.)

To escape the grip of the *jouisseur*, of figures like Walter, Žižek suggests inverting the anal Father to arrive at the Father-*logos*.[22] The fundamental problem for all these myths of the Father is that the Father in each is ultimately deceased, and in both of the films discussed thus far this appears to be the narrative resolution in at least some sense. The myths of the Father that Žižek takes from Freud and Lacan are myths of parricide where the subject comes to subjectively relate to the symbolic universe by overcoming the agent of the Symbolic who is legitimated by the order of the symbolic universe. This is compounded by Žižek's post-Althusserian-*cum*-Heideggerian promotion of the idea that we are riven by the empty place of the Father after the overcoming of each myth, because subjectivity is founded on a lack. Thus a tension emerges between subjectivity and possibility, the symbolic designation/identification of a subject in social reality veers away from open possibility at the same time that it instates the promise of a subject being authentically subjective.[23] The subject therefore appears to manifest within a crack in Being between the symbolic designation of the signifier and the signified promise of the designated object as sustaining a meaning. In this framing, the subject-as-creative-individual attempts to sate the lack at the core of being a subject. A lack which is concomitant with the crack in Being that reduces the subject to an individual, extant, reified object, a being that is an unassimilable remainder in Being.

The Father-*logos* cracks the universal order of Being for us, but this act is neither out of kindness nor malevolence, it just 'lets in some fresh air' precluding

22 *Ibid.*, pp. 328–329.

23 S. Žižek, *The Fragile Absolute – Or Why the Christian Legacy Is Worth Fighting For*, London: Verso, 2000: pp. 69–82.

total predetermination, *a propos* of Irigaray's critique of Heidegger.[24] The ego of the subject is thus the indicator of presence or, more precisely, the presence of a clearing in Being. Under the name of his commitment to German idealist philosophy, Žižek takes up this clearing through the eyes of Hegel as the 'absolute negativity' of the subject.[25] This negativity is absolute insofar as the arbitrary cut of the symbolic designation is not relative but universal in its radical difference. In practical terms this is what defines the human from other creatures and one another for Žižek: the human subject is the living thing that can pretend to pretend.[26]

Could such a radical difference ordained by the Father-*logos* maintain a primacy of the human even though humanity has been exposed as a Real-Thing? A first step to answering this question is to place emphasis on the absolute negativity of the subject. If human rights are to subjectivise the human, then this cannot be considered commensurate with the subjectivity of the subject engendered by such a move. The preclusion of the human subject's over-determination rests on their manifestation within a crack in Being between the symbolic designation of the signifier and the signified promise of the designated object as sustaining a meaning rather than as an object of discourse. This manifestation facilitates an understanding of the Human Real Thing in a pre-symbolic and symbolic space co-extensive with Žižek's understanding of the Real's operation in the *logos* of Being.

Žižek's conception of the Real's operation in *The Ticklish Subject* identifies it as a thoroughly symbolic register. Herein Žižek reads *logos* with the *mythos* of the Father-*logos*'s autonomous origin. Such a reading reveals the transition from the pre-symbolic *mythos* to the symbolic *logos* that renders the present neither totally in our control nor hopelessly predestined.[27] The Father-*logos* shows up the distinction between the God of philosophers *qua* the universal structure of the universe in its totality as pure becoming and the God of theologians *qua* the 'dark God' of capricious irrational Fate.[28] In the myth of the Father-*logos* we kill the Father without realising His universality. We misrecognise the demand of our ethical duty to care for the Father/Other as the contrived manipulations of the *jouisseur* trying to steal our enjoyment.[29] Tragically we realise all too late that the Father we killed, the Father Nietzsche accosts us for killing, demanded our care because He was at once destitute of agency and excessive in structure. Here, the manifestation of ethics with care spares us the torment of being free to act without a reason. With the eclipse of the Father-*logos*, the symbolic universe sustaining social reality is cast adrift in the meaningless abyss of the Real where the ontological meaning assured by *logos* is now supplemented by the creative

24 L. Irigaray, *The Forgetting of Air in Martin Heidegger*, M. B. Mader (trans.), Austin: University of Texas Press, 1999, pp. 133–134.

25 S. Žižek, *For They Know Not What They Do: Enjoyment as a Political Factor*, London: Verso, 1991, pp. 36–37.

26 This ethological point undergirds Lacan's 'mirror-stage' (Lacan, *op. cit.*, pp. 75–81)

27 Žižek, *The Ticklish Subject: The Absent Centre of Political Ontology*, *op. cit.*, pp. 317–319.

28 *Ibid.*, pp. 317–318.

29 *Ibid.*, p. 326.

imagining of the subject that does not recognise the scission between their 'Real' body as a Cause and its psychical doubling by the designation of it as a 'body' by the Symbolic, only the binary pairing of the two.

Yet, according to Žižek, this tragic realisation dawns on us by virtue of reflection. Žižek presupposes reflection as the terrain of interpretation, the place where we connect the dots separating binary opposites into distinct signifiers. In reflection, interpretation moves us from the Imaginary register to the Symbolic register. The dots need connecting because what is Real always-already exists as the vortex in which our little bits of something float, teasing our desire. In the Imaginary register these object-causes of desire, or *objets petits a*, over-determine subjectivity in the form of a Jungian archetype. The shift to the register of the Symbolic transubstantiates this archetype as a series of meaningless symbolic objects that cannot be translated back into the shared symbolic universe of social reality because they remain a semblance of imagining in place of a signifier of signification. Herein the object marked by the signifier becomes an *objet petit a* by undergoing an ontological shift which is reflected in a corresponding shift in the epistemological status of the object. These shifts disrupt the intersubjective status of social reality because the subjectivity of the subject functions as a blind-spot in the symbolic universe: subjectivity is neither a signifier nor a signified. However, overcoming the Father-*logos* appears to draw the subject into the position of the master-signifier, the signifier for which there is no signified meaning. Thus the *objet petit a* seems to transcend the registers of Being (Imaginary, Symbolic, Real) when the subject takes up the position of determining their own subjective possibility, and yet this is delusional because it elides the scission of the body counted in the Symbolic formal logic of rights and the Real Thing in all its horrifying, meaning-depriving excessiveness.

For Žižek, this quasi-transcendence of the *objet petit a* is indicative of the *jouissance* that exceeds the threshold of homeostasis in a self-regulating world of universal order. Such *jouissance* appears as the 'Imaginary-Real', the mysterious *je ne sais quoi* that allows the sublime dimension to shine through an ordinary object in the symbolic universe.[30] Such a Real-image manifests itself in the imagined 'us and them' opposition between liberal democratic nation-states and other forms of government wherein the sublimation of 'the art *(techne)* of democracy' magically elevates the value of democracy as the only dignified procedure of governing, even though democracy is still a form of government akin to those which it is imagined to be opposed against, such as totalitarianism.

The shift from the Imaginary to the Symbolic reinterprets the nuances of the *objet petit a* as a 'Symbolic-Real'. Herein the consistency of the transcendence of the *objet petit a* is questioned to the extent that the multiplicity of *a* may be abstractions with no concrete relation to our everyday life-world where we are engaged with social reality. Žižek's preferred version of the Symbolic-Real

30 Žižek, *The Fragile Absolute – Or, Why is the Christian Legacy Worth Fighting For?*, *op. cit.*, p. 30.

is the senseless formulae of quantum mechanics, which resist integration into the common-sense observations of the life-world;[31] for example, quantum field theory suggests that when your car keys are lost and you can't see them, they are actually everywhere but where you are currently looking.

This transition from the order of the Imaginary to the order of the Symbolic does not totalise the subject within an abstract homeostasis bound by these *objets petits a*. Where we find a subject in their entirety as an abstract symbolic entity, a Master of their own Signifier, they are atrophied as an unassimilable remainder in the symbolic universe because their subjectivity – that allows them access to the quasi-transcendental *objet petit a* – exceeds the Symbolic register of experience. And yet, as Lacan tells us, in negotiating the symbolic universe, subjectivity doubly removes the subject from the object in itself because the arbitrary 'self-designation of the subject' in the subjective assertion of a 'self' is obfuscated by the misrecognition of the symbolic designation of extant objects in the primal baptism of naming.[32] This misrecognition occurs because symbolic designation does not give the object without first symbolically encoding it; rather, the symbolic universe understands objects through its own system of signification, and perpetually attempts to assimilate objects into this process. Hence Lacan designates the symbolic world the world of machines and not of subjectivity, but the machines of the symbolic universe remain irreducible to the Order of the Symbolic Law.

In light of this, one should also add that for Žižek's ideology-critique the symbolic universe is composed of constellations of *techne* (techniques, crafts, skills, etc.) without these constellations being necessarily ontological. For example, when Fate draws the character of a novel or play to their destiny, should the character exceed the judgement of 'thou art that!', they no longer have reference to the separation of a name from its meaning. All meaning is thus inscribed too soon, therefore the ontological dimension loses its tension with everyday epistemological existence and the subject is reduced to an algebraic sign that is null. Because *techne* is given primacy by the Symbolic register which allows understanding to flourish and ontology to be reduced to material for symbolic inscription, *techne* differentiates itself from meaning on the one hand, and subjectivity on the other.

The differentiation of *techne* from subjectivity is given strong emphasis in the ancient Greek theatre of Sophocles, for example. When Oedipus seals his destiny at Colonus, fulfils his fate, he reaches a senseless space where he is neither dead nor alive: dead to the Symbolic Order but still alive and breathing.[33] In a way Sophocles' *Theban Plays* (1947) are the tale of a transition from '*homo sucker* to *homo sacer*', following Žižek's crass observations on Giorgio Agamben in *Welcome to the Desert of the Real*.[34] Oedipus begins by fulfilling his destiny through the active assertion of

31 Žižek often remarks that 'modern science touches the Real' in this senseless way.
32 Lacan, *op. cit.*, p. 6.
33 Žižek, *The Ticklish Subject: The Absent Centre of Political Ontology*, *op. cit.*, pp. 160–161.
34 Žižek, *Welcome to the Desert of the Real: Five Essays on September 11 and Related Dates*, *op. cit.*, pp. 83–111.

his subjectivity/creative individualism in the field of the symbolic Other/Fate. He is duped by the Fates, marries his mother, murders his father, and so forth. Upon achieving these fateful acts Oedipus is then reduced to living with no destiny as an old man with a private eternal past of grotesque deeds and no hope for the future when death comes upon him at Colonus. Oedipus is deprived of the possibility of the master-signifier because his own subjective assertion of agency is revealed as a sham, its independence was merely an illusion produced by the symbolic fictions of the social reality in which he found himself. Abandoned by the symbolic universe, Oedipus is left with the unassimilable remainder of his subjectivity that the Symbolic could not reinscribe into itself. Yet, as the scene at Colonus displays, that which the Symbolic cannot overwrite is also that which resists the liberating power of *techne*. The fate of Oedipus thus draws our attention to the forced choice of being 'to be', to become, rather than the regressive essentialism of being 'having' existence as a type of material quality. Herein, 'being' is the ground of the materiality of the subject of the Other's (Fate's) authority.

The revelation of the forced choice of existence by the predestination of Oedipus also shows that necessity pre-exists the being in its becoming. Against essentialism, necessity refers to a becoming without being. This becoming is revealed by the withdrawal of the symbolic universe and *techne*. In this retraction we are confronted with that which resists symbolisation, a kind of 'Real-Real'. Taking this pre-existence to itself, the Real-Real reveals the primordial Thing embodied by Ridley Scott's alien in the film *Alien* (1979). This creature is a grotesque being solely devoted to the consumption of life, whose very blood seems to corrode reality, supposing a constant cycle of decay. To this extent the primordial Thing and the abyssal vortex of Chaos in which Oedipus finds himself at Colonus coincide. We cannot know the being *qua* thing-in-itself without the register of the Symbolic. Yet the very persistence of necessity hints at an eternal past, a *mythos*, from whence it emerged into the becoming of Being *(logos)*. To elucidate this shift, Žižek borrows a term from Schelling to encapsulate the transition from the pre-symbolic to the symbolic proper: *Ent-Scheidung*. This term encapsulates the passage from *mythos* to *logos* that posits *mythos* as an eternal past and the predestination of the future as impossible and yet necessary.[35]

This positing of *mythos* as an impossible limit structurally impedes any attempt to impose the Thing of human rights on a reading of *Minority Report* or *The Recruit* without recognising the formal set of background conditions, the paternal function, that enables the possibility of human rights. For the Oedipal or anal Fathers, the human subject of human rights is foremost a subject of the Symbolic: the subject of separation in the Oedipal order and the subject of over-determination by the *jouisseur*'s archetypes in the theatre of the Imaginary. While many psychoanalytically minded jurisprudential readings of Sophocles' final Theban play *Antigone* have tangled with its *logos*, it is often overlooked how the primal

35 Žižek, *The Fragile Absolute – Or, Why is the Christian Legacy Worth Fighting For?*, *op. cit.*, p. 71.

decision that takes place in its precursor, *Oedipus at Colonus*, grounds the agency of Antigone in the burial at Thebes through the *mythos* of her Father, itself perhaps an indictment of ancient Greek patriarchy and the patriarchal tone of the philosophical foundations of human rights.

What then of the interpretation of this impossibility in the Symbolic Law of psychoanalysis? Žižek theorises that the invention of rules and regulations has become the never-ending task of today, 'even for sacred texts we must decide how it speaks to us *now*.'[36] Of course, with the certainty achieved by the Symbolic undermined by its endless contestability, any interpretation cannot be conclusive, and Žižek goes so far as to suggest that it remains absurd in itself.[37] Interpreting the world thus becomes a most 'useless art' *(techne)* yet one we are doomed to for being a subject as such, hence the Father/Other manifests as the Master of the signification of this interpretation.

The uselessness of interpretation finds its redemption in practice by unhinging what Žižek calls, following Judith Butler, our 'passionate attachments'.[38] In the myth of the Oedipal Father, where the Father is the cruel agent of superego prohibition, passionate attachments function as the price we pay to enter socio-symbolic space. We pay the price for the social link by betraying our little bits of *jouissance (objets petits a)*. These kernels of the Real belong to the subject as an organism engaged in the symbolic universe of ethics, aesthetics, and so forth. More precisely, this is the subject in their subjective assertion as a 'me' and not as an 'I' designated by the Symbolic Order.[39] What makes the Oedipal Father cruel is not that he invokes some 'irrational guilt', but that, as the superego, he manipulates the subjectivity of the subject to betray the fundamental passionate attachment to the pre-Symbolic Real where the incestuous maternal Thing resides.[40] The maturity of the subject developed by the transition through the Oedipal matrix thus comes at the price of desire for/of the mother who belongs to the Father. The mother is inscribed into the symbolic universe by the paternal function, and is therefore held apart from the subjectivity of the subject. In the Lacanian psychoanalytic frame: the promise 'to have' the mother is transmuted to the Father who functions as an abstract/symbolic stand-in for the subject, thus the subject is alienated and decentred from the relation. This decentration gives the subject their lack (desire) so that the subject can be jealous of the theft of their enjoyment by a symbolic authority instated to supposedly allow them compensation in place of the incest taboo. The paternal function thus opens onto fulfilling our fantasies by approving/disapproving our desire. In the absence of guilt we are left with the recognition from the agent of the Symbolic, which binds us ever tighter to the authority of the Father, as per the supremacy of recognition in Lacan.

36 Žižek, *The Ticklish Subject: The Absent Centre of Political Ontology*, *op. cit.*, p. 333.
37 *Ibid.*, pp. 61–62.
38 *Ibid.*, pp. 265–269.
39 *Ibid.*, p. 266.
40 *Ibid.*, p. 268.

Žižek's examination of the Other through the modes of the Father reveals the swerve around the Real which our recognition of symbolic authority undertakes. Such a swerve suggests errancy is older than truth because we do not realise how much we need prohibitive symbolic authority until it is gone. This is the structure of the truth-event. For the subject to be 'human' and not merely an animal possessed of reason *(zoon logon ekon)*, Žižek follows Lacan insofar as he relies on the ethological presupposition that we have the capacity to pretend to pretend. At the same time this indicates that Žižek is not free of the ancient Greeks and their Promethean myth of human technological independence, which at the same time carries this cycle of falsifying error. It is the comparative similarities and differences between Žižek and these ancient Greek philosophical forebears that reveal how the locus of one's creative individuality is enmeshed with our relation to symbolic authority in their very separation.

The gap between Žižek and the sense of singularity prevalent in pre-Socratic cosmology and epic poetry, Hesiod's *Theogony* for example, becomes apparent when we look more closely at the three Fathers.[41] To overthrow the Oedipal Father is to create an empty place where the symbolic efficacy of the Symbolic Order is invoked by the superego, the master-signifier. This allows the agent of symbolic prohibition to be polymorphous, embodied by a variety of things and not merely another speaking being. The art of overthrowing the agent of the paternal function is not without its difficulties, however. The very *techne* that revolts against the Oedipal Father can herein also embody the paternal function as an agent of the Symbolic. When the subject of this agent's prohibitive cut attempts to assume the empty point where the Symbolic legitimates itself, they find that they cannot wholly subsume it and become the Oedipal Father anew because they desire. This is so because, for the subject to be a subject engaged in a symbolic universe, they must already be marked by the cut of the Symbolic. Herein the game of prohibition is wrecked, because when I take up the mantle of the master-signifier and assume the position of the Other, I shed the ideal purity of this position, reducing the position to that of the small other, an alter-ego with the same propensity for desire as the subject. As the small other, the agent of prohibition is a sadist who takes delight in my pain because the symbolic authority has been substantialised and subjectivised, given intentionality.

This point is also retroactive. We realise in retrospect that we were duped all along, that the Other was always out to hurt us. Žižek's idealist philosophical reading of this consists of the Universal entering its own set of particular conditions *a propos* of the violent force of abstraction tearing apart every particular condition and subsequently sundering universality from within.[42] The polymorphous aspect of the Other becomes universalised, domesticating symbolic authority in

41 J. Barnes, 'Introduction' in J. Barnes (ed.), *Early Greek Philosophy*, Harmondsworth: Penguin Books, 1987, pp. xxxviii–xl.

42 S. Žižek, *The Puppet and the Dwarf: The Perverse Core of Christianity*, Cambridge, MA: The MIT Press, 2003, p. 87.

the fantasised form of some substantial entity. To Žižek's reasoning this is the process whereby the Universal is made concrete (in *techne*), but the situation can also operate as an analytic of the transition from the mysterious agent of prohibition, the Other as Oedipal Father, to the polymorphous agent of limitation that is my imaginary rival.

According to Žižek, this analytic shift is revealed by the function of Ferrero's *Kinder Surprise*. The allure of the chocolate-cased toy is brought about by our inability to access it. Once we make do with the chocolate casing and have access to the object (toy) at its core, the toy is no longer endowed with the same magical kind of allure because we come to focus on the empirical object rather than the enigma of what it might be: we know the Other *qua* Ferrero knew all along what type of toy was to be had, and now we know too.[43] The subject realises that their fate to have the particular empirical object was predetermined all along by a capricious, irrational Fate. This is Ferrero as the *jouisseur*, an imaginary rival we cannot defeat because free-action is circumspect, and all is predetermined.

In the case of the *jouisseur*, the Father becomes our imaginary rival for control of the primal horde.[44] When we overthrow this anal Father, however, we again find we cannot fully assume his symbolic mandate because the rivalry took place along the axis of Imaginary-Symbolic, the anal Father as a kind of Jungian archetype.[45] To kill the anal Father then is to destroy an origin of us. Where the demise of the Oedipal Father promises emancipation but delivers enslavement to our raw drive, the ruin of the anal Father deprives us of our *jouissance*.[46]

We can observe this consequence in today's post-political societies. To exist in these societies without *jouissance* is to become a mere *zoon logon ekon*, or perhaps a sociopath. And yet Žižek's Lacanian disposition means we are never free of *jouissance* as it is contained by the subject's own self-image or *imago*. This vital point suggests an image of a follow-up film to *The Recruit*, after Pacino's character Walter is captured by the CIA and Farrell's character James has the lie of his existence up to that point legitimated by the CIA itself whereby he is devoted to serving them. Herein one can also envisage that the cinematic obverse of this would be a film like *Taxi Driver* where Travis – Robert de Niro – is the sociopathic vigilante *par excellence* adhering to his own schizoid order.

Most disturbing of all is the demise of the Father-*logos*. Here we have killed the Father under the assumption he was the *jouisseur*, our rival, the one who did not want us, who hated us. What we realise after the fact is that he was the Real-Thing. He was the insubstantial 'it' to caffeine-free Diet Coke, the men's bathroom to Duchamp's *Fountain*, the Human Thing to human rights. The myth of the Father-*logos* shows up the veil of misrecognition included with the ego-ideal:

43 *Ibid.*, pp. 145–151.

44 Žižek, *The Ticklish Subject: The Absent Centre of Political Ontology*, *op. cit.*, p. 313.

45 *Ibid.*

46 As in a scene from the film *Fight Club* where the protagonist played by Edward Norton loses control of his hand, and it takes on a life of its own, beating him incessantly. Yet by the end of the film this excess activity is gone.

we misrecognise what the Other desires as a substance, as a theft of our substantial enjoyment.[47] However, what the Other wants is an enigma because it is the existence of the Other that is questionable *a priori* as an enigma proper. Thus the 'substantial enjoyment' imputed to the Other covers over the lack in the Other, their questionable status as the beginning of 'being' in its recognition. This misrecognition herein produces revenge as the beyond of the loss or mourning of the Father-*logos*, *techne* becomes a type of 'revenge' for our symbolic castration by the *logos*. What the model of the Father-*logos* therefore shows us is that we begin from the revolt of an undifferentiated Real and not our particular fantasies and desires entertained in the field of the Other.

Over the course of this chapter we have charted the variety of authorial economies through the psychoanalytic modalities of the Father deployed throughout Žižek's analyses. These modes revealed that the position or voice that a subject is able to assume in language varies, and this has also shown that the Human Thing of human rights is always a 'subject': subject to the order of rights but excessive and revolutionary. We might then conclude that of the three Freudian myths of the Father considered by Žižek, it would appear that the anal Father, the *jouisseur*, is the most likely candidate for a myth of authority grounding post-modernity as it locates the *jouissance* of humanity at the heart of the authorisation of human rights *per se*. Yet while the *jouisseur* offers the passion for the Real that defined the twentieth century, it also presents a further inversion in the form of the Father-*logos*. It is this alighting toward the dead figure of the Father-*logos* – universal structure which is ruined by the misrecognition of the subject – that performs the important task of breaking out of the vicious circle of representation and relativism instantiated by post-modernity and the potentially endless double movement of deconstructing the antijurisprudence of Law and Economics and developing a positive jurisprudence that gives the human primacy. In post-modernity it is the *jouisseur* who grounds power and authority through *jouissance*, excessive enjoyment. But for Žižek, this is not the whole story because the *jouisseur* is destined to be overcome by the self-consciousness of the subject, the critical awareness of ontology and its differentiation from the *techne* supporting the symbolic universe of social reality. However, any such 'revolutionary turn' invites the properly psychoanalytic criticism that its aggressivity is an infantile clawing of the Father's corpse. The Freudian Fathers in Žižek's work – and he is no stranger to revolution, be it soft or violent – show us that the variation in the place of 'the human' as a subject, in a subject, or by a subjection, alters the fundamental coordinates of revolutionary space. Revolution is at the core of every experience of authority, be it in the hothouse of 'the family' (however defined), the institutions of 'the state' or the physics of nature. These two critical points are also supported by the Lacanian observation that that which does not break with the Other will be doomed to repeat it. Žižek's critique of the eclipse of prohibition in the *jouisseur*'s colonisation of enjoyment clearly demonstrates the

47 Žižek, *The Puppet and the Dwarf: The Perverse Core of Christianity*, *op. cit.*, pp. 79–80.

danger for being unwilling to confront the all too Human Thing from the inner space of human rights. But the further step into the combustion of Being is the movement that opens onto the revolution at the core of authority itself. This, I dare say, is both the beginning and end of the excessive humanity contained by human rights and the confrontation with an impossible limit in the necessity of the force of Law as a Thing-in-itself.

CHAPTER 10

The legal and the erotic in *True Blood*

Law and enjoyment has undergone a supernatural renovation in recent years with the publication and adaptation of Charlaine Harris' magical realist series *True Blood*. In its adaptation to an episodic television series by HBO the narrative of *True Blood* has found itself among the tides of contemporary popular culture's ardour for vampires, zombies, werewolves and other fantastical representations. But unlike some other narrative attempts to show vampires and werewolves as bureaucratic secret societies, the HBO series reflected the novels' emphasis on mass media society and the impossibility of not incorporating other current Western fairytale horrors once vampires are announced. *True Blood*'s supernatural cast has gradually built up across each novel and season of the television series. By the end of the first season we have an inkling that vampires may not be the only supernatural manifestations out there, and the cast of 'supes' continues to grow. *True Blood* does well to ape the structure of the orthodox view of fairtytales as stories that shield us from the unknown, as it gives Harris some narrative purchase on an otherwise purely illusory cast of characters. Harris' series inverts this usual screening of horror to demonstrate that the stories themselves are true. Like a bad infinity, the train of supernatural creatures stretches out to include just about any enigma that the social structure produces in the story cycle.

The legal content of the series is structured by several antagonisms. At the level of politics the arbitrary, feudal order of vampire society contests the *petit bourgeois moralité* of the humans in the town of Bon Temps. More existentially, the absence of human purpose as humans try to get on with their lives is antagonised by the survival ethics of the supernatural denizens. Ethically, the mundane utilitarian world of use and abuse is contrasted by the erotics of seduction, blood and hubris that engineer much of the melodrama. There is also a queer antagonism between the demands of phallocentric human society as against the ethic of polymorphous desire in the open set of many different supernatural societies. Racism and speciesism are persistent features of the delivery of these dualisms in the narrative, cannily set in the American south. However, these racist attitudes are not confined to one species' or cross-species' sexuality: racism functions as the cloak to hide what is supernatural, as much as it is countered by an all too human race critique by characters such as Tara and Lafayette. These antagonisms will be explored in more depth below.

Law is constitutive of the social ordering of enjoyment in the narrative's antagonisms listed above. But in this analysis, rather than rely on oft-cited examples of lawyers, police and politicians, I want to turn to the romantic overtures of *True Blood*. Specifically, this discussion will examine the way in which the romance and betrayal of Sookie Stackhouse and the vampire Bill Compton captures the essence of what binds these two characters together as if in a contract. It is not that contracts are drawn up in *True Blood per se*, but rather that the grounds that give rise to the expectations of promises for the common law of contract are plainly shown by the romantic melodrama of the series. Here our gambit is that this romance and erotics in *True Blood* can be instructive for understanding the problem with viewing satisfaction of a contract/promise as materially complete because an underlying need may objectively persist. Love, as that shared between Sookie and Bill, is a very unusual contract, a limit case that is worth exploring.

The adaptation of *True Blood* for television is a unique strand in the current weaves of contemporary popular culture's vampire fantasies. Based on the Sookie Stackhouse novels, the *Southern Vampire Mysteries* by Harris, the narrative focuses on the lives of the residents of a small, fictional Louisiana township called Bon Temps. In the first season the *zeitgeist* of the town is marked by a gentile racism that has found a new sublime object for its abjection: vampires. Built on the idea that vampires have come 'out of the coffin', *True Blood* stakes its claim to an erotics that involves blood, seduction and carnivalesque violence, which are the thematic concerns of much modern vampire fiction since Joseph Sheridan le Fanu's *Carmilla* and Bram Stoker's *Dracula*. The seasons of *True Blood* that have aired each exhibit a deft series of narrative twists and a melange of tropes from horror and suspense film history also.

The story of the first season circulates around the Stackhouse family – brother and sister Jason and Sookie and their grandmother Adele – and the 173-year-old vampire Bill Compton who has returned to Bon Temps in an effort to 'mainstream' and gain social acceptance. Coinciding with Bill's return to Bon Temps, a serial killer makes his way through the town, and it is not revealed until the final episodes whether the numerous deaths that fill the first season's narrative arc are due to the vamps, the tramps or mundane humanity.[1]

The second season weaves a tale of Dionysian chaos as the town is held in the thrall of violent, anarchic pleasure. This season also suggests that there are more supernatural things ready to come in from the cold and make themselves known. The cause of the chaotic madness that flowers in Bon Temps is the second season's central antagonist, a *maenad* called Maryann Forrester, who attempts to summon the wily dark god of nature, hubri, and ecstasy, Dionysus. For the purposes of

1 It is worth recalling here that moral evil can be banal, ordinary and mundane, as argued by Hannah Arendt's *The Origins of Totalitarianism*, San Diego: Harcourt, Brace, Jovanovich, 1973.

gaining some critical purchase on this text, this analysis will be limited to the consistent and prominent protagonist of *True Blood*, Sookie Stackhouse, and some key questions about the nomological ontology of Sookie's erotics. Herein special emphasis will be given to how Sookie has a privileged link to the undergrowth of enjoyment in Bon Temps' otherwise polite southern gentility, not only through the trait of her psychic ability to read other people's thoughts but also through the formal critique of phallocentrism that she employs to deal with the eclipsed male sexuation of Bon Temps.

To gain purchase on law and enjoyment as they intersect in Sookie and Bill's romance, let us turn to the ontological connections of the commons of Bon Temps as it sustains and rearranges expectations of law in the series. By analysing the undergrowth of enjoyment in *True Blood* we can examine Sookie's place within this structure, but why is this important? At its simplest, the undergrowth of enjoyment is a formal process deployed by a socio-political order to create a subject through the subject's assumption of a norm and, in doing so, alienates this subject from this order (the subject is always within the prison house of this symbolic order or language) and from the pre-symbolic space that precedes this differentiation of the subject from a background of general indistinction.[2] The undergrowth of enjoyment is the general background of fantasies, silent prejudices and other *étoffes du moi* that give body to the narratives that the subject tells themselves about their place in this socio-political order.

In terms of the *True Blood* narrative, this undergrowth of enjoyment represents law for the characters in the story in some typical ways. We see a sheriff's department struggling to contain the excessive power of the broadening population of Bon Temps. We also see news media portraying legislation, the legislature and lobbyists regarding vampire rights. There are also atypical encounters with law as Bill moves to reclaim his family home as a vampire, Sookie's psychic abilities give her evidence of motives of a serial killer that could not be recognised by current real-world standards of evidence, and vampire blood becomes a narcotic that exists in a grey area of general use and illegality.

We ought to pause here for a moment to consider how we may understand this 'subject and norm' pairing as a gender relation. Through the gaze of gender criticism the subject is erected against the organic ground that gave rise to it: all subjection becomes a problem of castration in service to the phallic norm. This castration complex is a fear of mortifying the generative ground that pre-exists the symbolic order lest it 'cut off' the head of the big Other – sovereign, authority, etc. – that unifies the subject with an illusory purpose or fantasmatic promise for some future enjoyment that entails the negation of 'dumb pleasure'. Law in the narrative universe of *True Blood* is thoroughly connected to this symbolic space of existential purposes and agency.

However, several features of *True Blood* serve as critical responses to such

2 See S. Žižek, *For The Know Not What They Do: Enjoyment as a Political Factor*, London: Verso, 1991, for a more sociological definition.

a construction of the gendered subject and norm. Firstly, the undergrowth of enjoyment in Bon Temps is supernatural and ontologically 'greater' than the normalised identity/object of socio-political reification that constitutes the town as a 'human' community. All socio-political orders are supranatural in the Nietzschean sense that they construct and impose a view of nature and what is natural, but the supernatural emphasis of Bon Temps' socio-political order privileges the non-human vampires as ineffable agents of phallic authority: they are threatening, they are powerful, and they are 'higher' than humans in the scale of survival. Secondly, Sookie's parents are deceased at the outset of the narrative, siting Sookie in a different domestic space to what Bon Temps' ostensibly racist and parochial social ordering proffers as an impossible phallic norm. This second condition is rendered throughout the narrative of *True Blood* in a series of failed Oedipal figures such as the narcissistic and child-like Jason Stackhouse, the impotent rage of the sheriff's deputy Andy, and the jealous and naïve evangelical preacher of the Fellowship of the Sun, Rev. Steve Newlin. And, thirdly, there is the enjoyable suffering or *jouissance* of life in Bon Temps that is ever-present in its social rituals and the supernatural agents of such rituals' dissolution. As preceding chapters have shown, *jouissance* is here not to be taken in the sense of pain, but rather in the sense of an ejection of pleasure, where pain is overcome through the commitment to an act rather than the action itself.

Throughout the narrative of *True Blood*, the undergrowth of enjoyment in Bon Temps is consistently radicalised into effervescent moments of *jouissance* that threaten this undergrowth with its own dissolution. This threat takes many forms, be it through the colonisation of the town by belligerent vampires whose violent excesses are succour to their devotion to this pleasure, Sookie's repetitive repression of her mostly uncontrollable telepathy in a commitment to be a 'normal' woman, or the revelation of the impossibility of the social norm across the early seasons of *True Blood* as most of the authority figures in Bon Temps fail to fully live up to their symbolic commitment, from Maxine Foytenberry's inability to prohibit Hoyt's romance with newly made vampire Jessica Hamby, to vampire sheriff Eric Northman's failure to tame the petulant Jessica.[3] In all three key features above – the undergrowth of enjoyment, the eclipse of paternal authority, and Bon Temps' *jouissance* – it is the embodiment of some fantasy in the undergrowth of enjoyment of Bon Temps that marks the characters of *True Blood* as social agents. The challenge here is between the social cohesion assured by rule of law and the erotics of *jouissance*.

Where then does Sookie reside in relation to the *jouissance* of *True Blood*'s narrative universe? To answer this we must understand that *jouissance* is a psychoanalytic concept that designates the auto-limitation of pleasure, the point where pleasurable sensation abdicates from what begins as a pleasurable activity. *Jouissance* is a limit-concept and as such stands for the failure of pleasure to meet

3 There is a curio over later seasons' representation of Jessica as a somewhat meeker figure, that is overlaid with a familial love of her maker, Bill.

the demand for satisfaction; satisfaction instead being sought through 'enjoyable suffering', as in the commitment to some symbolic mandate that renders this mandate 'enjoyable' in a more mundane sense. *Jouissance* is not and should not be understood as an excess but rather as an excessivity inherent to pleasure's composite lack of satisfaction.

In terms of law, *jouissance* arises in moments where the legal is constituted by enjoyment rather than systemic power or sovereignty. For example, the threat of the colonisation of the town by belligerent vampires is brought into relation with law on two fronts: by their transgression of laws against homicide as well as by law inherent to vampires as a self-governing social group. The agency of vampires in the undergrowth of enjoyment in Bon Temps is continually submitted to higher purposes of survival, attempts to reinstate the rule of law as a civil peace. These are moments where law seems to have a life of its own, guiding the characters through chaotic suspense and melodrama.

This concept of *jouissance* can provide a way to understand Sookie's unusual position in the narrative of *True Blood*. On the one hand, her telepathy is at once too little to satisfy the normative criteria of the human community of Bon Temps wherein she is socially coded as a 'freak', and too much for her to bear or understand as she neurotically acts out attempts to regulate this 'obscene' or 'unhuman' excessivity that lets her hear the thoughts of other people. What Sookie telepathically hears, herein, is the subjection of the population of Bon Temps, the undergrowth of enjoyment embodied by these social agents in service to Bon Temps as a kind of big Other that brings the townspeople's lives meaning.

On the other hand, Sookie's erotic and romantic relationships are links to the supernatural, such as her vampire-lover Bill Compton, and these subvert the old phallic Other by exposing the insufficiency of Bon Temps as an 'organic' community. Aside from her obvious erotic and romantic relationship with Bill, in the first season Sookie encounters such an exposé when she accidentally reads the mind of her boss, Sam Merlotte, only to discover a rapid train of affectionate thoughts and feelings more akin to the dog Sam shape-shifts into, rather than the empathetic male authority figure he stands for as the forlorn romantic interest and owner of the local public bar in Bon Temps. Here even the regular, mundane phallic authority figure of Sam is proven as 'weird' and out-of-joint with the symbolic status he holds as a 'nice, normal guy'.

There is a touch of the perverse about Sookie's erotic relationship with the vampire Bill, but such a 'perversion' is only possible because Bill stands out against the background of Bon Temps' undergrowth of enjoyment in eclipsed phallocentrism as a new version of the phallic authority – literally *'père-version'*, a new version of the Father. Indeed, Sookie's erotic liaison with Bill becomes an effort to codify the *jouissance* that Bill embodies as a vampire living beyond death, and Sookie structures this through her unwanted telepathy: their relationship begins with Sookie's inability to read Bill's thoughts (because he's 'dead') and revolves around her attempts to normalise Bill's place in Bon Temps' social order with varying degrees of success. It is also marked on HBO's part that the erotic encounters between Sookie and Bill often resemble an idealised heterosexual couple and incorporate elements of Bill's vampirism such as biting as passion rather than kink.

In the elaboration of Sookie and Bill's erotics, it is interesting that the variation of Sookie's attempts to subjectively normalise her erotic relationship with Bill consistently subjects these erotics to romanticisation or what we can more critically term a sporadic deferral of pleasure in favour of some access to *jouissance*. These attempts create a space for Sookie and Bill to consent to an agreement where such an agreement is the love that they share, yet its satisfaction is unnecessary. This agreement is of a radically different sort to a common law 'contract' as the erotics are part of time and their love is constituted in the context of their unfinished relationship. That is to say, it is a contract *in situ*; it is in process. In practice, the agreement is satisfied but the need for love remains.[4] This is important for the unfolding of *True Blood* as a melodrama because it facilitates a time for love and trust on the site of what began as an erotic encounter. Yet the weakness of such an emphasis is that it overlooks the paradoxical creation of some future enjoyment from the past of deferred pleasures. In a certain sense, then, the future of Sookie and Bill's relationship intervenes between the past that contains all of their pleasures, deferred or otherwise, and the present in which Sookie is immediately engaged. This is perhaps what makes Sookie a 'Lacanian woman', if I may deign to use such a phrase: Sookie sees through the fantasy of pleasure's satisfaction to the contingency of *jouissance*; she can laugh at Bill's failed attempts to control her, she can constantly flit between different subject-positions depending on given contextual demands – just think of her negotiation of the vampire hotel in Dallas during season two – precisely because, as a subject of feminine *jouissance*, Sookie is able to see the illusory phallic *jouissance* promised to the eclipsed masculine subjects of Bon Temps as the fake that it is. Numerous effects of phallic *jouissance* ruminate in *True Blood*, including Sookie's perverted uncle Bill's awkward anachronistic morals, Jason's naïve narcissism, Lafayette's nymphomanic bravado, the Bon Temps sheriff's utter lack of personality, the sheriff's deputy Andy's unrationalised alcholism, and the list goes on. Something unusual herein is how the vampire 'men' are almost always represented as 'fuller' masculine subjects than their frail, all too human, counterparts. Contrarily, in the character of Sookie we get to glimpse something of a devotion that perforates the socio-political order of Bon Temps by radicalising the masquerade of social identity: masks aren't just put on, there is nothing behind them, the masks constitute a partial-truth that Sookie directly accesses through her telepathy, through what Lacan has called feminine *jouissance*.

The two forms of *jouissance* – feminine and masculine – are most obvious in the way that *True Blood* exaggerates its cast of characters. If we examine the central romantic couple, Sookie and Bill, we can observe *jouissance* as the modulator of the contract of their relationship. Bill embodies masculine *jouissance* and it is

4 The formula for love developed by Lacan is 'the demand for pleasure without need for satisfaction'. See D. Nobus, *Jacques Lacan and the Freudian Practice of Psychoanalysis*, London: Routledge, 2000.

not only his uncanny status as a vampire, a type of living dead, that reveals this. The tireless efforts of Bill to regain the authority he once enjoyed when he was alive in Civil War America echo a gallant conservatism that thrives on negating future possibilities. In his relationship with Sookie he is often the one to rely on ceremony and meaningful gestures that resist further discussion. Sookie contrarily embodies what Lacan calls 'feminine *jouissance*'; Sookie experiences her relationship with Bill often without or against the knowledge of what this relationship means for the parochial ethics of Bon Temps.[5] Sookie has a future by way of her demiurgical deferral of some of her erotic encounters with Bill, whereas Bill is often trapped in his rules about such relations and needs Sookie to lead him to the erotic encounter.[6] Obviously, it would be an oversimplification to limit femininity or masculinity to the sex or gender of Sookie or Bill, but what is at issue here is the way their heterosexual relationship reverses the male chauvinist phrase of film noir, 'the only good woman is a dead woman', by placing Bill beyond death as a type of living dead; 'the only good man in Bon Temps is a living-dead man'.

What is most important in Freudian terms for *True Blood*, then, are those times when Sookie and Bill are erotically engaged, because it is these engagements that signal the satisfaction of some *jouissance*. A naïve view would suggest that Sookie is compromising her desire because such erotic encounters are somehow exploits of pleasure rather than the ground of the relationship in the first place. For example, when I discussed this chapter with a colleague, they laughed off *True Blood* as HBO's attempt at soft-core pornography, an exploitation of erotics on screen. But such a view misses the melodramatic ecstasy that Sookie finds in the erotics she shares with Bill at the formal level of the narrative. Such ecstasy is beyond the conservative narrative regimen of pornography where the minimum of narrative is treated as ridiculous or perfunctory to the objectification of bodies.

Contrarily, the melodrama of *True Blood* retains a sense of the camp carnivalesque where everything hints at the ridiculous sublime of the living dead. This is where death is overcome and everyone gets the best sex that they have ever had. Here, in their living deadness, vampires are stronger, faster and more cunning, and humans, in their dynamic living, have a depth of feeling attached to a claim to life that is denied to the vampire because such life is always a 'past life'; yet both overcome the limitations imposed by their difference by behaving as the other would and arrive at an ideal erotic encounter that mediates and subsumes this difference. You can never have too much melodrama in *True Blood* because you can never have enough of this sublime synthesis.[7]

It is precisely at this point of the ridiculous sublime of melodrama that *True Blood*'s characterisation of Sookie anachronistically questions the validity of some

5 There is a critical race theory discussion to be had about how *True Blood* recasts, complicates and displaces the racism of the American south.

6 This is about the world agreed upon and constituted by their relationship.

7 From a Freudo-Lacanian perspective, the synthesis is ongoing because this difference is the mark of the absence of a sexual relationship that is refracted through the logic of the Subject.

applied ethical analyses of the series. The problem with these ethico-philosophical analyses is that they often read the erotics of Sookie and Bill's relationship in a gender-neutral frame, be this framing Kantian, realist, liberal or even Aristotelian. As Luce Irigaray and others have criticised, the universal subject of philosophy is masculine: it questions existence as though reality were erected against an abyss of pre-ontological nothingness, it humanises questions of meaning into dynamic word-games, it hopes for the transcendental and prays for the ontological, and it theorises affect. Such 'phallic habits' of philosophy were neatly summed up by Lacan as philosophy's tendency to create totalities or grand metaphysical systems.[8] While such a process might satisfy those subject to the rule of masculine *jouissance*, it does not account for the effervescent masquerade of feminine *jouissance*. From a psychoanalytic perspective, Sookie is not engulfed by the socio-political order of Bon Temps on virtue of her amplified femininity (amplified by the genre of melodrama) that allows her to 'see the fakes' telepathically. In these philosophical studies of *True Blood*, however, there is a tendency to reduce Sookie to a universal subject where every character in *True Blood* is humanised. The philosophers really will 'think bad things with you', but these are bad precisely because they commit to abstraction in place of embodiment.

And is such an entertaining of bad thoughts by coding them in abstract terms not the legislative move par excellence? Legislation and statutes appear as attempts to domesticate logics of rules and parliamentary intent through the abstract formulation of language that may not entirely account for the substance of what is said. We can see this incompleteness in the function of extrinsic materials and how they are used to clarify statutory provisions. Attempts to think *True Blood* philosophically similarly lapses into this reticence about the immediacy of the narrative on show.

Such criticisms of philosophy run parallel to Sookie's comparative juxtaposition to the masculine subjects of Bon Temps. Between Sookie and Bill, for example, a mutual exclusivity develops across the first two seasons of *True Blood*. Initially, when they meet in Bon Temps Sookie is drawn to Bill because she cannot hear his thoughts. Bill is bewildered by Sookie's unusually empathetic acceptance of him as a 'person' (read: subject) where vampires such as he are so often objects of ridicule in the undergrowth of enjoyment that sustains the fictionalised American south. Bill, contrarily, after his initial bewilderment, rapidly constructs the social, ethical and political edifice of a relationship with Sookie that invents a series of boundaries, the most melodramatically emphasised of these involving Sookie's safety and their shared sexual practices, such as Bill sinking his fangs into Sookie's neck while having intercourse. Drawing blood during an erotic encounter is certainly not anything new nor particularly supernatural, but it is interesting to note that in the same season that Sookie plays, at times sarcastically, Bill's game of

8 See J. Lacan, 'Subversion of the Subject and the Dialectic of Desire in the Freudian Unconscious' in *Écrits*, B. Fink (trans.), New York: W. W. Norton & Company, 2007, pp. 671–702.

consent, Bon Temps is overrun by a Dionysian mania that radically divides erotic sanguination from blood-letting sexual practices where the latter is given a violent overtone.[9] The third season of *True Blood* continues to develop this juxtaposition of Sookie and Bill, with the former trapped in a coma of mystical experience wherein Sookie finds something akin to divine Truth (what Jacques Lacan might have called 'the truth of *jouissance*') while Bill is faced with the seemingly endless stream of existential dilemmas of phallic authority as he becomes embroiled in the affairs of the vampire king of Louisiana.

The erotics of *True Blood* can tell us something about law. As the erotism of Sookie demonstrates, what we enjoy is often structured around a deferral of pleasure. And more than this, this deferral of pleasure is enjoyed as the subjective gesture of the subject. For a lovers' contract to function, this deferral is not static but ongoing, and it is this promise of some future satisfaction that creates the temporality of their contract. Two basic systemic problems emerge from this. On the one hand, the melodrama of *True Blood* amplifies *jouissance* in a gendered frame wherein masculinity is eclipsed or failing and femininity stands as another name for the inconsistent Other of Bon Temps as a hierarchical political community that produces a series of phallic women who sacrifice their femininity in service to the *jouissance* of the Symbolic Law, such as Maxine Foytenberry. The critical problem with this framing, and the systemic problem driving the *True Blood* series, is not how these phallic subjects falter and fail – although this does provide a great deal of narrative purchase – but how alternative figures emerge who are not submitted to the prevailing Symbolic Law and its undergrowth of enjoyment: Sookie with her telepathy short-circuits the normative rules conditioning subjecthood in Bon Temps by accessing a feminine *jouissance* that sees through the façade of the Other, and Maryann Forrester embodies and enlists the primordial chaos around which Bon Temps circulates as a political community keeping this chaotic and avowedly phallic *jouissance* at a distance through causalities or 'naturalised' relations in public etiquette, to name but two. It is curious to note that when Maryann is impaled by Sam in the form of a white bull at the end of season two, Maryann suddenly assumes the discourse of a sacrificial victim sacrificed for a higher phallic Other. Sookie fits into the narrative universe of *True Blood* as a feminine subject who is beyond the Law gestured to by Maryann. Sookie is able to fully assume the burden of *jouissance*. It should come as little surprise to us then that the third season of *True Blood* suggests that Sookie is not as human as she otherwise appears to be. Such a narrative move is *ad idem* with how *True Blood* constructs law and enjoyment as political objects for Bon Temps in the category of *jouissance*. Sookie is not another failing 'masculine' fake, but a subject proper who is able to assume her *jouissance* as the partial-truth of her place in Bon Temps. Law's encounter with Sookie highlights the need to rethink future promises of satisfaction in matters of contract between people and their others.

9 The 'game of consent' meaning that Bill feels incapable of biting Sookie until she permits him to, particularly after an early failed attempt that Sookie rejected.

CHAPTER 11

Power and *jouissance* in *The City & The City*

This chapter approaches the construction of law in China Miéville's *The City & The City* and the *jouissance* therein, both of the law-like construction and the narration of this construction.[1] Herein, the discussion will examine Miéville's deployment of law in *The City & The City* by beginning with its phenomenological unfolding; phenomenological in the precise sense that what we encounter in Miéville's writing is the essence of law: command and prohibition. The encounter with this essence of law may seem deceptively simple to a legal-trained eye, but this runs the risk of overlooking the important reworking of the phenomenal experience of law in which Miéville's novel deals: the command is silent, the prohibition irreducible, and both are enjoyably suffered. This silencing of the command that law enjoys in *The City & The City* will be the focus of the psychoanalytic reading to come.

Miéville is an author of speculative and weird fiction as well as a voice of Marxist interpretations of international law. This background provides ample critical reference points for his fictionalisation of the law, as is made apparent by the fabric of the plot in *The City & The City*. *The City & The City* is a work of detective-noir fiction, and takes the reader through a hard-boiled narrative set in a city split in its manifestation, cognitive mapping and in its core: Besźel-Ul Qoma.[2] *The City & The City* is written from the vantage of Tyador Borlú, a detective of the Besź *policzai*, and we learn very early in the narrative how the law of the split city requires he un-sense the world around him, ostensibly erasing even the very trace of the alternative city to the one he finds himself in 'grossotopologically'.[3] Borlú informs the reader that to not un-sense and un-think the other city is to commit

1 A previous iteration of this discussion was published in *Law, Culture and the Humanities*, 9, 2013.

2 Miéville references other split cities such as Berlin, Jerusalem, etc., throughout the narrative to reinforce the pertinence of this story's links to 'really existing' politico-historical situations.

3 This is Miéville's neologism to designate the way the two cities, Besźel and Ul-Qoma, inhabit identical topological space but differ in their mental geographies as interpreted by the citizens and denizens of each city.

'breach', and from here a shadowy extra presence hovers threateningly beyond the edges of Borlú's gaze. The question, thus, is how does Borlú do his detective work if he must persistently un-detect the world around him to varying degrees? How can this agent of the law be the enforcer that his position demands of him?

Borlú's relation to the law in Miéville's *The City & The City* is constructed through a seemingly phenomenological account that renders the world from Borlú's narrated point of view. A constant hum weaves through the narrative as Borlú un-senses parts of the world around him as he goes about his detective work and negotiates – but mostly bends – the writ of the law to reveal a hidden conspiracy. But this phenomenal condition of unsensing goes far deeper: it transvaluates Borlú himself, breeding a hierarchisation of value not only in his perception but in his way of being, and this complicates his relation to the law as its agent because it is marked by this fundamental, schizoid, inconsistency that refuses the law the opportunity to penetrate certain spaces.[4] Conceptually speaking, this is why the unsensing of *The City & The City* is ontological rather than merely phenomenological: it gives the order of being to the subject-Borlú prior to the letter of the law and its affects. As an ontological action, unsensing is onto-genetic to the extent that it informs Borlú of a pre-history that exceeds his private subjective universe, it tells a story, a *mythos*, about the primal decision that split Besźel-Ul Qoma in two and the archaic Law of Breach that emanates from this dark moment of pre-history as the event of rupture. Whatever expedient rationalisations Borlú offers the reader, whatever phantasms of sense-perception manifest at the edge of his sight, hearing, smell, taste or touch, the Law of Breach remains Real: impossible, archaic, negative. The Law of Breach is thus distinct from the common law of the cleaved cities: rather than structuring something of 'the commons', it ruptures and crosshatches the jurisdiction of the common laws of Besźel and Ul-Qoma; it accounts for but is unaccountable to the common law; it dominates the command of law through a terrifying silence.

The Lacanian psychoanalytic concept of *jouissance* can be helpful in understanding the way that Borlú enjoys (and destroys) – *jouir* – his position as a detective given this Law of Breach that dominates the narrative. In its simplest definition, *jouissance* is the pleasure taken from suffering and most often this suffering is the result of some symbolic limit or law-like injunction that prohibits and entices certain actions on the part of the subject.[5] Borlú's world is quite similar

4 This phenomenality of Borlú's encounter with and relation to the law is consistent with the views upheld by many notable writers on law and culture, a view most recently presented by W. P. MacNeil, *Novel Judgments: Legal Theory as Fiction*, London: Routledge, 2014, R. Salecl, *The Tyranny of Choice*, London: Profile Books, 2011 and A. Young, *The Scene of Violence*, London: Routledge, 2010.

5 As Jacques-Alain Miller has pointed out, *jouissance* is haunted by time, never arriving on time but rather always out of synchronicity, out of joint ('Introduction to the Erotics of Time', B. P. Fulks (trans.), *Lacanian Ink* 24/25, 2005, pp. 22–23). The problem for Borlú as an agent of the law is thus when to enact his position as an agent (of law) rather than a (human) subject.

to our own with a symbolic universe of meaning that pushes the consumption of pleasure that tells the human-subject, 'You may!' Here the core problem that will drive our discussion further is that in this permissive symbolic network of morals, etiquette and meaning, all enjoyment is already enjoyed by the symbolic authority when the symbolic universe is conditioned by the rule of the *jouisseur*, suffocating the subject who is 'meant to enjoy' with endless calls to consume pleasure according to the 'Yes!' of this permissive post-modern authority. The enjoyment of the subject can be read as 'enjoy-meant' by this permissivity of the *jouisseur*. This absence of enjoyment is the desert of legal realism in *The City & The City* wherein the invisible actions of authority figures are part of the capacity for judgment, echoing the phrase attributed to Jerome Frank: the law is what the judge ate for breakfast.[6] But the *jouisseur* is not Breach. Instead, the *jouisseur* is the Beszź rule of law as it is ridden with the *jouissance* of Breach: the inflection of positive law within natural law.

Yet, paradoxically, this perverse rule of law becomes enjoyment without enjoyment, *jouis-sans*, as the subject is confronted with no pleasure of their own, i.e. even enjoying the most agonising of discomforts are ordained by the *jouisseur*'s perverse order of *jouissance* that tries to draw out *jouissance* from 'desolate' reality.[7] The fixation of the rule of law in both Besźel and Ul-Qoma is the Law of Breach that sticks to every aspect of life in the twin cities. Not a moment goes by in Miéville's narrative where the Law of Breach does not stain the scene.

This imagined relation between the subject and the authorial other becomes the axis of *j'oüis-sens* because it substitutes the symbolic universe that is over-flowing with pathological pleasures perverted by the touch of the *jouisseur*'s 'enjoy-meant'.[8] Herein the subject engages in a sublimation of natural Law *(logos)* because of the conditioning axiology of the *jouisseur*'s anality: *logos* becomes the speculative Ideal that 'binds' reality, the pre-Symbolic unity of the One in a time before Breach. Indeed, *The City & The City* is ostensibly driven by a plot for the unification of Besźel-Ul Qoma. The construction of the law in *The City & The City* is thus a dialectic of *jouissance*: the Law of Breach, dark and archaic, splits the city and the common law into two sites known as Besźel and Ul-Qoma but stains these sites as a taboo, the prohibition of some forbidden *jouissance*, realised in practise as dissensation or 'unsensing'; Borlú's experience of the law as a detective, an agent of the law, experiences the Law of Breach and its associated dissensation as a

6 This critical insight into the *jouissance* sustained by legal realists' approach to the law adds an interesting interpretative dimension to the literature. See J. Frank, 'Excerpts from *Law and the Modern Mind*' in M. D. A. Freeman (ed.), *Lloyd's Introduction to Jurisprudence*, London: Sweet & Maxwell, 2007, pp. 827–830, and also William P. MacNeil, *Lex Populi: The Jurisprudence of Popular Culture*, Stanford: Stanford University Press, 2007, pp. 81–84.

7 S. Freud, *On Sexuality*, J. Strachey (trans.), London: Penguin Books, 1991, pp. 80–82.

8 For a full analysis of the structural modes of *jouissance* see: L. Chiesa, 'Lacan and Artaud: *j'oüis-sens, jouis-sens, jouis-sans*' in S. Žižek (ed.), *Lacan: The Silent Partners*, London: Verso, 2006, pp. 336–364.

series of inconsistencies and gaps in Besźel that limits the power he enjoys *(jouir)* as an agent of the law; and, lastly, the agents of Breach require the cities insofar as they are a totem of their power, the Law of Breach as a *logos* binds together the reality of Besźel-Ul Qoma through a speculative and ideal past, a *mythos*, that promises unity before the Law, but this myth can only be accessed through a permanent sacrifice of the common law of each city in the present through the maintenance of a taboo, i.e. to never commit a breach of the Law. This latter stage knits together the taboo of the thesis of the Law of Breach with the inconsistencies of the common law experienced by Borlú to reveal a construction of law in Besźel-Ul Qoma that is the site of *j'ouïs-sens*: the sacrifice of *jouissance* assures its persistence as a taboo.

The twin cities of Besźel and Ul-Qoma circulate around a government building known as Copula Hall which houses the Oversight Committee and deals with matters involving both cities. Copula Hall is also the spatial locus of legitimately crossing between the cities, and it is marshalled by border-guards and checkpoints. Miéville's narrative makes this the site of political negotiations between the cities and the place where the Law of Breach can be invoked. Herein, *The City & The City* distinguishes two interstices of the Law of Breach: on the one hand it is a spontaneous and shadowy event that occurs 'on the street' and, on the other hand, it is a discretionary power invoked rather than exercised by the Oversight Committee.

However, to simply focus on these two modes of the Law of Breach is to commit to a banal representationalism that is reminiscent of some cultural studies discussions of Lacan's Law of the Other during the 1980s and 1990s. The problem herein is that we only read the Law in its seemingly wild and spontaneous Imaginary intervention 'on the street' (there are the people and then there is the Law) and in its precarious symbolic position wherein the Law of Breach sustains the distancing and connection of Besźel-Ul Qoma through its discursive practices. This bi-fold view reminiscent of the dualism of primary and secondary rules of law in Hartian postivism[9] misses the way that the Law of Breach stains both of these scenes as their negation: on the street the Law of Breach is absent but ever-present and in Copula Hall the Law is irreducible to the bureaucratic apparatus that negotiates its invocation – as Major Yorj Syedr, one of Miéville's right-wing Besź nationalists sitting on the council, says: 'Breach is an [...] *alien power*, and we hand over our sovereignty to it at our peril. We've simply washed our hands of any difficult situations and handed them to a – apologies if I offend but – a shadow over which we have no control.'[10]

9 Hart's system of rules provides the law with some coherent consistency. The self-referential recognition between the institution of law and the agents of the law, but Miéville's construction of a dark natural law jurisprudence in the Law of Breach sustains such consistency through the negation of the institution of law rather than by its recognition as in H. L. A. Hart, *The Concept of Law*, Oxford: Clarendon Press, 1961.

10 C. Miéville, *The City & The City*, New York: Random House, 2009, p. 64.

Using the voice of Syedr, Miéville is here craftily gesturing to the tension between the post-political politics of bureaucratic administration and the necessity of some ideal Good or Cause that is formulated by natural law. The Oversight Committee on which Syedr is sitting when he makes the above remark is part of a political apparatus that assures the rule of law for the commons of both cities. But this common law is a positive law, and quite distinct from the natural law discourse of Breach. The Law of Breach stands here in tension to the political institutions that govern and legislate the twin cities' existence: it is simultaneously the negation of these cities and their foundation. Although Hart's concept of law does account for the interaction of law and politics, it does so with a positivist eye that presents the law objectively, literally positing the law as an object. Miéville's narrative shifts the focus to the foundation and negation of law in itself, in its very possibility to be law, and this is how we can preliminarily approach the Law of Breach.

However, what these two scenes of the Law of Breach miss is the foundation of *jouissance*, what Jacques Lacan calls the Real. The Real is the site of Breach in Miéville's *The City & The City*: it renders its description meaningless, it constitutes the point of impossibility for detective Borlú's unsensing by dwelling in the dissensation itself, and it threatens to swallow reality whole by enjoying an excessive and mysterious power or *jouissance*. The Real is the locus of *jouissance*, the limit of pleasure and enjoyment beyond which lies the promise of endless enjoyment. I say here 'promise of endless enjoyment' because *jouissance*, like Breach, intervenes in enjoyment rather than adding to it. It is void, unseen, a stain upon polite *plaisir* and the puppeteer of desire: the limit.

The law of *jouissance* is the pervert's law of intervening in desolate reality to incite small moments of excessive pleasure; the pervert is the tool of the Other's enjoyment. 'Breach *intervenes*,'[11] says detective Borlú's interior monologue; but we should also add the Lacanian–Miévillian subtext to Borlú's statement: Breach is both the pervert and the whip. When Miéville introduces us to the agents of Breach at the end of *The City & The City*, they are consumed by *jouissance*, beings represented as black-clad figures with phallic sigils who move mechanically, and fiercely debate courses of action through a bare minimum of movement. The only regulatory principle that guides the Cause of Breach is to police and punish those who contravene its Law, the law of *jouissance*.

The danger of Breach in detective Borlú's unsensing is the appearance of the *jouisseur*, the agents of the positive law ridden with *jouissance*, on the streets of Besźel-Ul Qoma. If the Law of Breach is the Law of the Other, the *jouisseur* is the tool of *jouissance*. The Law of Breach is hated by the *jouisseur*s of Miéville's novel: Besź and Ul-Qoman nationalists despise it, but oddly none of the characters in *The City & The City* loves it. Even the agents of Breach seem to attend to the Law of Breach without attraction, pleasure or want. In both cases, the Law of Breach is the quilting point that provides the nationalists and the agents of Breach with

11 Miéville, *op. cit.*, p. 65.

ontological consistency – the nationalists instrumentalise *jouissance* whereas the agents of Breach tirelessly attend to the law of *jouissance*.

Yet it is the nationalists who function as a threat to the stability enjoyed by the rule of the Law of Breach. As a perverse authority or *jouisseur*, the Besź nationalists in Miéville's narrative are an unmitigated danger to the polity of Beszél-Ul Qoma that threatens to rupture the Law of Breach and instate a new Law. But, as Russell Grigg points out, 'any practice that does not rupture with the big Other will be condemned to repeat one or other of the practices made possible by the Other itself.'[12] In this nightmarish scene the *jouissance* of the *jouisseur*-as-Other condemns those subject to the Law to wild ideation 'on the street' as martial law, a law without the sense *(jouis-sans)* endowed by linking the imaginary effects of experience (i.e. unsensing) to some symbolic chain that 'binds and orients them'.[13] Ultimately, the nationalist revolution for unification in Miéville's narrative necessarily failed because its vision of the law was strictly positive: it posited the institution and made itself the source of law *(nomos)* as Law *(logos)*.

The conclusion of Miéville's narrative presents precisely such a scenario. In the final throes of the narrative, unificationists terrorise the Law of Breach and a chaotic orgasm of forces bursts forth from both cities. Breach overcomes this chaos and manages to conserve its Law because it is not limited to a positivistic modality. But it is interesting that Miéville's narrative only moves toward the conservation of the Law of Breach when it appears to be at its most facile and meaningless, when the systems of surveillance and policing of the limit of prohibition fail.[14] At the end of *The City & The City* we have a return to a calmer, normative order of things, but only after Borlú is shown the Law of Breach as a fantasised reduction to 'pure' representation, i.e. the sensorial manifestation of the agents of Breach to the populations of Beszél and Ul-Qoma retains the insignia of Breach, their phallic inscription behind which they invisibly dwell in the urban populace's dissensation. In these late stages of the narrative, the symbolic universe of Beszél-Ul Qoma is now centralised around the imaginary locus of the ineffable Breach as an attempt to paper over the desolation of reality with the imagining of a pre-Symbolic Beyond, the realm of the un-sensed becomes primary although it is derivative. This paradox is normalised by the reinstantiation of a taboo that protects Breach's access to a *jouissance* that is forbidden to the commons of the cleaved cities.

Miéville is herein presenting his readers with the danger of Breach: if the subject attempts to overcome the perverse injunction of polymorphous enjoyment by the *jouisseur*, they may fall into the role of a Dostoyevskian idiot, plagued by

12 R. Grigg, 'Absolute Freedom and Major Structural Change' in G. Boucher, J. Glynos and M. Sharpe (eds), *Traversing the Fantasy: Critical Responses to Slavoj Žižek*, Farnham: Ashgate, 2005, p. 193.

13 J. Lacan, 'Seminar on "the Purloined Letter"' in *Écrits*, B. Fink (trans.), New York: W. W. Norton & Company, 2006, p. 6.

14 This is an unusual twist for Miéville, given that most of his novels tend toward a narrative of successful revolution, whereas it is usually his short stories that weave tales of conserving a dark, primoridal Law.

moments of mystical experience when enjoyment evaporates in the confrontation with 'desolate' reality before the Law. Staying within the process of all-consuming enjoyment, however, also exposes the subject to a situation reminiscent of Slavoj Žižek's reading of *The Brothers Karamazov*: 'If God doesn't exist, then everything is permitted: nothing at all is permitted – not even the most innocent pleasures of eating, drinking, and smoking.'[15] Such a concomitant betrayal of reason suggests a nihilistic gap in the imagined relation between the subject and the Law. A question therefore arises as to whether the subject can overcome their condemnation by the *jouisseur* or if recourse must always be made to a 'higher' Law as per Miéville's construction of the law and revolution in *The City & The City*? Furthermore, if such a gap does exist, would its effects remain confined to the imaginary relation between the people of Besźel-Ul Qoma or is this rupture the nihilistic infiltration of some excluded piece of the Real on the orders of the Imaginary and Symbolic that the subjects in terroristic support for the unification of the cities misrecognised as *jouissance* beyond the Other?

Both of the aforementioned questions suggest a speculative critique of positivism insofar as all 'positive modes' posit their object in some way. Miéville is careful to avoid positivising the Law of Breach in *The City & The City*, although the narrative does posit the authority of the police or *policzai* as well as the nationalist relation to the Law of Breach. The difference between these two positive relations is in their respective connections to the Law of Breach. For the nationalists aiming at the unification of Besźel-Ul Qoma, the Law of Breach is 'nonsense on stilts': a series of effects that can be calculated, economised and negated. The brilliant play of unsensing in Miéville's narrative is disavowed by these nationalist-unificationist characters. Yet they only see this Law return in the fantasy field of the globalised lie that sustains their disavowal: that Besźel-Ul Qoma can be unified because the agents of Breach are merely alter-egos to compete with.

The positive relation of senior detective Borlú to the Law, however, is quite different. Rather than disavow the Law of Breach, Borlú experiences the Law of Breach as a (un)conscious compulsion to repeatedly un-sense those 'other' elements in his environment. This is underscored by Borlú's denotation as a senior detective of the *policzai* in Besźel: he has a particular place in the rule of law designated through this symbolic demarcation as an agent of this authority. However, his relation to the Law of Breach is uneasy and borders on the mystical. Whereas the nationalist-unificationists antagonise the Law of Breach by positing a false distance between their present circumstances and an imaginary unified future,[16] the character of detective Borlú is plagued by the Law of Breach as a spectre just beyond his gaze, a power beyond his powers as a senior detective.

Borlú's positive relation to the Law of Breach is mystical; it searches for the Good at one remove. The narrative of *The City & The City* is consumed by Borlú's

15 S. Žižek, *The Art of the Ridiculous Sublime: On David Lynch's Lost Highway*, Seattle: The Walter Chapin Simpson Center for the Humanities, 2000, p. 65 n27.

16 I.e. they both negate the law and claim to be the source of authority.

search for the *jouissance* of Breach, the *jouissance* of the Law. But as Lacan tells us: there is no *jouissance* of the Law, only the law of *jouissance*.[17] Borlú only comes to the recognition of this when he breaches, when he transgresses the limit of the law of *jouissance*. Borlú's shift from an agent of the Besźel *policzai* to an agent of Breach is a further removal from the immediacy of his phenomenological engagement with the effects of positive law. Initially, Borlú's unsensing facilitates his disavowal of Ul-Qoman law, the law of the other city in its identical legal-jurisdictional functioning. But when Borlú breaks the Law of Breach and is taken away by the agents of Breach, he enters the space of dissensation, of *jouissance*.

This shift paradoxically indicates that Borlú's escape into the mysticism of unsensing is inevitably marked by the betrayal of his 'being' *(jouis)* because the anality of the Law of Breach – its tireless attentiveness to the prohibition of its transgression – is predicated upon a 'positive principle of being' that posits the existence of Borlú as a subject-able-to-breach-the-Law *(j'ouïs-sens)*. This positing of Borlú negates the opening to an ontological encounter with Borlú's incongruent place in the Law of Breach *(jouis-sens)* in all its antagonistic excessiveness as the autonomous choice for transgression. Borlú does transgress the Law of Breach in *The City & The City*, but this transgression is a question of *jouissance* instead of desire. The positive space that Borlú inhabits before he commits breach is the jurisdiction of the *policzai* and the positive law of Besźel in its black letters and institutions. But this space creates a gap between the Law of Breach and the positive laws of Besźel-Ul Qoma that is filled out by Borlú's negation (*jouis-sans*) of the Law of Breach through unsensing. Herein Miéville's narrative discloses Borlú's subjectivisation as 'a subject' through the support of a speculative identity that stands at the interstices of transmutation between the authority of the Law of Breach (wherein the agents of Breach become a perverse Order, a tool of the Law that enacts its *jouissance* because it cannot avow this *jouissance*) and the subjectivity of Borlú as Besźel *policzai*.

This gap iterates the ontological difference between natural law and positive law, between the Law of Breach and the laws of Besźel-Ul Qoma, between the law of *jouissance* and the law of desire. On the side of positive law, Borlú fears the transgression of the Law of Breach. More specifically, he fears failing to fail to sense both cities to be limited by the taboo nowhere written in the letters of the positive law. Where the rule of desire is that it invites its own transgression, the law of *jouissance* is the limit itself. In Miéville's narrative, Borlú's transgression of the Law of Breach is driven by his desire to know the *jouissance* of the Law of Breach at one remove. The event of Borlú's breach is a vanishing mediator, and he seems to immediately flip from the space of positive law to that of natural law. From this new ontological position at the close of *The City & The City* a realisation

17 J. Lacan, *The Seminar of Jacques Lacan, Book XI: Four Fundamental Concepts of Psychoanalysis*, J.-A. Miller (ed.) and A. Sheridan (trans.), New York: W. W. Norton & Company, 1998, p. 92.

dawns on Borlú that the law of *jouissance*, the Law of Breach, is what provides an invisible consistency to the positive laws of Besźel-Ul Qoma. The Law of Breach thus becomes a 'real illusion', a fantasy space just beyond the unsensing of the populations of Besźel-Ul Qoma that is necessary for the polity of the cleaved cities. But this position is a properly speculative one, it rests on the liminal limit between desire and its transgression; it is *jouissance* as *jouis-sens*, 'enjoy-meant' and not 'enjoy-ed'. As Breach, Borlú only comes into existence when the Law of Breach is transgressed through its positing: the loss of dissensation as the breaching agent fails to fail to sense.

To conclude, I would like to offer some arguments for what we can learn from the plight of senior detective Borlú in *The City & The City*. First off, I find that Miéville's narrative offers an explicit criticism of a purely positivistic interpretation of law. The consistency of the Law is herein maintained by its reason for being, its ontological place, and not by the material structures it fosters. When the Law is viewed from these material structures, our gaze becomes blinkered by the ontological difference that separates the limit of the prohibition in its liminality from the transgression of this limit or the desire fostered by the prohibition.

Secondly, the scission of the cities in Miéville's narrative – Besźel-Ul Qoma – is a real illusion. In this sense a binary opposition of positive and natural law is an opposition that is imaginary and open to speculative critique as the opposition can only be maintained by recourse to the ontological difference that opens up the gulf of desire. As I tried to show, the attempt to reduce the character of Borlú to his descriptive actions misses that the very possibility of his having an identity is held in tension to its positing as a culpable agent. The ontological horizon of meaning for the black letters of the Law inheres in the *jouissance* of their principality: that is to say, the identity of Borlú only exists insofar as his identity is etched into the world through his recognition of the Law. This recognition does not have to be positive, and indeed Miéville's narrative demonstrates how the law abides its own ignorance to provide ontological consistency.

The encounter with this dissensation of the Law inverts Lacan's reading of Joyce. The inventiveness of Joyce's language, especially in *Finnegan's Wake* (1957), carries within it a kind of raw violence: we *must* interpret the text, otherwise it is un-readable (un-conscious).[18] The unusual feature of Miéville's *The City & The City* is that it shows a way of being that actively pursues this un-consciousness, and herein one can begin to see the traction that Lacanian critiques gain on legal positivisms: by refusing the interpretation of the law through its limits, legal positivisms admit a kind of raw violence that obscures the positing of difference inherent in the 'place' of the law. This Lacanian catch-cry is aptly announced by Grigg as 'any practice that does not rupture with the big Other will be condemned to repeat one or other of the practices made possible by the Other itself.'[19] And here rests the kernel of Miéville's critique of the law in *The City & The City*.

18 J. Joyce, *Finnegan's Wake*, New York: Viking Press, 1957.

19 Grigg, *op. cit.*, p. 193.

CHAPTER 12

Contract and conflict in *Eve Online*

This final analysis examines the systemic politics of enjoyment created by the contractual provisions and licence arrangements that commodify and sell pleasures on a massive scale with powerful consumer investment: massively multiplayer online videogames, or MMOs. Focusing on the science fiction MMO *Eve Online* (hereafter *Eve*), this discussion locates the way that players move between the socio-legal *milieux* created by the contract and licence of CCP Games (hereafter CCP) and player interactions in *Eve*. Taking the semiotics of the game and metagame spaces seriously, this discussion explores the place of *jouissance* and law in player revolt,[1] CCP's consolidation of political power through licence arrangements, and the way such things are wedded by the contractual obligations imposed by the game itself.

How is law presented in the interactions between the *Eve* community and the proprietor of the game service CCP? Is the fact that *Eve* bears the burden of entertainment value reason enough to consider the legal questions as questions of desire? Most likely not in general, but as we have so far seen, desire and law are intimately connected. Perhaps the question would be better posed in its reversed form: how does desire inform the legalities of *Eve* as entertainment? There appears a chain of significant points in reply: the lore of the fictional universe creates a semiotic background that gives the virtual objects and geography within the game world a coherent sensibility; the game's end-user licence agreement frames, promotes and restricts the use of the game world within and beyond the game itself; the right to enjoyment *a propos* the entertainment value of *Eve*; the 'right enjoyment' imposed by the ideological relationship of the game's licensing; the sensibility of the game world and its use by players and the meta-game community; and the politics of enjoyment in the licenced relationship when players transgress the bounds of the licence or stage a revolt to hold CCP to account for their marketing and under-delivery of promised features.[2]

1 A useful outline of the game and these tribulations was filmed at 2013's Eve Online Fanfest: *A Tale of Internet Spaceships*, http://www.youtube.com/watch?v=IB1M9ZVuWtM.

2 Does the company's insistence that its employees take on a unique mantle such as CCP Falcon, CCP Punkturis, CCP Nullarbor, etc., indicate a machine for ideology at

In the barest terms *Eve* is a science fiction MMO set in a fictional far-flung future. The lore of this mythical universe tells of a wormhole from Earth and a mass migration. With the unexpected collapse of the wormhole, the Eve Gate, the colonies were cast adrift and left to fend for themselves. Only a handful of the colonies survived and have become the distinct cultural identities that the players encounter upon entering the game world. CCP, the creator of *Eve*, perhaps could not have foreseen just how closely this fictional backstory reflects the beliefs and attitudes that many players hold about the game, how it is played, the public image of CCP and other players.

Moreover, the legal challenge for CCP reflects the trend of intellectual property holders who wish to control their work while profiting financially from its use. These challenges are coloured by CCP's avowedly for-profit interest in the game. Contractual controls over content, API data sharing, real money transactions and misrepresentation[3] are all regular topics of conversation for players in the game's online space colloquially termed 'the metagame'. Yet the uniqueness of *Eve* is that its narrative space is largely reliant upon the players' generation of emergent content, such as the clandestine sharing of intelligence about other players' activities, scams involving in-game currency, elsewhere termed InterStellar Kredit (ISK), and the infiltration of player corporations to the ends of spying, espionage and theft, that make up much of the entertainment value of the game. Alongside more orthodox MMO activities such as exploration and harvesting resources, quest/mission running or player versus player combat, the player-generated content of *Eve* is its central draw card for CCP.[4] In effect, the players build the attraction and profitability of *Eve* on its chaotic and un/intended use. This double-edged use constitutes its appeal as entertainment, or, as Tracey Lien writing for *Polygon* calls it: 'Eve: the most thrilling boring game in the universe.'[5]

The intellectual property aspects of *Eve* reflect the simple problem of how to best authorise the use of an authored work when the author has limited knowledge of how the audience intends to use their work. Information about *Eve* and related

its most effective? These titles given to developers and other CCP staff are the primary device through which players learn to associate the development of the game and the operation of CCP with their own conduct and production/gameplay. The one exception to this rule, in a predictably corporate totalitarian shift, is the CCP CEO Hilmar Veigar Pétursson, who retains his own name.

3 While *Eve*'s *Terms of Service*, discussed in detail below, begin by prohibiting hate speech and harassment, by the seventh provision it introduces trademark and intellectual property regulations, while the eighth provision centres on CCP's proprietary rights.

4 It is worthwhile resisting the now traditional distinction of 'linear' and 'emergent' gameplay here. What is at stake for both these pre-planned and open gameplay models is users' *playing* of the game.

5 T. Lien, 'Eve: The Most Thrilling Boring Game in the Universe', *Polygon*, 2014, http://www.polygon.com/features/2014/2/24/5419788/eve-online-thrilling-boring.

matters are publically thrashed out in the 'meta-game': the realm of player-made podcasts, websites, wikis, blogs, programs, and so forth that function as a socio-legal imaginary for the game, binding the players ever closer to the intellectual property of CCP. This imaginary is as much an echo chamber for statistics and facts about the game and its patch notes as it is for speculation and rumour about CCP, other players or the gameplay itself.[6]

A cursory glance at the meta-game space shows its heavy reliance on binary oppositions that exhibit little rational purpose beyond attendance to the entertainment offered by *Eve*, from the sublime to the ridiculous. This is perhaps best demonstrated by the immense volume of information that a new player must learn upon first entering the game.[7] Despite the best efforts of CCP to improve the new player experience, the learning curve of *Eve* is notoriously steep and its 'learning cliff' enjoys some infamy among the player community, journalists and meta-game websites such as *Massively*, *Kotaku*, *Polygon*, *Kugutsumen* and *Something Awful*.[8] The boundary to understanding *Eve* is thus not sorting the fiction from the truth but in fact trying to not be overwhelmed by the fragmented edifice of the game itself. Coupled with its constant demands for players' *Ursprüng* engagement, the meta-game imaginary is a sort of 'dream state' for *Eve*. The meta-game of *Eve* operates as a theatre where a wild play of images can revolve around and stumble upon the experience of the game. This meta-game imaginary is a space for 'remembering and working through' the troubles of life in the game. It can often serve to bring new players to the medium, popularise and sustain the market for *Eve*, or resolve antagonisms with the game by interrogating polemics such as '*Eve* is dying'.

6 See in particular the attempts by the alliance 'Rooks and Kings' to turn their enterprises into a cogent narrative using YouTube: https://www.youtube.com/watch?v=XrYe_4vHzgE. While unusual for the way that this video turns the player versus player action into a concise and partly fictionalised narrative, many in the meta-game space rate Rooks and Kings' videos amongst the exemplars of PvP in the game.

7 Other mainstream games in the sandbox MMO genre such as *World of Warcraft*, *Rift*, *TERA*, *Guild Wars 2*, *WildStar*, *Archeage*, *Star Wars: The Old Republic* or *Final Fantasy FFXIV: A Realm Reborn*, have markedly more intuitive and comprehensible tutorial systems for new players. *Eve* is generally more fragmented and more reliant on players connecting the dots between similar and often identical objects or processes in the game than these other titles, and the changing face of Eve's tutorial experience signals the gap in which the player must intervene. In a way, the gameplay of *Eve* is a sort of player-centred occasionalism in the spirit of Malebranche's philosophy where the player rather than God forms the sinews of narrative reality through their intervention in the probabilities of success or failure in the game.

8 The Something Awful community has a significant connection to the player group known as Goonswarm, whose cynical motto, to paraphrase their leader Alex Gianturco (aka The Mittani), is: 'We're not out to ruin *the* game; we're out to ruin *your* game.'

1. The lore of the game world

Like many online communities, the meta-game of *Eve* promotes connections and tensions between members of the community. This sociality is both a strength and weakness of the virtual world. The game mechanics used in *Eve*, such as player-claimable sovereignty over certain territories, player-generated structures and corporations, and meta-game politics in the guise of player coalitions and regional economies, provide a superficial sense of belonging. The strongly libertarian ethos of *Eve* opens this belonging to abuse and subversion by means of theft, espionage and attacks without cause against your allies. Such attacks, known in-game as Awox-ing after the activities of a player character named Awox, present the player-versus-player experience that *Eve* primarily aims to achieve.[9] At its core *Eve* is a player-versus-player environment and its best mechanics focus this competitive energy towards creative destruction, often resulting in the loss of in-game assets and generating further demands for the in-game economy to satisfy. In an echo of Freud's analysis of the incest taboo and civilisation, the formation of *Eve* corporations rests on not blowing up each other's ships, just other people's ships. Freud argued that the incest taboo was effective because civilisation compensates with a promise, however fantasmatic, of some greater happiness in the consenting collective rather than the autonomous individual.[10] There is no necessary reason why the collective would provide greater happiness, however, and it often produces the opposite phenomenon: discontent. The heavy satire and irony of some *Eve* players' reflections on the game points to the fragility of this promise of cooperation and the ease with which it can be subverted.

Given its strong adversarial emphasis in its player activity and game mechanics, one way to understand the gameplay of *Eve* is to look to the way that the players often act in accordance with this social link that simultaneously enacts and sunders attachment to virtual objects in the game. An ethics of *Eve* would appear to parallel the Lacanian motto of the *objet petit a*: 'I love you, but inexplicably I love something in you more than you, and therefore I destroy you' (Seminar XI). For both Freud and Lacan, the alienation of an individual psyche is partly written by its pursuit of its own appetites and desires. CCP often totes a narrative of 'risk versus reward' for in-game activities in *Eve*, but there is more to this logic in light of psychoanalysis. 'Risk versus reward' is an attempt to entice desire to gain

9 In a centrist turn, CCP Games recently flagged that it was considering implementing an in-game 'instant death' for the Awox perpetrator after some discussion of how to remove intra-corporate Awoxers from player corporations if they are not docked at a station at the onset of nightly downtime. While not removing this 'exploit' entirely, it may reduce its risk in high security space. See CCP Games, *CSM 9 Meeting Minutes, 17–19 September*, 2014, http://cdn1.eveonline.com/community/csm/CSM9Summer_Minutes_2014.pdf, p. 82.

10 S. Freud, *Civilisation and its Discontents*, J. Strachey (ed. and trans.), New York: W. W. Norton & Company, 2010.

something more quickly than by other means. Historically there have been opportunities for large player coalitions in control of some of the riskiest/most rewarding parts of the game world – from player-controlled space, to wormhole systems detached from the regular map, and faction warfare systems – to manipulate the outcomes of this design philosophy.[11]

However, this ethic is curiously absent from the grand narrative of the fictional world that pits four empires against one another. The imperial conflict between the Amarr, Gallente, Caldari and Minmatar empires is shot through by numerous pirate factions, the Angel Cartel, Guristas, Serpentis, Blood Raiders and Mordu's Legion, and other hostile sentient artificial intelligence entities such as Rogue Drones and Sleepers. As discussed at the outset of this chapter, *Eve*'s grand narrative imagines a flight from a fictional Earth through a wormhole to a previously uncharted region of space. The wormhole comes to be known as the Eve Gate. By the time that the Eve Gate collapses, a significant interstellar colonisation has taken place on the other side of this vortex, a region of space named New Eden. With the loss of a connection to Earth many colonies perish. And so in the succeeding fifteen millennia human civilisations lose contact with one another and begin to rediscover high technology and space flight. The Amarr civilisation is the first to regain interstellar travel and is depicted as a fundamentalist monarchy embarking on a *jihad* to renew the civilisations of the universe and bring their culture and living god to all. Like many a tale of colonisation, the Amarrian *jihad* results in the enslavement of the people of the neighbouring Minmatar region. The Gallente Federation appears soon after the Amarr begin their interstellar rediscovery, and is ascribed a system of liberal confederacy that values freedom as much as scandal. The more economically ruthless Caldari State eventually secedes from the Gallente Federation in a bitter civil war. The Minmatar also rebel against their Amarrian slave masters and so the four empire factions are created: the imperial and zealous Amarr, the liberal and mediacratic Gallente, the corporate and utilitarian Caldari and the tribal and liberated Minmatar. An unsteady peace is established between the four factions in 23230 AD with the institution of the Consolidated Cooperation and Relations Command (CONCORD) peace-keeping organisation and proclamation of Eve Standard Time (YC). In YC105 cloning technology is said to advance to a degree that grants an instant transfer of consciousness to a cloned body upon the moment of death, effectively achieving

11 Most notably, before a recent patch to the game, several player coalitions sometimes at odds with each other organised a monopoly over all of the moons, that provided an advanced item (technetium) necessary for the production of a massive proportion of often-used items in the game world. The agreement was known as 'OTEC' (Organization of Technetium Exporting Coalitions), a pun on 'OPEC' (Organization of Petroleum Exporting Countries). It took a major change in game mechanics by CCP to break this monopoly in 2012. (The Mittani, 'Sins of a Solar Spymaster #78: The Extortion Empire', *TenTonHammer.com*, http://www.tentonhammer.com/node/230860/page/2.)

immortality in terms of both biology and memory. Players are then inserted into the narrative through one of the four empire factions – into a star cluster at war.[12]

In such a maze of conflicting factions, new players begin life in the 'safe' reaches of high security space patrolled by either the non-player controlled (NPC) security force CONCORD or the similarly NPC empire customs vessels. As per the functioning of garrisons and police in regular life, *Eve*'s security forces will only intervene after players commit a transgression, which can be constituted by either player action or the 'criminal' history of a character that may exclude them from these high security territories. There are a handful of transgressions that have made international headlines outside the game, but the vast majority of transgressions remain mundane or par for the course of a player versus player environment. Many headlines, such as the BBC's 'Billions Stolen in Online Robbery', tend to misrepresent the unique circumstances of this environment by imposing a general construction of transgression.[13] Whether transgression is considered from without or within the contractual terms and narrative universe of *Eve*, the crucial question that interests us here is why transgress in *Eve* at all?

A first answer may come from the lore itself. In a strange parallel, the religiousness of the Amarr reads the medievalism of Lacan's work that idealises the scientific study of desire.[14] For both the Amarr and Lacan, a desired object is constitutive of the desire itself; the science of desire is a study of pure desire. In the narrative universe of *Eve* the desire involved in the Amarrian enslavement of the Minmatar tribes positions these tribes as a desirable object (e.g. labour force) that is constructed by the Amarr's Orientalist spiritual vision. This Orientalism constructs the Minmatar as 'primitive' and of lesser status, and therefore, for the Orientalist Self, legitimately able to be enslaved because they are not simply a 'lesser' alter-ego to be exploited but are desirable to the Amarr in the way that they are viewed; their racism is endemic and systemic.[15] But the desire to enslave is a separate issue to the desire that elevates the ordinary object into an object of desire. The Amarr, as it were, have read their Lacan, but the price of this reading is a certain blundering around their own narrative that confuses desire with the desire for something. In this frame transgression is all too often cast as a moral issue, a desire for transgression. Instead, let us turn to transgression in itself, as a

12 For more information see CCP Games 'New Eden Cluster' entry in *Evelopedia*, 2014, https://wiki.eveonline.com/en/wiki/New_Eden_(cluster).

13 'Billions Stolen in Online Robbery', BBC News, 3 July, 2009, http://news.bbc.co.uk/2/hi/technology/8132547.stm.

14 E. F. Labbie, *Lacan's Medievalism*, Minneapolis: University of Minnesota Press, 2006, p. 177.

15 One is reminded of the elementary racist logic slavery exposed by Herman Melville's novella *Benito Cereno* where the European sailors are caught off-guard by the slave Babo's cunning and genius, and the 'regular' Eurocentric master–slave relationship typified by the ship's motto 'follow your leader' is universalised such that 'leader' becomes an empty place for any autonomous agent to fill out with their perspective and threat of violence for non-compliance.

phenomenon constitutive of the construction of the limit or lack that desire rests upon: the limit of the law.

2. The law of the game

The law of *Eve* manifests to its players most often when it does not work. In this misfiring of *Eve*'s law, transgression is frustrated by the incompetence of the Other to secure the promised enjoyment of the game through its prohibitions. Meta-game discussion of various aspects of the rules governing the game are most frequent when they do not work to elicit enjoyment of the game, when they under-deliver on their promised outcome or when they run counter to the conservative entropy of the collective desire of the community to enjoy the game.

How then can we first frame what is going on at the level of observation and experience when the law misfires? The well-worn example of the broken hammer from Heidegger's *Being and Time* may serve as a preliminary guide here. A broken hammer loses its practical function but at the same time exposes that the tool use usually associated with a hammer that is *present-at-hand* and able to be used as a hammer in fact relies upon the hammer's constitution as an ontological Thing; 'hammer' is not just a name, hammering is not just an activity, there is a given way to use this Thing for an existential purpose or *raison d'être*. It is the suppositional given-ness of the hammer, its *presence-at-hand*, that comes to light when it breaks. In the uninterrupted use of the hammer, however, its ontological conditions are hidden by its empirical/existential usefulness for a task. Similarly, in the uninterrupted use of *Eve*, its usufruct status as a legal Thing is papered over. The bending or transgression of the legal rules of enjoying playing *Eve* is therefore not so much about what is condoned by its licence and its provisions, but rather it is about the legal grounds that give rise to this right to use/enjoy the game service. Law and ontology are intimately connected for the *Eve* universe. If desire and transgression are constitutive of enjoyment, then in a similar way for law and ontology it is only where enjoyment falters, where *Eve* really is at its most boring and idiotic, that its desire is laid bare.[16]

There are moments of law and desire in *Eve* too numerous to mention here. The exemplary moments, however, are those in direct connection with the licence of the game. The licence presents *Eve*'s structure as intellectual property that is aimed to be shared with and used by others. Examples include the power to ban players from the game, the prohibition against trading in-game assets for real money, the rejection of automated gameplay that makes use of bots and scripts, the prohibition against in-game names that reflect real world entities, and the injunction against actively bringing grief to new players by destroying or scamming them out of their in-game assets.

16 S. Žižek, *Enjoy your Symptom! Jacques Lacan In Hollywood and Out, Revised Edition*, London: Routledge, 2001.

There are two documents that control the usufruct value of *Eve* for the players. The *End-User Licence Agreement (EULA)* gives players limited reign over the game.[17] The *Terms of Service (TOS)*, on the other hand, handles the existential use of the game.[18] The difference between the two agreements reflects a typical Western legal division between entitlement and use; being entitled to something may not necessarily confer exclusive rights to enjoy it. What is curious, however, is the way that the *TOS* condones in-game activities that are either frowned upon or bannable offences in competing intellectual franchises and the broader social community. These include scamming, hostile takeovers, espionage, theft, and so on.[19] Other socio-legal critics have handled questions of theft[20] and governance[21] in virtual environments, but our inquiry here hinges on the legal-*cum*-psychoanalytic question of desire and the politics of this enjoyment.

The usufruct value of *Eve* is not a matter for speculation alone. Clearly stated in the *EULA*, the right to enjoyment is stated in a tellingly constructive jurisprudential way:

> Access to the System and playing EVE is intended for your personal entertainment, enjoyment and recreation, and not for corporate, business, commercial or income-seeking activities. Business entities and anyone who is acting for or on behalf of a business or for business purposes may not establish an Account, access the System or play EVE. Accessing the System or using the Game for commercial, business or income-seeking purposes is strictly prohibited.

It is not only the usufruct value of *Eve* that is enforced by this agreement: the prohibition against business is punitively constructed as a limit to the enjoyment. The construction here simultaneously posits enjoyment and how it is intended to be enjoyed, silently foreshadowing a range of prohibited enjoyments under the banner of 'corporate, business, commercial or income-seeking activities'. Yet notice the shift in the language of the beginning and conclusion of the clause that excludes corporate interest from the final list of purposes. How are we to approach this erased corporate purpose in the voiding of corporate activities?

17 http://community.eveonline.com/support/policies/eve-eula/.

18 http://community.eveonline.com/support/policies/eve-tos/.

19 *Eve*'s *EULA* and *TOS* both enjoy plain language and relative brevity and may rank well in some critics' measures of accessibility. The question or problem that we address here, however, is how much weight the enigmatic owner CCP exerts in these terms when reserving all matters to its own discretion, prejudice and corporate language. The contract of *Eve* constructs an politico-moral world within a legal world; it is in between law, morality, politics and the hearts and minds of its players.

20 W. Rumbles, 'Theft in the Digital: Can you Steal Virtual Property?', *Canterbury Law Review* 17, 2011.

21 M. de Zwart, 'Contractual Communities: Effective Governance of Virtual Worlds', *University of New South Wales Law Journal* 33(2), 2010.

The community-driven meta-game of *Eve* can offer some insights into this conundrum. A not-for-profit organisation like an advertising-free community radio station or dedicated *Eve* podcast enjoys a collective purpose. The multitude of people and their actions serving the collective form the corpus of the radio show or podcast channel. Technically a para-legal corporate activity, podcasts profit from the virtual property and intellectual property of *Eve*. However, while free, many podcasts do not identify as not-for-profit. The hidden focus of the licence is then on what profit is gained by a collective of individuals engaged in a group purpose without legal incorporation. While straightforward enough, the focus of the licence here rests on a contest between the profit of CCP and the profit of the *Eve* community. The profit of the community must not be a monetary one, as such a profit is forbidden by the *EULA*. This challenges the loyalty that a subscription-based game like *Eve* needs to inspire in order to survive in a competitive market. The paradox of the usufruct clause is thus that it admits and prohibits enjoyment attached to the intellectual property of the game outside the virtual world while leaving open the types of pleasure that players may take from the game. This is a moment of law where it is not entirely prohibitive but in fact the rules imagine a space for legitimate enjoyment.

The power of CCP's prohibition, including its possibility for failure, in the *Eve EULA* and *TOS* has a spectrum of outcomes from warnings to lifetime bans from the game. The power to ban players from the game by cancelling their accounts with impunity is given to CCP under the terms of the licence. This extends from acts connected to *Eve* but not necessarily conducted inside the game. This is, as Ronald Dworkin has shown, where the writ of law becomes the trappings of policy. We might even say that the *EULA* is really a legal-moral doctrine of sorts. The shift from writ to policy was openly demonstrated in a forum post by game developer CCP Falcon in early May, 2014:

> Hey guys
>
> It's with a heavy heart that I have to speak in relation to the damage that was done to the EVE Universe Monument just four days after it was unveiled.
>
> Firstly, I'll say that the fact that the monument was vandalized is an insult to the entire community, not just to the individual who's [sic] name was directly targeted by the vandalism. Thankfully with the assistance of a number of members of the community, including some of those who were involved with the incident and other members of their own alliance, we've been able to make headway in identifying those responsible.
>
> Secondly, we would like to reiterate that we do not tolerate this kind of behavior and will continue to operate a zero tolerance approach to dealing with harassment and victimization in the EVE Universe.
>
> As such, three individuals have been permanently removed from the EVE Community. A total of 7 EVE Online accounts, and 1 DUST 514 account belonging to them have been permanently banned. Another individual who was indirectly involved in the vandalism has received a 6 month ban from EVE Online on their sole registered account.

> The four individuals involved are also blacklisted permanently from attending future Fanfest events.
>
> While the community has been justifiably outraged and a number of people have requested that we release the ingame identities of those who carried out the act, we feel that this would be contrary to our privacy policies. As such we will deal with this incident in line with our current policies, and the identities of those responsible will remain confidential.
>
> With this in mind, we now consider this issue resolved within the EVE Universe, and any further action taken outside the virtual world relating to criminal damage or recovery of costs for repairs to the EVE Universe Monument will remain confidential between CCP Games, the authorities, and those involved.
>
> This thread will be left open for discussion, be sure to keep it on topic, with no personal attacks and finger pointing. This is a pretty sensitive subject for some members of the community, and as such people who break the rules will lose their forum posting privileges.
>
> Thanks.[22]

The problem here cuts in several interesting directions. Firstly, the *EULA* and *TOS* that supposedly target the handling of the game and its virtual world are extended to the vandalism of a physical object *associated with* rather than *present inside* the virtual world of *Eve*. In effect, the bundle of rights that make up CCP's proprietary interest in *Eve* have been asserted as a maximal matter of policy: 'an insult to the entire community'. Secondly, the application of the rules is here discretionary as highlighted by the absence of any coherent test for a measure of damages in either the *EULA* or *TOS*. Thirdly, rather than simply being an official announcement, the thread was left open to elicit feedback with strict rules of compliance that would effectively give CCP its own message in an inverted form from those receiving it. This is weirdly similar to one of the offender's admonitions about the incident that included a photograph of a defaced name on a fake Twitter account designed to raise suspicion about another party: '@Xenuria found your name and lost it again. #tweetfleet #eveonline #evefanfest You're welcome, everyone in eve! pic.twitter. com/rQ5hnkRe8V.'[23] And, fourthly, for all of the emphasis on CCP's policies about the game, the developer's missive resorts to slipping in a reference to a really existing legal apparatus. In effect, all but the fourth point mentioned here suggest that the civil politics of CCP's response to the vandalism of its monument is the over-determining factor with regards to how the corporation wants to incorporate law, rather than law being imposed by a sovereign, as might be suggested by the late inclusion of the legal apparatus, a little bit of the extant legal

22 CCP Falcon, 'A message regarding vandalism of the Eve Monument', 2014, https:// forums. eveonline.com/default.aspx?g=posts&m=4563345, posted 2014.05.07 15:56.

23 Gaius Homerson (@The_Real_Gevlon), https://twitter.com/The_Real_Gevlon/statuses/463002069989736448, 4 May, 2014.

state poking through the totalitarian circuit of CCP's discretionary interest. While everything is spoken from a civil law position, here the turn to law proper is the turn to law at its most codified and retroactive: criminal law.[24]

The appeal to the community of Eve by CCP Falcon in his forum missive signals the construction of the community as a *civitas* of players. For ancient Rome, the *civitas* was comprised of the citizens of Rome unified by law and endowed with rights from this law. But further, it required the citizen to internalise the prohibitions of law even if it went against their wishes. As classicists have noted, citizenship was a sought-after status in the ancient Roman empire, partly because its imperial cosmopolitan development rejected citizenship for conquered populations. The result was that it was a difficult process to acquire citizenship or be naturalised as a Roman. For *Eve*, however, all that it takes to gain entry into the players' *civitas* is the price of a subscription. It should come as little surprise, then, that the majority of exclusions and prohibitions in its *TOS* rely on economic particulars rather than unilateral reasons.

These economic prohibitions target a curious selection of actions. The prohibition against trading in-game assets for real money grants CCP exclusive control over the force that may make up its revenue stream. This prohibition also attempts to distance real world economic power from a direct intervention into the community. Yet this also contradicts CCP's own Pilot Licence Extension items (PLEX) that can be purchased with real world currency and be converted into either more subscription time or an in-game item that can be exchanged on the in-game markets for in-game currency. One may effectively play *Eve* for free if one earns enough in-game currency, as has been the running joke since PLEX was first introduced in 2008: you can pay for a paid subscription-only game with its own in-game resources. At base, the regulation of real money trading is an attempt to limit the player community to what CCP can control and it positions the narrative universe of *Eve* as the sort of ideal legal-economic state for these manipulations.

The licence arrangements push this statehood of *Eve* further by rejecting the automation of gameplay by players themselves. The use of bots and scripts to automate gameplay has been toted as a political issue of fairness for paid subscription players. The main activities of such 'botters' have historically been the harvesting activities of the game. While very difficult for CCP to police, players have taken it upon themselves to hunt these botters using a test reminiscent of the Voight-Kampff test used to locate replicants in *Blade Runner*. The practice, like the famous scene in the film, relies on biological responses, a basic question of 'how human are you?' But such questions are problematic for a screen space

24 Late in his life Derrida argued that the process of judging criminal law relies on a future recognition of a past indiscretion that then applies statutory measures to punish someone in the present rather than restore proven inequities, some of which may be unrecoverable. An award of reparative damages can only work in some instances. The challenge, for Derrida, is to forgive the unforgivable and reconcile with the neighbour who harms you.

where users can manipulate multiple accounts at the same time in a legitimate way. The only channels of communication in the game itself are how players' ships behave to another presence in their immediate vicinity and how a text chat between a hunter and a miner can coherently avoid preformed responses. The fear of being confused with a bot has driven some to create events like 'Hulkageddon', where the premiere mining ship for a long time, the *Hulk*, was used almost exclusively by botters and advanced industrial players alike. The *Hulk* was exclusively targeted by attackers using temporary characters (one account has three character slots) in very cheap, high-damage ships known as destroyers that would likely be blown up by CONCORD upon destroying the miner. Significant prizes were offered for those who could take down large numbers of *Hulk*s and so the reward on offer made the activity very profitable for some.[25] The fear of being 'discovered' to be a replicant, the narrative distortion of Deckard between various versions of *Blade Runner* for instance, is complicated in *Eve* in that Hulkageddon does not discriminate between replicants and players, although it has for some years adopted an anti-botter rhetoric. Hulkageddon is mostly about blowing up other people who might be ill equipped or unskilled to deal with a player versus player engagement, the supposed core of the *Eve* game mechanics.

Hulkageddon's success since 2009 may be attributed to the way that it adapts two strong solutions to the problem of legitimate gameplay sanctioned by the *EULA* and *TOS*. On the one hand, all miners are initially treated as replicants and are therefore legitimate targets. The possibility to be mistaken for a bot is maximised as the view that you *cannot not* be mistaken for a bot: all players are riven with the spectre of bot-ness if they mine. In effect the in-game activity of mining ventriloquises the player as a bot. On the other hand, not all risks are avoidable for players. As discussed above, the larger player coalitions inhabit the 'lawless' areas of greatest risk and reward and they unsurprisingly arise as the major supporters of events like Hulkageddon because the shift in the in-game supply to the markets elevates prices for those who can supply demand, although the velocity or throughput of currency and commodities in the game may wane as some miners simply log off for the period of Hulkageddon, as they might for organised aggression by other players' declarations of war that are regulated by time paid for with ISK.[26] In recent years, Hulkageddon has become a quasi-permanent feature of *Eve*, and the *Kronos* patch brought with it a reorganisation of attributes for mining ships, partly to adapt the ships to the players' use of them and partly to improve their survivability.

The spectre of bots raised above hides a deeper truth of the *Eve* political economy. If all player accounts can create up to three characters, then even the aggressors of Hulkageddon are subject to the same logic of bot depiction.

25 The prizes listed on http://www.machine9.net/?p=882 demonstrate this quite well. An average attacking destroyer may cost around one million ISK (http://eve.battleclinic. com/loadout/54971-Catalyst-300DPS-23day-Train-Hulkageddon.html), while the rewards reach into the several billions.

26 This connection to large player coalitions is mentioned in the official *Evelopedia* entry for Hulkageddon: https://wiki.eveonline.com/en/wiki/Hulkageddon.

All of the characters are robotic copies of 'copies' of users' data held by CCP's accounts department. The charge of bots in the *EULA* is thus a legal fiction akin to the economics of real money discussed previously: the only bots and scripts permitted belong to CCP, and the only money traded through the virtual infrastructure of *Eve* is for the benefit of CCP. The visceral pleasure of a raised heartbeat and adrenal release while hunting other players in the player versus player fantasy role-play environment of *Eve* is elicited for the benefit of this big Other: CCP. And perhaps here is a lesson that law can take from the study of this videogame: role-play and faking it can be as real for eliciting enjoyment as what is empirically evidenced. In fact, the fantasy of role-play, even in its most cynical out-of-character flavour for which *Eve* is well known, is just as capable of spawning economic, political and social networks of affects and effects as real life, from comradery to anxiety.

The legal narrative of *Eve*'s fantasy role-play, particularly its rules regarding character, corporation and alliance names, presents the distance between the legal fictions of the *EULA* and *TOS* and the players themselves. Role-play relies on the recognition and identification with an extant symbolic universe. Out-of-character role-play relies on suspending the usual rules of role-play to speak in a second voice: 'we all know this is a fictional universe but here's what I really think about it.' Yet the *EULA* extends legal culpability to both the fictional and personal voices:

> You are encouraged to use a pseudonym, but you may not choose a name that violates anyone's trademarks, publicity rights or other rights. Acceptance of a pseudonym by the System does not mean that your chosen pseudonym does not violate anyone's rights. You are responsible for any liability incurred by yourself, CCP or anyone else due to the pseudonym you choose. CCP retains the right to reject any pseudonym it determines, in its sole discretion, is unlawful, indecent, obscene or otherwise violates standards of good taste.[27]

The clause insists on distinguishing between the user, 'you', and the pseudonym in the game world. But when we exercise a simple logical reversal and ask how CCP, the legal owner with exclusive rights to *Eve*, registers this transgression imagined by the clause, we can begin to see the problem devolve into two categories: the pseudonym and the person deciding. What is being regulated by this clause is not the intent to create an obscene pseudonym in bad taste but in fact to articulate a system of taste by localising the power to decide what is tasteful within the discretion of CCP.

Section D of the *EULA* similarly aligns these masters of taste, with the discretionary interest to decide what is and is not offensive but pleads ignorance of player communication. The prevalence of sexually violent language to describe activities and tactics in the game world, which would be highly offensive in most other *civitas*, perhaps speaks to the barbarism inherent in trying to regulate taste:

27 *EULA* Your Account sB.

the threshold of acceptability is arbitrarily decided by CCP and may be manipulated and extended as we saw in the example of vandalism to a monument to the players above. The treatment of player communications through the view of indemnity strikes an unusual moment for *Eve* as, again, the terms that CCP serves to its players provincialises one form of narrative communication, pseudonyms and role-play, while ghettoising another, open communication. The very zone of social sentiments that might construct an aesthetics of taste as we have known it historically is traded away for the enigmatic *obiter dicta* of CCP's private counsel. CCP constructs the shift from players' legal right to enjoyment to *the right enjoyment* through law.

3. The right to enjoyment

At the barest level of description, *Eve*'s *EULA* and *TOS* serve to frame and delimit the terms through which the game may be enjoyed. More than this, as a game, enjoyment would appear to be the logical aim of *Eve* as a commercial product. So far we have seen how law guides and frustrates this aim through a select series of examples drawn from the *EULA* and *TOS*. But the issue remains of how this use-value of *Eve*, entertainment, is coded by these terms.

Given its paid subscription model, regulation of money traded through its infrastructure and insistence on letting players openly communicate within certain limits of acceptability, one may wonder if CCP is interested in incorporating players into its fold. Customer loyalty is, after all, good for business longevity. Yet the *EULA* states:

> You have no interest in the value of your time spent playing the Game, for example, by the building up of the experience level of your character and the items your character accumulates during your time playing the Game.[28]

Eve has an interesting training mechanic governing this investment in the game. Unlike traditional MMO models where avatars in the world must do some activity to earn experience points that increase the status of the avatar as they are accumulated, *Eve* instead utilises passive skill training. In its model, CCP has chosen to grant training on a clock that runs even when the player is not online. The player can pause or queue more skills to train as they wish, but the game will keep 'playing' itself while the player is logged off. One might recall the story about Niels Bohr who had a horseshoe hung above his door in superstitious fashion. When asked by a friend why the famed physicist, a *premier* mind of rational thinking, would hang such an irrational totem above his door, Bohr replied that he had heard that it would work even if you did not believe in it. *Eve*'s skill training exhibits an identical structure to Bohr's horseshoe logic: even if you don't play the game, if you never undock from the glass prison of a space station, even if you

28 *EULA* Proprietary Rights sB.

forget to log in, the game will keep training as long as a skill is queued, as long as a horseshoe is hung. Paid subscription time thus takes on a special meaning for *Eve*: even if you do not play the game as it is structurally intended, as a player versus player fantasy role-play, your avatar can still progress. The clause cited above, however, converts this player investment in the game into the profit of CCP rather than the player. Enjoyment of *Eve* is thus really the Other's enjoyment; the desire to achieve something in the game's system of small victories and *les petites morts* (kill reports for eliminating other players' ships) are the province of CCP rather than the players playing the game. No bots, no players; just *Eve*.

4. The right enjoyment

At this point it would be fair to wonder why anyone would bother playing *Eve* at all. To phrase this more affirmatively, what does the total control of CCP offer players that they themselves cannot produce? CCP controls the black box of taste that is the right enjoyment, but how are players included into this enigma of the Other's desire? The *EULA* tries on several occasions to map the right way to enjoy *Eve* for the players. The first is its teen rating with the Entertainment Software Rating Board (ESRB).[29] Several ages are mentioned in the *EULA* that loosely trace the consenting ages of various Western jurisdictions including Iceland from where CCP hails, e.g. thirteen, eighteen, etc. The *EULA* also defines the right enjoyment of *Eve* by weakly regulating in-game communications with the same strong approach to discretionary interest and deciding penalties.[30] Both of these clauses take aim at the surplus of the contractual terms promoted by the *EULA*: law lived by the players' use of the game service.

Rather than coding the dead letter of law as something predatory and undead, laying in wait for a player's transgression, the right enjoyment of *Eve* means that the legal apparatus of the *EULA* invisibly 'walks' with the use of the game service. The surplus of the *EULA* and *TOS* is therefore the human element, the player who plays and enjoys in the fantasy role-play of *Eve*. It is telling when a game service will indemnify itself from those it services and, simultaneously, elevate its own discretionary interest to totalitarian heights. What is CCP so afraid of that it must shield itself from its customers? Rather than transgressions, which are retroactively created by the association of some action with the terms of the *EULA* or *TOS*, the issue here is that players are playing the game too well, taking *Eve* to the limits of what it can do.

This affirmation of *Eve* is inscribed into the fabric of CCP's conduct and communication policy. The clause from the *EULA* reads:

> CCP may establish Rules of Conduct (discussed below) for players accessing the System and may, but is not obligated to, monitor and take action

29 *EULA* Your Account sC(2).

30 *EULA* Your Account sD.

> regarding inappropriate conduct. Nonetheless, it is possible that at any time there may be language or other material accessible on or through the System that you may consider inappropriate or offensive to some users. You acknowledge that other players may transmit communications or content, or access to content, that you may consider inappropriate or objectionable. CCP does not, as a matter of policy, prescreen the communications or content transmitted by each player and is in no way responsible for the communications and content transmitted by players of the Game.[31]

Some factors in this clause weigh heavily on players' construction of the right type of enjoyment, including the unannounced surveillance of players' conduct and communication to the toleration of conflicting viewpoints by the players themselves. Yet this clause also contains a counter-intuitive policy argument to disentangle CCP from any duty of care to survey player communication and therein monitor or moderate inappropriate or offensive content. The *EULA* of *Eve* thus constructs the right enjoyment for players on three fronts. Firstly as enjoyment that ambiguously may or may not be corroborated by CCP, i.e. if you transgress you may not be caught. Secondly, a certain type of enjoyment is nonetheless demanded by the terms of the contract between players and CCP. And lastly, this enjoyment relies on an abstraction of policy that self-consciously governs the application of the rules that players should abide by, which the players must themselves paradoxically internalise as a customary measure for what is the 'right' enjoyment in a space oriented as a locus of interpersonal adversity and strife.

5. The politics of enjoyment

The politics of the right enjoyment for *Eve* is a politics of its legality. Moreover, this legality relies on the interaction of humans with a computer. This pair, human and computer, face one another as an interface that is thoroughly ridden with the potential for il/legal pleasures. But this legality of the contract between players and CCP is also rigorously customary, relying heavily on players' internalisation and submission to the agreement. At base, the law of *Eve*, and perhaps cyber contract law in general, is thoroughly psychic. The topology of the legal relations of Eve discussed above are in fact psychic relations of self with an Other, of egos with alter-egos, of human subjects culpable in the eyes of the law with depersonalised policy expectations and terms of usufruct use. But does the law of *Eve* make the right enjoyment a safe choice? After all, the trope of *Eve* players is, as one commentator put it: 'These people actually live *for* the game. I mean, talk about obsession.'[32]

31 *Ibid.*

32 Mythos comment to Evan Narcisse, 'How Fan Revolt in *EVE Online* Gave Birth to its Latest Expansion', *Kotaku*, 7 December, 2011, http://kotaku.com/5865930/how-fan-revolt-in-eve-online-gave-birth-to-its-latest-expansion.

Lacanian cybertheorist André Nusselder has argued that the human–computer interface, such as that required to play *Eve*, creates virtual objects that 'allow us to control and manipulate the world, to make it "emotionally safe"'.[33] Nusselder goes onto argue that the limit case of video game addiction exemplifies this screening of anxiety: 'the game is a compulsive, pleasurable repetition of a life-and-death performance in which the player's anxiety can never be finally mastered.'[34] However, we should pause here to note that the structure of this repetition is not in itself pathological. The insight that psychoanalysis brought to repetition is that it may be unintentional, pleasurable or burdensome but that it remains beyond the simple seeking of ever more pleasure. Due to its transitory status, one cannot merely stack pleasures. Nusselder argues that attempts to repeat pleasure, or more appropriately to repeat the symbolic coordinates of where pleasure once was, is a repetitive attempt to grasp the real through the symbolic artifice of language.[35] However, the repetition is doomed to failure because every attempt to symbolise the real relies on an extant symbolic network of language and signification. One does not get out of language, so to speak. Yet the more interesting point here is that the real is an absent cause for symbolic repetition; the fleetingness of pleasure itself heralds something lost.

Following Nusselder, we may read the politics of the right enjoyment of *Eve* as a politics of *mimesis*. These seemingly endless repetitions decay and change over time. They also entail that player revolt, an increasingly common feature of the community of *Eve* players, is not so much a revolutionary act as it is an acting outside the repetitions that promised some security from anxiety without delivering it. Player revolt in *Eve* was most notable around the 'Jesus feature' of virtual avatars walking around a private 'captain's quarters' after docking in the in-game space stations with the 2011 release of the *Incarna* expansion.[36] The player reaction became organised under the banner 'Summer of Rage' where in the previous year, 2010, CCP had seemed 'an untouchable powerhouse in the games industry'.[37] The *Incarna* feature was a radical shift away from a game built on virtual spaceships and interpersonal conflict. The quarters only ever allowed a single player themselves to be present. In this virtual space the human–computer interface underwent a doubling as in-game computer screens displayed game information to the avatar. Yet the payoff of alleviating anxiety was strangely absent.

The *Incarna* captain's quarters feature was not game changing, precisely because it ignored the basic locus of what makes *Eve* a game *per se*: player versus player strife. The strife itself arose in an economic way as a large number of players

33 A. Nusselder, *Interface Fantasy: A Lacanian Cyborg Ontology*, Cambridge, MA: The MIT Press, 2009, p. 108.

34 *Ibid.*

35 *Ibid.*, p. 109.

36 CCP Games, *Incarna – 21 June 2011*, 2014, http://www.eveonline.com/expansions/incarna.

37 Brendan Drain, 'Eve Evolved: The Human Casualties', *Massively by Joystiq*, 2011, http://massively.joystiq.com/2011/10/23/eve-evolved-the-human-casualties/5.

suddenly unsubscribed from the game. In the words of then senior producer Arnar Gylfason, 'It wasn't a complete surprise. But, at the time, we were shocked at the magnitude of the backlash and dissatisfaction.'[38] The strange resignation from Gylfason can be explained partly from the totalitarian discourse generated by the terms of the agreement between players and CCP. And moreover, the way that this discourse was about a totality of enjoyment centred upon what was the right enjoyment for *Eve*. The *Incarna* expansion erred precisely because it ignored what the legal contract had created in the hearts and minds of the players themselves. Law, at least in the case of *Eve*, is never without narratives and social customs to support it and maintain its function.

Conclusion

In a recent developer missive about the upcoming (as of this writing) expansion *Hyperion* from CCP Fozzie, a subtitle reveals the lesson that CCP had to learn from *Incarna* in order for *Eve* to survive as a successful MMO: 'No plan survives contact with the players: let's talk about emergence.'[39] But perhaps more than learning from the *Incarna* experience, this emphasis about plans and players emphasises the core tension of *Eve* as an intellectual property: regulating the hearts and minds of the players. The social interactions and legal constructions spawned by *Eve*'s *EULA* and *TOS* demonstrate that law is about power and its impotence: powers constructed on the side of law will come to naught unless these obligations are internalised, not merely accepted or tolerated, by those subject to law. Acceptance details some private space in which I am able to accept or reject the rule *a priori*; thus it remains fundamentally incomplete and open to change. Tolerance on the other hand is decidedly one sided as *Eve*'s licence arrangements do not tolerate a player's dissent from the rules, but it is instead the player's tolerance of the rules that will sustain the dominance of law and the property holder CCP Games. Instead, and as we have seen above, the *EULA* and *TOS* insist on the usufruct use of *Eve* as something reliant on CCP's absolute discretion. It is curious that the other side of this narrative universe so heavy with libertarian ethics in its mechanics and official narrative is totalitarian control over enjoyment or, more appropriately, enjoy-meant (by CCP). In short, enjoyment is at one level a part of the legal construction of *Eve*'s licence arrangements and at another deeper level a unilateral structure of desire that law in itself intends in the form of the owner's exclusive rights. *Eve* is an MMO, a 'sandbox' game about spaceships with a libertarian ethic at its core. Yet it nonetheless intends a particular way of enjoying the game. The legal narrative of the licence herein moves from 'a right to enjoyment' to the politics of 'the right enjoyment'.

38 Narcisse, *op. cit.*

39 CCP Fozzie (2014) 'Into the Known Unknowns: Wormhole Updates in the Hyperion Release', 2014, http://community.eveonline.com/news/dev-blogs/into-the-known-unknowns/?_ga=1.183055456.753417130.1405299146.

Conclusion

When I first set out to consider legal philosophy, I was struck by its invisibility and pervasiveness. Statutes and judgments embodied modes of thinking about law, random events were narrativised into something law could recognise on its own terms, what was legal seemed at once irrational and logical, and even the most quotidian and suburban of small pleasures seemed to gain a certain prestige or infamy when subjected to a legal gaze. Yet there was something missing in this complex web of rules, tests and recognition: the psyche. Unlike mind or brain, psyche is the idea that agency is part of the chaos of life; it is inseparable from one's body, and today, after the lessons of psychoanalysis, it is also anti-humanistic.

The invention of psychoanalysis in the nineteenth century moved the psyche from the ancient frame of Hellenic society to modernity. For Freud, dreams are a kind of story, and they have a psyche; they live, they trip up, they repeat things in odd ways, and they have something to say. For post-Freudian thinkers today such as MacNeil and Žižek, law also has a psyche. And where the psyche of telling a story exhibits a certain pleasure in telling that story, law also seems to enjoy in telling its stories.

The psychic tales of law may appear to put pleasure at law's edge. In the discussion of anarchy we saw how knowledge of law contaminates all attempts to seek a space outside law. The parallax of anarchy against and beyond law speaks to a realm of pleasure beyond the legal reality of modernity that is impossible for law to think. In the discussion of jurisprudence as a *Wissenschaft* the vocation of enjoying the ways of legality signalled that part of what locks down thought for law is both the limitation of legal knowledge as a form of rational knowledge and the interpretative activity of jurisprudence. Law is not a hard science, but the evocative technicalities emphasised by legal positivists do tend to erode the vestiges of jurisprudence as little more than armchair philosophising about the deeper structure of the rules with no worldly application. Yet even such a positivism would have to admit that it has a certain way of viewing the world, a certain psyche or system of how the law is and is not. Even at its most positivist, law is part rule, part understanding those rules, and part a persistence of those rules even if we ignore them, wilfully or unconsciously. These facets of positive law may not always meet on equal terms, and this problem partly stems from the rational construction of law as against the rationality of lawyers, jurists and jurisprudes.

The discussions of the narratives of *Coraline*, *Minority Report*, *True Blood*, *The City & The City* and *Eve Online* all tried to come to terms with this antagonism by examining the disjuncture between legal knowledge and rational authority. By shifting the frame of the discussion from law to law *vis-à-vis* culture, the gaze upon the law is refreshed and transformed. This transformation pointed to enjoyment or, more particularly, the enjoyment wrought by rational authority and the ontology of law. Several features of enjoyment became clear in the inquiry into these narratives: enjoyment is not always about pleasure; the limit of enjoyment is also the site of power for law's psychic life; law's psychic life has a temporality and modulation that rearticulates those who are recognised in law; and the legal codification of enjoyment may undo the authority that maintains such a usufruct right. Unlike strictly legal analyses, comparative critical reading of these cultural texts produced a complex view of enjoyment in law and enjoyment intended by law even if such enjoy-meant remained oblique, screened by the rationalism of legal authority.

Thus law and enjoyment are intimately connected. The case of *Eve Online* presented a particularly crucial insight into the way that contractual obligations for an entertainment platform that supposedly assures a usufruct right rigorously codifies all enjoyment through a right way to enjoy. The basis for this normative order of legal enjoyment is constructed by the legal narrative of what enjoyment is.

The discussion of Miéville's *The City & The City* offered a glimpse of the grounds of the legal narrative of enjoyment. To be precise, the problem that Miéville's narrative shows is the hegemony of the legal narrative of enjoyment: 'any practice that does not rupture with the big Other will be condemned to repeat one or other of the practices made possible by the Other itself.'[1] This critical point underscores the problem with legal positivism in a post-positivist discussion: legal positivism's rejection of interpretation presents a violent obscuring of the source of law and the place of what is 'legal'. The contractual terms of *Eve Online* are especially instructive on this: law constructs a normative view of the world where such a regime imposes a right way to enjoy without offering arguments for why it ought

1 R. Grigg, 'Absolute Freedom and Major Structural Change' in G. Boucher, J. Glynos and M. Sharpe (eds), *Traversing the Fantasy: Critical Responses to Slavoj Žižek*, Farnham: Ashgate, 2005, p. 193.

to be enjoyed. This obscuritanism of law was especially evident in the promise of a future satisfaction for Sookie Stackhouse in *True Blood*.

There are critical problems for the construction of legal narratives of enjoyment. At the forefront is the enjoyment of our humanity in a legal order. Human rights, for example, martial the Thingliness of the human that undermines the stable empowerment of the individual through legal rights. The problem for the discourses of human rights is thus how to orient authority to this Human-Thing through the legal machinery of rights rather than an appeal to a natural order or *logos* of law. The discussion of Gaiman's *Coraline* showed that this other space of law, its familial scene, to echo Agamben, is diffuse. For Coraline to come before law and enjoy human rights presents a partial arrangement: I am human in and out of law.

This inside and outside of law is the motor of law's adversarial structure problematised by Kafka and restorative justice alike. For Kafka, the Thing outside law, Ordradek, remains attentive to legal-symbolic order nonetheless; it becomes a perverse tool of law's enjoyment that threatens to undo the coherent account of law as a system. Restorative justice discourse similarly highlighted that in the changing face of legal practice, lawyers are losing traction as agents of acquiring justice as practice moves outside the legal institutions towards mediations and conferencing between offenders and victims. The curious feature of this mediation process was the way that both the offender and victim were victimised by the legal apparatus *a priori* to the mediation, and where this victimisation is redoubled for the victim of child sexual assault discussed by Daly – situating such a human person in a worse position than normative victimhood *per se*. This outside space of law, the para-legal, is the realm of the Thing rather than polite and discrete objects. The difference hinges on the way that objects are coordinated within a discourse whereas the Thing identified by psychoanalysis resists any such codification of difference. Rather than difference and division the Thing is subject to the law of *jouissance*, a drive towards pleasure that exists at the intersection of civilisation and organic life.

Exactly how law approaches this intersection of civilisation and organic life was discussed through the analytic of legal knowledge. It was observed how the university discourse of modern law schools construct an approach to knowledge that promises rather than delivers on satisfaction, effectively creating a false distance between enjoyment and knowledge that returns in seemingly meaningless objects and gestures such as grading regimes. At base, the positioning of jurisprudence as *Wissenschaft* in the vocational pursuit of modern legal training creates a difficult paradigm where the promise of some satisfaction is of more realistic value to pursuing legal knowledge than the mechanics of the pursuit itself. Moreover, such a jurisprudence belies the philosophical contingency at the core of any possible *logos* that can teach what law is and is not. Ultimately, what modern law schools cannot teach its students to enjoy is the other scene of law, its reverse. This is the fantasmatic thicket of law and enjoyment today, the imbroglio of legal knowledge and any legalism that it may spur.

Whatever the angst about psychoanalysis today, the method's fascination with narrative, law and how civilisation promises happiness and its vicissitudes makes it an indispensable tool of legal philosophy. The rich tableau of ways to think of law and its place in the world is not only one of totalising systems and higher orders, it is also sceptical and materialist. Psychoanalysis enables us to read law differently, to see law in and outside its institutional frame. This is important because law is ineffective without enforcement, and even less so without some minimum of belief in the rule of law. This belief is generated within law itself and is a common thread to representations of the legal. Psychoanalysis lets us excavate the structures and stories that come before law and give us access to interpreting law and its broader meanings for the way we live, no matter the trouble that civilisation causes us. At the very least, psychoanalysis lets us listen to legal narratives and narratives about law. To hear the tics and blunders, the repetitions and symptoms that make law a coherent feature of our modern existence fraught with choices large and small, is to learn how we tell stories about law for ourselves.

We still tell these stories about law, even if we don't really believe them. What does it mean to enjoy these fictional tales about law, much less legal fictions? This book tarried with this question and resolved to argue that fictionalisation can serve to make rational authority more than palpable: to make it enjoyable for a range of encounters, to even make it a vocation. Enjoyment is at the centre of law, the core of the subjects who make up its lived existence. But nonetheless these subjects, these interpreters and storytellers of law, are at the edge of law like a penumbra. This discussion has tried to shine a light on how law is narrativised and uncover some of the *jouissance* that stains both the legal and the cultural alike.

Bibliography

'Graphesis: Perspectives in Literature and Philosophy', *Yale French Studies* 52, 1975.

Arendt, H., *The Origins of Totalitarianism*, San Diego: Harcourt, Brace, Jovanovich, 1973.

Arthur, L., 'Does Case Management Undermine the Rule of Law in the Pursuit of Access to Justice?', *Journal of Judicial Administration* 20, 2010.

Balay, A., '"They're Closin' Up Girl Land": Female Masculinities in Children's Fantasy', *Femspec* 10(2), 2010.

Barnes, J., 'Introduction' in J. Barnes (ed.), *Early Greek Philosophy*, Harmondsworth: Penguin Books, 1987.

Beiser, F., *The Romantic Imperative: The Concept of Early German Romanticism*, London: Harvard University Press, 2003.

Benjamin, W., *Charles Baudelaire: A Lyric Poet in the Era of High Capitalism*, H. Zohn (trans.), London: Verso, 1983.

Benson, S., 'Introduction', in S. Benson (ed.), *Contemporary Fiction and the Fairy Tale*, Detroit: Wayne State University Press, 2008.

Birke, R., 'Neuroscience and Settlement: An Examination of Scientific Innovations and Practical Applications', *Ohio State Journal on Dispute Resolution* 25, 2010.

Braithwaite, J., 'Doing Justice Intelligently in Civil Society', *Journal of Social Issues* 62, 2006.

Braithwaite, J., 'Narrative and "Compulsory Compassion"', *Law and Social Inquiry* 31, 2006.

Braithwaite, J., 'Restorative Justice and Therapeutic Jurisprudence', *Criminal Law Bulletin* 38, 2002.

Buck-Morss, S., *Origin of Negative Dialectics: Theodor W. Adorno, Walter Benjamin, and the Frankfurt School*, New York: The Free Press, 1979.

Chiesa, L., *Subjectivity and Otherness: A Philosophical Reading of Lacan*, Cambridge, MA: The MIT Press, 2007.

Chiesa, L., 'Lacan and Artaud: *j'ouïs-sens, jouis-sens, jouis-sans*' in S. Žižek (ed.), *Lacan: The Silent Partners*, London: Verso, 2006.

Cook, C., Crekyke, R., Geddes, R and Hamer, D., *Laying Down the Law, 8th Edition*, Chatswood: LexisNexis Butterworths, 2012.

Copjec, J., *Read my Desire: Lacan against the Historicists*, Cambridge, MA: The MIT Press, 1994.

Copjec, J., 'The Orthopsychic Subject: Film Theory and the Reception of Lacan', *October* 49, 1989.

Cossins, A., 'Restorative Justice and Child Sexual Offences: The Theory and the Practice', *British Journal of Criminology* 48, 2008.

Daly, K., 'Setting the Record Straight and a Call for Radical Change: A Reply to Annie Cossins on "Restorative Justice and Child Sexual Offences"', *British Journal of Criminology* 48, 2008.

Daly, K., 'Restorative Justice and Sexual Assault: An Archival Study of Court and Conference Cases', *British Journal of Criminology* 46, 2006.

Daly, K., 'Restorative Justice: The Real Story', *Punishment and Society* 4, 2002.

Danto, A. C., *Mysticism and Morality: Oriental Thought and Moral Philosophy*, London: Basic Books Inc., 1972.

Dean, J. 'Žižek on Law', *Law and Critique* 15(1), 2004.

Debreuil, C., *The Right to Water: From Concept to Implementation*, Marseilles: World Water Council, 2006.

Deleuze, G. and Guattari, F., *Kafka: Towards a Minor Literature*, D. Polan (trans.), Minneapolis: University of Minnesota Press, 1986.

Dews, P. and Osborne, P., 'Lacan in Slovenia: An Interview with Slavoj Žižek and Renata Salecl', *Radical Philosophy* 58, 1991.

Dolar, M., *A Voice and Nothing More*, Cambridge, MA: The MIT Press, 2006.

Dostoyevsky, F., *The Brothers Karamazov*, S. McReynolds Oddo (ed. and trans.), New York: W. W. Norton & Company, 2011.

Douzinas, C., *Human Rights and Empire: The Political Philosophy of Cosmopolitanism*, London: Routledge-Cavendish, 2007.

Esposito, R., *Communitas*, T. C. Campbell (trans.), Stanford: Stanford University Press, 2010.

Felstiner, W., Abel, R. and Sarat, A., 'The Emergence and Transformation of Disputes: Naming, Blaming, Claiming …', *Law and Society Review* 15, 1980–1981.

Fichte, J. G., *Foundations of Natural Right*, F. Neuhouser (ed.) and M. Baur (trans.), Cambridge: Cambridge University Press, 2000.

Fink, B., *A Clinical Introduction to Lacanian Psychoanalysis*, London: Harvard University Press, 1997.

Flieger, J. A., *Is Oedipus Online? Siting Freud after Freud*, Cambridge, MA: The MIT Press, 2005.

Foster, T., *The Souls of Cyberfolk: Posthumanism as Vernacular Theory*, Minneapolis: University of Minnesota Press, 2005.

Foucault, M., *The History of Sexuality: 1 – The Will to Knowledge*, R. Hurley (trans.), London: Penguin Books, 1978.

Frank, J., 'Excerpts from *Law and the Modern Mind*' in *Lloyd's Introduction to Jurisprudence*, M. D. A. Freeman (ed.), London: Sweet & Maxwell, 2001.

Freeman, M. D. A. (ed.), *Lloyd's Introduction to Jurisprudence*, London: Sweet & Maxwell, 2007.

French, B., 'Dispute Resolution in Australia – The Movement from Litigation to Mediation', *Australasian Dispute Resolution Journal* 18, 2007.

Freud, S., *Civilisation and its Discontents*, J. Strachey (ed. and trans.), New York: W. W. Norton & Company, 2010.

Freud, S., *Beyond the Pleasure Principle and Other Writings*, J. Reddick (trans.), London: Penguin Books Ltd, 2003.

Freud, S. *New Introductory Lectures on Psychoanalysis*, J. Strachey (trans.), London: Penguin Books, 1991.

Freud, S., *On Sexuality: Three Essays on the Theory of Sexuality and Other Writings*, J. Strachey (trans.), London: Penguin Books, 1991.

Freud, S., *The Origins of Religion: Totem and Taboo, Moses and Monotheism and Other Works*, J. Strachey (trans.) and A. Dickson (ed.), Harmondsworth: Penguin Books, 1985.

Freud, S., *The Interpretation of Dreams*, Harmondsworth: Penguin Books, 1958.

Gabriel, M. and Žižek, S., *Mythology, Madness and Laughter: Subjectivity in German Idealism*, London: Continuum, 2009.

Gaiman, N., *Coraline & Other Stories*, London: Bloomsbury Publishing, 2009.

Gibson, W., *Mona Lisa Overdrive*, London: Harper Collins Publishers, 1988.

Gibson, W., *Count Zero*, London: Harper Collins Publishers, 1984.

Gibson, W., *Neuromancer*, London: Harper Collins Publishers, 1982.

Glynos, J., 'Radical Democratic Ethos, or, What is an Authentic Political Act?', *Contemporary Political Theory* 2, 2003.

Gooding, R., '"Something Very Old and Very Slow": Coraline, Uncanniness, and Narrative Form', *Children's Literature Association Quarterly* 33(4), 2008.

Goodrich, P., *Oedipus Lex: Psychoanalysis, History, Law*, Oakland: University of California Press, 1995.

Goodrich, P. and Gray Carlson, D., 'Introduction' in P. Goodrich and D. Gray Carlson (eds), *Law and the Postmodern Mind*, Ann Arbor: University of Michigan Press, 1998.

Goss, J., 'The Mother with the Button Eyes: An Exploration of the Story Construct of the "Other-Mother"', *Papers: Explorations into Children's Literature* 19(1), 2009.

Grigg, R., 'Absolute Freedom and Major Structural Change' in G. Boucher, J. Glynos and M. Sharpe (eds), *Traversing the Fantasy: Critical Responses to Slavoj Žižek*, Aldershot: Ashgate, 2005.

Grigg, R., 'Guilt, the Law and Transgression', *Cardozo Law Review* 24(6), 2003.

Grigg, R., 'From the Mechanism of Psychosis to the Universal Condition of the Symptom: On Foreclosure', in D. Nobus (ed.), *Key Concepts of Lacanian Psychoanalysis*, New York: Other Press, 1998.

Hardt, M. and Negri, A., *Multitude: War and Democracy in the Age of Empire*, Harmondsworth: Penguin Books, 2005.

Hardt, M. and Negri, A., *Empire*, London: Harvard University Press, 2001.

Harris, N., Walgrave, L. and Braithwaite, J., 'Emotional Dynamics in Restorative Conferences', *Theoretical Criminology* 8, 2004.

Hart, H. L. A., *The Concept of Law*, Oxford: Clarendon Press, 1961.

Hayes, H., 'Apologies and Accounts in Youth Justice Conferencing: Reinterpreting Research Outcomes', *Contemporary Justice Review* 9, 2006.

Heidegger, M., 'Poetically Man Dwells', in A. Hofstadter (trans.) and M. Stassen (ed.), *Martin Heidegger: Philosophical and Political Writings*, New York: Continuum International Publishing Group Inc., 2003.

Heidegger, M., 'The Question Concerning Technology', in *Basic Writings: from Being and Time (1927) to The Task of Thinking (1964)*, D. F. Krell (ed.), San Francisco: HarperCollins Publishers, 1993.

Heidegger, M., *The Basic Problems of Phenomenology*, A. Hofstadter (trans.), Indianapolis: Indiana University Press, 1982.

Hesiod and Theognis, *Theogony, Works and Days, and Elegies*, Harmondsworth: Penguin Books, 1976.

Hourigan, D., 'Breach! The Law's *Jouissance* in *The City & The City*', *Law, Culture and the Humanities* 9, 2013.

Hourigan, D., 'Postmodern Anarchy in the Modern Legal Psyche: Law, Anarchy and Psychoanalytic Philosophy', *Griffith Law Review* 21(2), 2012.

Irigaray, L., *The Forgetting of Air in Martin Heidegger*, M. B. Mader (trans.), Austin: University of Texas Press, 1999.

Johnston, A., *Badiou, Žižek and Political Transformations: The Cadence of Change*, Evanston, IL: Northwestern University Press, 2009.

Johnston, A., 'The World Before Worlds: Quentin Meillassoux and Alain Badiou's Anti-Kantian Transcendentalism', *Contemporary French Civilization*, 33(1), 2009.

Joyce, J., *Finnegan's Wake*, New York: Viking Press, 1957.

Kafka, F., 'The Cares of a Family Man' in N. Glatzer (ed.), W. Muir and E. Muir (trans.), *The Complete Short Stories of Franz Kafka*, London: Vintage, 1999.

Kennedy, D. 'Legal Education as Training for Hierarchy' in D. Kairys (ed.), *The Politics of Law: A Progressive Critique, 3rd edition*, New York: Basic Books, 1998.

King, P., *Private Dwelling: Contemplating the Use of Housing*, London: Routledge, 2004.

Knapp, S. and Michaels, W. B., 'Against Theory' in *The Norton Anthology of Theory and Criticism, 2nd edition*, V. B. Leitch (ed.), London: W. W. Norton & Company, 2010.

Labbie, E. F., *Lacan's Medievalism*, Minneapolis: University of Minnesota Press, 2006.

Lacan, J., *Le Séminaire, livre XIX: ... ou pire*, Paris: Seuil, 2011.

Lacan, J., *The Seminar of Jacques Lacan Book XVII: The Other Side of Psychoanalysis*, R. Grigg (trans.), New York: W. W. Norton & Company, 2007.

Lacan, J., *Écrits*, B. Fink (trans.), New York: W. W. Norton & Company, 2006.

Lacan, J., *The Seminar of Jacques Lacan, Book XX: On Feminine Sexuality, the Limits of Love and Knowledge, 1972–1973*, J.-A. Miller (ed.) and B. Fink (trans.), London: W. W. Norton & Company, 1998.

Lacan, J., *The Seminar of Jacques Lacan, Book XI: Four Fundamental Concepts of Psychoanalysis*, J.-A. Miller (ed.) and A. Sheridan (trans.), New York: W. W. Norton & Company, 1998.

Lacan, J., *The Seminar of Jacques Lacan, Book III: The Psychoses*, J.-A. Miller (ed.) and R. Grigg (trans.), London: Routledge, 1993.

Lacan, J., *The Seminar of Jacques Lacan, Book I: Freud's Papers on Technique*, J. Forrester (trans.), New York: W. W. Norton & Company, 1988.

Laurent, E., 'The Purloined Letter and the Tao of the Psychoanalyst', in V. Voruz and B. Wolf (eds), *The Later Lacan: An Introduction*, Albany: State University of New York Press, 2007.

Logan, M.-R. (ed.), 'Graphesis: Perspectives in Literature and Philosophy', *Yale French Studies* 52, 1975.

Lysy-Stevens, A., 'Unconscious and Interpretation', *Hurly-Burly* 1, 2009.

MacNeil, W. P., *Novel Judgements: Legal Theory as Fiction*, London: Routledge, 2012.

MacNeil, W. P., *Lex Populi: The Jurisprudence of Popular Culture*, Stanford: Stanford University Press, 2007.

Marcuse, H., *One-Dimensional Man*, London: Sphere Books Ltd, 1972.

Maxwell, G. and Hayes, H., 'Restorative Justice Developments in the Pacific Region: A Comprehensive Survey', *Contemporary Justice Review* 9, 2006.

Maxwell, G. and Morris, A., 'Youth Justice in New Zealand: Restorative Justice in Practice?', *Journal of Social Issues* 62, 2006.

Meillassoux, Q., *After Finitude: An Essay on the Necessity of Contingency*, R. Brassier (trans.), London: Continuum, 2008.

Melville, H., 'Benito Cereno' in *Melville's Short Novels*, D. McCall (ed.), New York: W. W. Norton & Company, 2001.

Meyer, C. (ed.), *Le livre noir de la psychoanalyse*, Paris: Les Arènes, 2005.

Miéville, C., *The City & The City*, New York: Random House, 2009.

Miller, J.-A., 'Interpretation in Reverse', in V. Voruz and B. Wolf (eds), *The Later Lacan: An Introduction*, Albany: State University of New York Press, 2007.

Miller, J.-A., 'Introduction to the Erotics of Time', B. P. Fulks (trans.), *Lacanian Ink* 24/25, 2005.

Miller, S., 'Lacan at the Limits of Legal Theory: Law, Desire, and Sovereign Violence', *Umbr(a): Ignorance of the Law*, 2003.

Murphy, P., 'Postmodern Perspectives and Justice', *Thesis Eleven* 30, 1991.

Nobus, D., *Jacques Lacan and the Freudian Practice of Psychoanalysis*, London: Routledge, 2000.

Nozick, R., 'The State', in E. Stringham (ed.), *Anarchy and the Law*, Washington D.C.: The Independent Institute, 2007.

Nusselder, A., *Interface Fantasy: A Lacanian Cyborg Ontology*, Cambridge, MA: The MIT Press, 2009.

Palahniuk, C., *Non-Fiction (True Stories)*, London: Vintage, 2004.

Parker, I., *Slavoj Žižek: A Critical Introduction*, London: Pluto Press, 2004.

Parsons, E., Sawers, N. and McInally, K., 'The Other Mother: Neil Gaiman's Postfeminist Fairytales', *Children's Literature Association Quarterly* 33(4), 2008.

Patterson, D., 'Postmodernism/Feminism/Law', *Cornell Law Review* 77, 1992.

Queensland, *Parliamentary Debates*, Legislative Assembly, April 23, 1975.

Richards, K., 'Police-referred Restorative Justice for Juveniles in Australia', *Trends and Issues in Crime and Criminal Justice* 398, Australian Institute of Criminology, 2010.

Roche, D., 'Dimensions of Restorative Justice', *Journal of Social Issues* 62, 2006.

Roudinesco, E., *Jacques Lacan: An Outline of a Life and History of a System of Thought*, Oxford: Polity Press, 1999.

Rumbles, W., 'Spectre of Jurisdiction: Supreme Court of New South Wales and the British Subject in Aotearoa/New Zealand 1823–1841', *Law Text Culture* 15, 2011.

Rumbles, W., 'Theft in the Digital: Can you Steal Virtual Property?', *Canterbury Law Review* 17, 2011.

Salecl, R., *The Tyranny of Choice*, London: Profile Books, 2011.

Salecl, R., *On Anxiety*, London: Routledge, 2004.

Salecl, R., *The Spoils of Freedom: Psychoanalysis and Feminism After the Fall of Socialism*, London: Routledge, 1994.

Sophocles, *The Three Theban Plays: Antigone; Oedipus the King; Oedipus at Colonus*, R. Fagles (trans.), Harmondsworth: Penguin Books, 1984.

Stavrakakis, Y., *The Lacanian Left*, Edinburgh: Edinburgh University Press, 2007.

Stavrakakis, Y., 'On Acts, Pure and Impure', *International Journal of Žižek Studies* 4(2), 2010.

Stavrakakis, Y., 'The Lure of Antigone: Aporias of an Ethics of the Political', in G. Boucher, J. Glynos and M. Sharpe (eds), *Traversing the Fantasy: Critical Responses to Slavoj Žižek*, Aldershot: Ashgate, 2005.

Strang, H., Sherman, L., Angel, C., Woods, D., Bennett, S., Newbury-Birch, D. and Inkpen,

N., 'Victim Evaluations of Face-to-Face Restorative Justice Conferences: A Quasi-Experimental Analysis', *Journal of Social Issues* 62, 2006.
Tyler, T., 'Restorative Justice and Procedural Justice: Dealing with Rule Breaking', *Journal of Social Issues* 62, 2006.
Tyler, T., 'The Psychology of Disputant Concerns in Mediation', *Negotiation Journal* 14, 1998.
van Stokkom, B., 'Moral Emotions in Restorative Justice Conferences: Managing Shame, Designing Empathy', *Theoretical Criminology* 6, 2002.
Weber, M., 'Science as a Vocation', in H. H. Gerth and C. Wright Mills (trans. and eds), *From Max Weber: Essays in Sociology*, New York: Oxford University Press, 1946.
Young, A., *The Scene of Violence*, London: Routledge, 2010.
Young, I. M., 'House and Home: Feminist Variations on a Theme', in N. J. Holland and Patricia Huntington (eds), *Feminist Interpretations of Martin Heidegger*, Pennsylvania: The Pennsylvania State University Press, 2001.
Žižek, S., *Less than Nothing: Hegel and the Shadow of Dialectical Materialism*, London: Verso, 2012.
Žižek, S., *In Defense of Lost Causes*, London: Verso, 2008.
Žižek, S., *Violence*, London: Profile Books, 2008.
Žižek, S., *The Parallax View*, Cambridge, MA: The MIT Press, 2006.
Žižek, S., *The Universal Exception*, R. Butler and S. Stephens (eds), London: Continuum, 2006.
Žižek, S., 'Is Psychoanalysis Really Outmoded? Apropos the 150th Anniversary of Freud's Birth', *Journal of European Psychoanalysis* 23, 2006.
Žižek, S., 'A Plea for a Return to *Différance* (with a Minor *Pro Domo Sua*)', *Critical Inquiry* 32/2, 2006.
Žižek, S., *Interrogating the Real*, R. Butler and S. Stephens (eds), London: Continuum, 2005.
Žižek, S., 'Odradek as a Political Category', *Lacanian Ink* 24/25, 2005.
Žižek, S., 'The Politics of *Jouissance*', *Lacanian Ink* 24/25, 2005.
Žižek, S., *Iraq: The Borrowed Kettle*, London: Verso, 2004.
Žižek, S., *Organs Without Bodies: On Deleuze and Consequences*, London: Routledge, 2004.
Žižek, S., 'The Lesson of Rancière' in J. Rancière, *The Politics of Aesthetics*, G. Rockhill (trans.), London: Continuum, 2004.
Žižek, S., *The Puppet and the Dwarf: The Perverse Core of Christianity*, Cambridge, MA: The MIT Press, 2003.
Žižek, S., 'Hitchcock's Organs Without Bodies', *Lacanian Ink* 22, 2003.
Žižek, S., 'What Some Would Call ...: A Response to Yannis Stavrakakis', *Umbr(a): Ignorance of the Law*, 2003.
Žižek, S., *Welcome to the Desert of the Real: Five Essays on September 11 and Related Dates*, London: Verso, 2002.
Žižek, S., *Enjoy your Symptom! Jacques Lacan In Hollywood and Out, Revised Edition*, London: Routledge, 2001.
Žižek, S., *The Fright of Real Tears: Krystof Kieślowski between Theory and Post Theory*, London: BFI Publishing, 2001.
Žižek, S., *The Art of the Ridiculous Sublime: On David Lynch's Lost Highway*, Seattle: The Walter Chapin Simpson Center for the Humanities, 2000.
Žižek, S., *The Fragile Absolute – Or Why the Christian Legacy Is Worth Fighting For*, London: Verso, 2000.
Žižek, S., *The Ticklish Subject: The Absent Centre of Political Ontology*, London: Verso, 1999.
Žižek, S., 'Death and the Maiden', in E. Wright and E. Wright (eds), *The Žižek Reader*, London: Blackwell, 1999.

Žižek, S., 'Kant with (or against) Sade,' in E. Wright and E. Wright (eds), *The Žižek Reader,* Oxford: Blackwell, 1999.
Žižek, S. 'The Obscene Object of Postmodernity,' in E. Wright and E. Wright (eds), *The Žižek Reader,* Oxford: Blackwell, 1999.
Žižek, S. 'From "Passionate Attachments" to Dis-Identification', *Umbr(a)* 1, 1998.
Žižek, S., 'Introduction: Cogito as a Shibboleth', in S. Žižek (ed.), *Cogito and the Unconscious,* Durham, NC: Duke University Press, 1998.
Žižek, S., *The Plague of Fantasies*, London: Verso, 1997.
Žižek, S., *Tarrying with the Negative: Kant, Hegel, and the Critique of Ideology*, Durham, NC: Duke University Press, 1993.
Žižek, S., 'In His Bold Gaze My Ruin is Writ Large', in S. Žižek (ed.), *Everything You Always Wanted to Know About Lacan (But Were Afraid to Ask Hitchcock)*, London: Verso, 1992.
Žižek, S., *For They Know Not What They Do: Enjoyment as a Political Factor*, London: Verso, 1991.
Žižek, S., *The Sublime Object of Ideology*, London: Verso, 1989.
Žižek, S. and von Schelling, F. W. J., *The Abyss of Freedom/Ages of the World*, Michigan: University of Michigan Press, 1997.
Zupančič, A., 'When Surplus Enjoyment Meets Surplus Value', in J. Clemens and R. Grigg (eds), *Jacques Lacan and the Other Side of Psycho-Analysis*, Durham, NC: Duke University Press, 2006.
Zupančič, A., *Ethics of the Real: Kant, Lacan*, London: Verso, 2000.
Zwart, M. de, 'Contractual Communities: Effective Governance of Virtual Worlds', *University of New South Wales Law Journal* 33(2), 2010.

Primary legal sources

Acts Interpretation Act 1901 (Cth).
Acts Interpretation Act 1954 (Q).
Criminal Code (Q).
Fair Trading Act 1999 (Vic).

Cases

Adler v George (1964) 2 QB 7.
Heydon's Case (1584) 3 Co Rep 7a.
Lacey v Attorney-General of Queensland (2011) 242 CLR 573.
Project Blue Sky Inc. v Australian Broadcasting Authority (1998) 194 CLR 335.
Royall v R (1991) 100 ALR 669.
Victorian Bar Inc. v CEM QC [2006] VCAT 1417.

Films

Dead of Night, A. Cavalcanti (dir.), Studiocanal, [1945] 2014.
Minority Report, S. Spielberg (dir.), 20th Century Fox Home Entertainment, [2002] 2003.
The Recruit, R. Donaldson (dir.), Buena Vista Home Entertainment, 2003.
Fight Club, D. Fincher (dir.), 20th Century Fox Home Entertainment South Pacific Pty Ltd, [1999] 2000.
Jacques Lacan la psychoanalyse réinventée, E. Roudinesco and E. Kapnist (writers), Paris: ARTE France, 2001.

TV series

True Blood: The Complete First Season, A. Ball (creator), USA: Home Box Office Inc., 2009.

True Blood: The Complete Second Season, A. Ball (creator), USA: Home Box Office Inc., 2010.
True Blood: The Complete Third Season, A. Ball (creator), USA: Home Box Office Inc., 2011.

Websites

@The_Real_Gevlon, Gaius Homerson on Twitter, https://twitter.com/The_Real_Gevlon/statuses/463002069989736448

ATOI Spaceships, 'A Tale of Internet Spaceships', *YouTube*, 2014, http://www.youtube.com/watch?v=IB1M9ZVuWtMBattleclinic, *Catalyst: 300DPS, 23day Train, Hulkageddon*, http://eve.battleclinic.com/loadout/54971-Catalyst-300DPS-23day-Train-Hulkageddon.html

Badiou, A., 'The Subject of Art', *Lacan.com*, 2005, http://www.lacan.com/symptom6_articles/badiou.html

BBC News, 'Billions Stolen in Online Robbery', 3 July 2009, http://news.bbc.co.uk/2/hi/technology/8132547.stm

Boson, H., *Hulkageddon Prize List Update (Over 16Bil Worth)*, 2012, http://www.machine9.net/?p=882

Campbel, T. C. (ed.), *Commonalities: Theorizing the Common in Contemporary Italian Thought*, 2010, http://commonconf.wordpress.com/

CCP Falcon, 'A Message Regarding Vandalism of the Eve Monument', 2014, https://forums.eveonline.com/default.aspx?g=posts&m=4563345

CCP Fozzie, 'Into the Known Unknowns: Wormhole Updates in the Hyperion Release', 2014, http://community.eveonline.com/news/dev-blogs/into-the-known-unknowns/?_ga=1.183055456.753417130.1405299146

CCP Games, *CSM 9 Meeting Minutes, 17–19 September*, 2014, http://cdn1.eveonline.com/community/csm/CSM9Summer_Minutes_2014.pdf

CCP Games, *Incarna – 21 June 2011*, 2014, http://www.eveonline.com/expansions/incarna

CCP Games, *Eve Online End User License Agreement*, 2014, http://community.eveonline.com/support/policies/eve-eula/

CCP Games, *Eve Online Terms of Service*, 2014, http://community.eveonline.com/support/policies/eve-tos/

CCP Games, *Evelopedia*, 2014, https://wiki.eveonline.com/

CCP Games, 'Hulkageddon', *Evelopedia*, 2014, https://wiki.eveonline.com/en/wiki/Hulkageddon

CCP Games, 'New Eden Cluster', *Evelopedia*, 2014, https://wiki.eveonline.com/en/wiki/New_Eden_(cluster)

Drain, B., 'Eve Evolved: The Human Casualties', *Massively by Joystiq*, 2011, http://massively.joystiq.com/2011/10/23/eve-evolved-the-human-casualties/5

Grant, G. J., 'Neil Gaiman Interview', *Indie Bound*, American Book Sellers Association, 2008, http://www.indiebound.org/author-interviews/gaimanneil

Lien, T., 'Eve: The Most Thrilling Boring Game in the Universe', *Polygon*, 2014, http://www.polygon.com/features/2014/2/24/5419788/eve-online-thrilling-boring

Narcisse, E., 'How Fan Revolt in *EVE Online* Gave Birth to its Latest Expansion', *Kotaku*, 2011, http://kotaku.com/5865930/how-fan-revolt-in-eve-online-gave-birth-to-its-latest-expansion

Rooksandkings, 'Rooks and Kings: Clarion Call 3', *YouTube*, 2011, https://www.youtube.com/watch?v=XrYe_4vHzgE

Something Awful: The Internet Makes You Stupid, http://www.somethingawful.com/

The Mittani, 'Sins of a Solar Spymaster #78: The Extortion Empire', *TenTonHammer.com*, http://www.tentonhammer.com/node/230860/page/2

Index